The Third World Security Predicament

Emerging Global Issues

Thomas G. Weiss, Series Editor

Published in association with the
Thomas J. Watson Jr. Institute for International Studies,
Brown University

The Third World Security Predicament

State Making, Regional Conflict, and the International System

Mohammed Ayoob

LYNNE RIENNER PUBLISHERS

BOULDER
LONDON

Published in the United States of America by
Lynne Rienner Publishers, Inc.
1800 30th Street, Boulder, Colorado 80301
www.rienner.com

and in the United Kingdom by
Lynne Rienner Publishers, Inc.
3 Henrietta Street, Covent Garden, London WC2E 8LU

ISBN 978-1-55587-576-3 (pbk. : alk. paper)

Printed and bound in the United States of America

The paper used in this publication meets the requirements of the American National Standard for Permanence of Paper for Printed Library Materials Z39.48-1992.

For
Robert O'Neill

Contents

Foreword

THOMAS G. WEISS

I identify with Mohammed Ayoob's views about the Third World's security predicament; and I commend this book to the attention of the wide readership I believe it deserves and am confident it will get.

Ayoob and I have been intellectual sparring partners for a number of years. It has always been professionally rewarding to have him as part of a conference or a collaborative book project. This past year it has been Brown University's and my personal pleasure to welcome him into our community. He has been in residence as part of a generous grant from the Ford Foundation to support ongoing work at the Thomas J. Watson Jr. Institute for International Studies. I would like to express my gratitude to Shepard Forman, director, and Geoffrey Wiseman, program officer, of the International Affairs Program, for having made it possible for Ayoob to have spent 1993 to 1994 at Brown University as the Ford Foundation Fellow in International Security.

This volume is the seventh in a Lynne Rienner book series entitled "Emerging Global Issues." However, using the term *emerging* in conjunction with the "Third World's Security Predicament" is a bit of a misnomer. Third World security has been very much on the policy agenda in one form or another since shortly after World War II; more so since the rapid decolonization of the 1950s and 1960s and the emergence of a distinct group consciousness among developing countries. As Ayoob notes, "The Third World was born into bipolarity and the Cold War." In fact, four of the previous six volumes in the series have touched directly upon elements of the Third World's security predicament.

With the tectonic shifts now underway in world politics, it is increasingly difficult to recall the roots of the rhetorical divisions between rich and poor, capitalist and communist, which dominated international discourse over much of the past five decades. The Non-Aligned Movement (NAM) and its conception of the Third World were born in the mid-1950s from the fertile and independent minds of Gamal Abdul Nasser, Josip Tito, and Sukarno in order to steer a middle course in the global ideological struggle between the United States and the Soviet Union. The founding members of this movement—as well as the host of African, Asian, and Latin American countries that became independent and joined afterward—were located in the Third World.

There is some discussion as to the first use of this term. The weight of opinion seems to be on the side of French demographer Alfred Sauvy (1898–1990) in *Le Nouvel Observateur #118,* August 14, 1952. His *tiers monde* referred to India and China as leading the struggle for decolonization at that point. His inspiration was a reference to the *third estate,* a term originally used by Emmanuel Sieyès in January 1789 to describe the struggling third force in the French Revolution that was combating the clergy and the aristocracy.

Third World was coined to describe an open-ended (its numbers continue to grow) and residual category for those countries not part of the Cold War division either of the so-called First World, the capitalist and democratic countries, members of the North Atlantic Treaty Organization (NATO) and the Organization of Economic Cooperation and Development (OECD); or of the Second World, socialist countries, members of the Warsaw Treaty Organization (WTO) and the Council on Mutual Economic Assistance (CMEA). The geographical location of the Third World was largely south of the equator, in contrast to the more advanced industrialized countries with either a market or a socialist orientation in the northern hemisphere.

Although the WTO and the CMEA have disappeared along with the communist bloc, Ayoob maintains—and I believe he is fundamentally correct—that the relative weakness of the state apparatus still distinguishes virtually all of the countries that constitute the Third World from those countries that once constituted the First and Second Worlds. Hence, their peculiar security problems remain meaningful in analytical terms. We need to understand them better as we prepare to deal with the widespread instability that permeates international relations at the dawn of the twenty-first century.

Ayoob and I approach Third World insecurity somewhat differently. In particular, I place more emphasis on the concept of human security, whereas his narrower focus is on political issues, which almost inevitably spill into military ones. My own work tends to be less state-centric and more concerned with the growing pluralism of world politics, especially of nongovernmental organizations. Moreover, I find it difficult to think of the Third World as a meaningful entity because this group of around 150 countries seems at least as heterogeneous as its 35 Northern counterparts. At the same time, attempts to cast analytical nets broadly have been messy and unsatisfactory, particularly since the inclusion into military security discussions of such variables as economic deprivation, environmental degradation, and human rights abuse, as well as a host of nonstate actors and more differentiation among various categories of states. To date, more comprehensive perspectives have led to more heat than light. And so I envy Ayoob's forest over all of my trees.

By focusing on the politico-military reality of the Third World's security conundrum, Ayoob has brought clearly into focus several central realities of our turbulent times. I wish to underline two important ones that emerge from his work, because they temper such optimism as has surfaced from the post–Cold War era. Initial euphoria has given way to a more realistic appraisal of the likelihood of ever-increasing ethnic, religious, and political fragmentation; Ayoob dumps even more cold water on the optimism.

The information and technological revolutions have indeed made borders more permeable and less significant, and traditional state sovereignty is under siege from many directions. In spite of the visceral rejection of the role of state structures as part of the stunning defeat of communism as a societal organizing principle, the crucial problem within the South, paradoxically, may well be "inadequate stateness." Drawing heavily on the state-building experiences of Europe since the seventeenth century, Ayoob is distressed by the appearance of a growing number of partially or totally failed states. Examining the human debris in Afghanistan, Somalia, Liberia, Lebanon, and Zaire, he argues that the tragedies of failed states constitute a greater threat to peoples than even autocratic—but functioning—states such as Iraq and Syria.

Another central reality is Ayoob's emphasis on the primacy of the domestic situations in Third World states. It is the internal frailties and vulnerabilities of these states, rather than regional or global dimensions, that essentially explain the high levels of violence and suffering in many parts of the Third World. In spite of the increasing number of possible roles for the United Nations and regional intergovernmental organizations in helping to pick up the pieces from armed conflicts, there is no real substitute for the time and resources to build greater societal cohesion and state legitimacy. Unfortunately, there are very few shortcuts in the process of state building. There is a contradiction at this historical juncture between the normative goals of extending state control and respecting groups and individuals who resist such control and dominion.

Too many readers in the Western world are bound to ask, "So what?" I would recommend heartily that U.S. citizens become familiar with the contents of this book. Four years after the official end of the Cold War, surveys of elite and public opinion in the United States indicate that when asked to identify the most urgent foreign policy priority, most Americans name a domestic issue, with special emphasis on the economy. Yet as Ayoob concludes, "In this era of nuclear weapons and jet travel, the core of industrialized democracies, despite its best efforts, cannot insulate itself from the conflicts and instabilities in the global periphery. There may be an element of poetic justice in this outcome after all."

The problems raised by Mohammed Ayoob cannot fail to interest both students and diplomats. The security predicament of the Third World is, after all, not just a concern for those who live in developing countries or who sympathize with them: It is ours as well. It has been my pleasant task to discover, before others, the extremely insightful contents of this book.

—*Thomas G. Weiss*

Preface

This book is a modest attempt to apply the classical approach to the study of one important aspect of international relations, an approach the late Hedley Bull described as "a scientifically imperfect process of perception or intuition [that is] characterized above all by explicit reliance upon the exercise of judgment."[1] In other words, it is an essay in judicious interpretation, which, as Stanley Hoffmann noted, is "the attempt to seize the meaning of what has been explained" and is "an artistic enterprise rather than a scientific one."[2]

The book sets out to interpret—that is, to dissect, reflect upon, and conceptualize—the Third World's security predicament. It is essential to understand this predicament in order to comprehend the role and place of the Third World in the international system. The case for the continuing relevance of the Third World as an analytical category in the post–Cold War era is made in the first chapter, as is the argument about the crucial importance of the concept of security in the analysis of the politics and international relations of the Third World.

The security predicament of Third World states is generated largely by the twin pressures of late state making and their late entry into the system of states. I conclude that a paradigm that does not make security its centerpiece will lack adequate power to explain the domestic or international behavior of Third World states. Simultaneously, I argue that just as it is essential to make security the central focus of any paradigm that attempts to explain Third World state behavior, it is also necessary to adopt the notion of state making as the point of departure for the study of Third World security. Analyses based on a clear understanding of the security variable's centrality and of the importance of the state-making process within that variable are likely to provide much richer comparative data and less ephemeral conclusions than those that adopt development or dependency as their basic organizing concepts.

I also analyze issues that have become increasingly salient following the end of the Cold War and the transformation in the global balance of power. I conclude that the Cold War did not ease the Third World's security predicament and that its demise could make that predicament even more acute. This could be the case because the end of the Cold War has removed certain constraints that were imposed by the superpowers on the conflictual behavior of Third World states to protect themselves from being sucked directly into conflicts on the global periphery. More important, the recent relaxation of international norms guaranteeing the territorial integrity of established and internationally recognized states, and the renewed legitimation of ethno-national self-determination following the end of the Cold War, are expected to adversely affect the security predicament of Third World states that are struggling to translate their juridical sovereignty into effective statehood.

In the book I provide the essential backdrop to the foregoing arguments by analyzing the impact of the emergence of the Third World on the system of states and that of the international system on the crucial task of state building currently underway in the Third World. It is impossible for a single author to provide complete answers to all of the big questions relating to the nature of the Third World's relationship with the international system. However, it is my hope that the unanswered, or partially answered, questions raised here will offer enough intellectual excitement to inspire other scholars to follow the inquiry lines I have not developed fully in this volume. If this book sets off such a scholarly chain reaction, it will have succeeded in its primary mission.

Let me point out at the outset that this study does not pretend to provide guidelines or policy prescriptions for statesmen or decisionmakers in the developed or the developing worlds. I agree with Hedley Bull that "the search for conclusions that can be presented as 'solutions' or 'practical advice' is a corrupting element in the contemporary study of world politics, which properly understood is an intellectual activity and not a practical one."[3]

It is not the job of serious international relations students to prescribe quick solutions for immediate problems. It is their obligation, however, to reflect upon, analytically dissect, and meticulously conceptualize long-term trends and tendencies in the international system in order to make considered judgments about them. This is a quintessential academic activity because it adds to the total fund of knowledge at our disposal about how the international system operates and makes it possible for the more discerning scholars to get to the roots of the fundamental problems that face the society of states. This reflection also helps to clear the air of wishful thinking, often posing as faddish analysis in pseudoscientific jargon.

I have touched upon some of the major themes contained in this book in articles in scholarly journals and in book chapters published earlier. Some of the ideas contained here have also been presented at various conferences and workshops in the United States, Canada, the Netherlands,

India, and Australia. I would like to thank the editors of those journals and books and the conference and workshop participants; their comments have enriched my understanding of the subject and improved the quality of this final product.

The book has been made possible by the generosity of various institutions and individuals to whom I am extremely grateful. Although I have been interested for a dozen years in conceptualizing both the role of the Third World in the international system and the security problematic of the Third World, I began to conduct sustained research on the central themes presented here in 1989–1990 at the Center of International Studies, Woodrow Wilson School of Public and International Affairs, Princeton University, where I spent eighteen months as SSRC–MacArthur Foundation Fellow in International Peace and Security. I would like to thank the MacArthur Foundation and the Social Science Research Council for funding the initial phase of this project. I am particularly grateful to Henry Bienen, then director of the Center of International Studies at Princeton and now president of Northwestern University, for extending the center's hospitality to me during that crucial phase of the project. Richard Falk, Richard Ullman, Atul Kohli, and Robert Gilpin also deserve my thanks for their intellectual input and constant encouragement during my time at Princeton.

Work on the project continued from 1990 to 1993 simultaneously with my teaching duties at James Madison College, Michigan State University—a truly unique institution that combines the ambience of a small college specializing in public and international affairs with all of the advantages of the large university within which it is situated. Many of the ideas that form the core of the book comprised major themes of my senior seminar, "Major Dimensions of Third World Security." I am greatly indebted to two groups of very bright students at Madison College who brought fresh perspectives to bear on this subject and helped me refine my arguments and sharpen my conclusions. I would also like to thank my colleagues at Michigan State University, Michael Schechter, Norman Graham, and Linda Racioppi, for acting as sounding boards for my ideas, sometimes without realizing they were performing this role. Kenneth Waltzer and William Allen, the former acting dean and the current dean of James Madison College, respectively, provided enthusiastic support in more than one way to enable the completion of this project.

I am very grateful to the Ford Foundation's Program on Peace and Security and to the Watson Institute for International Studies at Brown University for awarding me the Ford Foundation Fellowship in International Security at the Watson Institute for the 1993–1994 academic year so I could complete the project. I am particularly grateful to Thomas G. Weiss, the associate director of the Watson Institute, for extending the hospitality of the institute, for his keen interest in the project, and for writing the foreword to this volume. His constant encouragement and perceptive advice contributed greatly to the completion of the project within the time frame of the fellowship. I would also like to thank Fred Fullerton, Mary Lhowe, and Susan Costa at the Watson Institute who worked hard to give this volume its final shape. I am grateful to Gia Hamilton and Cheryl Carnahan at Lynne Rienner Publishers for their very professional handling of the editing process.

I am extremely grateful to my wife, Salma, who has been a constant source of unstinting support during the years I have worked on this project, as she has been in all my academic endeavors.

Finally, as a token of appreciation for his friendship and support, I dedicate this book to my very good friend and former colleague at the Australian National University, Robert O'Neill, currently Chichele Professor of the History of War at All Souls College, Oxford, who has been a great source of inspiration to me intellectually and in many other ways during the two decades we have known each other.

—Mohammed Ayoob

Notes

1. Hedley Bull, "International Theory: The Case for a Classical Approach," in Klaus Knorr and James N. Rosenau (eds.), *Contending Approaches to International Politics* (Princeton: Princeton University Press, 1969): 20.

2. Stanley Hoffmann, "International Society," in J. D. B. Miller and R. J. Vincent (eds.), *Order and Violence: Hedley Bull and International Relations* (Oxford: Clarendon Press, 1990): 17.

3. Hedley Bull, *The Anarchical Society: A Study of Order in World Politics* (New York: Columbia University Press, 1977): 319–320.

■ 1 ■

Concepts and Definitions: "Third World" and "Security"

The Third World has a multidimensional relationship with the international system. The most fundamental dimension of this relationship is a direct result of the Third World's weakness toward what Robert Gilpin has called the two organizing principles of international social life—the sovereign state and the international market.[1] This weakness is manifested at both of the levels at which the Third World interacts with the international system: as a group, and as individual sovereign states.

Many scholarly attempts to explain this weakness have been made from many different perspectives. These attempts include the world system critique of the current international order, which provides the philosophical foundation on which much of the dependency literature is based;[2] the reformist prescriptions for improving the position of the developing world by co-opting the more important countries, particularly the more important socioeconomic strata within those countries;[3] and the neoconservative justification of inequality embedded in that order.[4] This entire spectrum of views, from the revolutionary through the reformist to the most ardent defense of the status quo, accepts the notion of Third World weakness and vulnerability, even though the proposed solutions range from radical restructuring of the international order to vehement opposition to even tinkering with it. Even more interesting is that few, if any, analysts of these various persuasions have taken their arguments to their logical end by concluding that Third World state behavior, whether at the individual or the collective level, is largely determined by the insecurity that is aggravated by the overwhelming feeling of vulnerability, if not impotence, among its state elites.

Stephen Krasner probably comes the closest to this conclusion in his analysis of North-South relations, which he terms *structural conflict* between the affluent, powerful North and the poor, weak South. He attributes this conflict primarily to the Third World's quest to change international regimes, especially those covered by the New International Economic Order (NIEO) agenda, by making such regimes more authoritative and thereby redistributing benefits (an economic value) and power (a political value) to the Third World through its numerical superiority in international forums.[5] However, even Krasner fails to capture the multidimensional nature of North-South relations because of his excessive preoccupation with the Third World's NIEO demands to the exclusion of many other issues. The neglected issues are found in the field of political and military security and also in the economic and technological spheres, including aid, trade, investments, and technology transfers. Economic and technological limits severely constrain the Third World's capacity to bargain effectively with the developed countries of North America and Western Europe, and they contribute to the South's multifaceted dependence on the North, as individual states and as a group. Economic and technological dependencies and political and military weaknesses therefore have greater bearing on North-South relations than the failed dialogue around NIEO. In fact, it is the vulnerabilities and dependencies in the political and military spheres that largely explain the South's failed attempt to get the North to accept its NIEO demands.

The main reasons for the lack of attention to security, which should be considered the major variable determining Third World state behavior both domestically and externally, are not difficult to decipher. In the case of the world system theorists, led by Immanuel Wallerstein, this lack of attention to security has arisen from the relative neglect of political variables in favor of economic ones and from the theorists' almost exclusive concentration on the systemic level of analysis at the expense of the unit level. Although one offshoot of the world system dependency school—that is, the dependent development subschool—does bring the state back as an explanatory factor, it does so in a reductionist form.[6] As Atul Kohli noted, commenting generally on the neo-Marxist analysts of the Third World and particularly on the dependent development subschool, "Even though the significant role of the state in development has been widely recognized [by them], varying explanations of this role share one blind spot: they insist that it must reflect the interests and goals, not of the political elite, but of specifiable economic actors."[7]

The neoconservative position, to which both Robert Tucker and Stephen Krasner subscribe in varying degrees, has distorted the major driving force behind the foreign policies of Third World states by misreading the relationship between security and power in determining such policies. Although Third World states, as with all states in the international system, seek to enhance their capabilities and to improve their standing within the international hierarchy, the primary objective of Third World state elites is not to substitute one type of inequality among nations for another (as Tucker argues) or to change the rules by which the game of nations is played (as Krasner seems to think) but to reduce the deep sense of insecurity from which Third World states and regimes suffer domestically and internationally.

Tucker's argument is far from convincing because of the obvious inability of Third World states to change the international pecking order in any meaningful fashion. This was demonstrated above all by the unrealistic euphoria surrounding the oil price rise of 1973 and 1974. This euphoria was considerably eroded by the end of the 1970s and was thoroughly dissipated by the mid-1980s with the crash in oil prices and the disagreement over production quotas among Organization of Petroleum Exporting Countries (OPEC) members. The Gulf War of 1990 and 1991 further emphasized the lesson that weak, one-product economies cannot hope to change international power equations because such rentier income does not significantly decrease their vulnerabilities—in fact, the situation throws their weaknesses into sharper relief. This was demonstrated in Kuwait and Saudi Arabia as well as in Iraq.[8]

Similarly, Krasner's thesis about the Third World's interest in changing the rules by which the international system operates misses the point that such an interest by developing countries is selective as well as instrumental. Their primary concern is to reduce their vulnerabilities; they may occasionally find authoritative international regimes attractive only because they believe such regimes may be able to help them inch toward the overriding goal of reducing state and regime insecurities individually and collectively. Furthermore, as Robert Rothstein has pointed out, the Third World campaign in favor of NIEO, on which much of Krasner's central argument rests, had already fizzled by the time Krasner's analysis was published in the mid-1980s, thereby demonstrating the ephemeral character of his argument.[9]

By concentrating on Third World attempts in the mid-1970s and late 1970s to tinker with the international economic regimes to make them more responsive to Third World interests, Krasner also glosses over the point that whereas Third World states may have a selective interest in changing certain norms in the international economy, their commitment to the central postulates of the international system—sovereignty, nonintervention, self-help, codes of diplomacy—has been strong. Third World commitment to these postulates is, in fact, stronger than that of the developed states of the West, which were initially responsible for the formulation and global dissemination of these governing principles of the international system.[10] In fact, Third World state elites have internalized the dominant values of the Westphalian system to such a degree that Western states find this increasingly exasperating as their own international agenda moves beyond the Westphalian framework.[11] The Third World state elites' commitment to Westphalian values is derived from their acute sense of internal and external insecurity. They see the Westphalian values in their pristine form as the greatest normative and ideological bulwark against both domestic and foreign threats to states and regimes in the Third World.[12]

Although there is an obvious relationship between power and security, for most Third World states power is not viewed exclusively or primarily as an end in itself but as an instrument to ease their security predicament. This viewpoint is related to two factors: the early stage of state making in which Third World states find themselves, and their late entry into the system of states in which they form the weak, intruder majority. Both of these dimensions of the Third World's security problematic are analyzed in later chapters.

The Third World state elites' major concern—indeed, obsession—is with security at the level of both state structures and governing regimes. As Ali Mazrui has pointed out, the predominance of insecurity and the preoccupation with security in the social life of the Third World state is primarily the result of the dissonance between "the defining characteristics of any state . . . the twin principles of centralised authority and centralised power."[13] In most Third World states there are competing locations of authority; these are usually weaker than the state in terms of coercive capacity but equal to or stronger than the state in terms of political legitimacy in the view of large segments of the states' populations. This situation reflects a lack of adequate stateness—defined as a balance of coercive capacity, infrastructural power,[14] and unconditional legitimacy[15]—on the part of Third World states; this lack of stateness prevents them from imposing a legitimate political order at home and from participating effectively in the international system.

Furthermore, a lack of adequate stateness makes the states acutely vulnerable to external pressures—political, military, economic, or technological—from other and usually more developed states, from international institutions, and from transnational actors, including multinational corporations, irredentist groups, and supranational movements.[16] These vulnerabilities and the consequent permeability of Third World states explain the obsession of Third World state elites with the notion of security, which is why it is not possible to construct a paradigm that has sufficient power to explain Third World state behavior internally or externally without the concept of security at its center. It is such a paradigm—an alternative to the developmental and dependency theses—that I attempt to explicate.

Western Concept of Security

Before proceeding further, it is necessary to define the two key concepts that pervade this book—namely, security and Third World. I define the concept of security in the sense that it is used here. Although the dictionary definition of the term—namely, to be free from danger, anxiety, and fear[17]—may be quite clear, the term has been endowed with a particular content when applied to the discipline of international relations. Therefore, to reach my definitional goal I must analyze the evolution of the concept and the ways it has been interpreted in international relations literature.

To begin with, as it has been traditionally used in international relations literature, the term *security* is based upon two major assumptions: one, that most threats to a state's security arise from outside its borders and, two, that these threats are primarily, if not exclusively, military in nature and usually require a military response if the security of the target state is to be preserved. These assumptions were summed up best in Walter Lippmann's celebrated statement that "a nation is secure to the extent to which it is not in danger of having to sacrifice core values, if it wishes to avoid war, and is able, if challenged, to maintain them by victory in such a war."[18] Lippmann's definition, according to Arnold Wolfers, "implies that security rises and falls with the ability of a nation to deter an attack, or to defeat it. This is in accord with the common usage of the term."[19] Similarly, the article on national security in the *International Encyclopedia of the Social Sciences* defines security as "the ability of a nation to protect its internal values from external threats."[20]

Even scholars who have differed from this starkly realist perspective and focused on *international* as well as *national* security have been primarily concerned with reconciling national security, meaning reducing external threats to a state, with the security of the international system as a whole. They have taken their philosophical cue from authors such as Martin Wight who argued that "if there is an international society, then there is an order of some kind to be maintained, or even developed. It is not fallacious to speak of a collective interest, and security acquires a broad meaning: it can be enjoyed or pursued in common."[21] Indeed, the earliest of the twentieth-century proponents of international security, the "idealists," who predated Wight by half a century, refused to distinguish the security of the parts from that of the entire system.[22]

The post–World War II breed of system-centered scholars has been more discriminating than its predecessors. These scholars have argued from the assumption that the various segments of the international system are interlinked to such an extent that their security and welfare depend upon each other.[23] Although much of the initial impetus for this line of argument came from the awesome concentration of nuclear weaponry in the hands of the two superpowers and the periodic crises in their relations—from the Berlin blockade of 1948 to the Cuban missile crisis of 1962—the economic problems the leading Western industrialized states faced from the early 1970s, including the two oil shocks of 1973–1974 and 1978–1979, led to the crystallization of the interdependence argument.[24]

Most interesting for our purpose is the fact that both of these dominant strands of security thinking (in their many variations) defined the concept of security in external or outwardly directed terms—that is, outside the commonly accepted unit of analysis in international relations: the state. This definition and the process by which it was reached were understandable because both reflected a particular trajectory of historical development that could be traced back at least to the Peace of Westphalia, if not earlier. In the three hundred years between 1648 when, to quote Martin Wight, the modern system of states "came of age,"[25] and 1945, the evolution of the European system of states and its interaction with the domestic political processes of national consolidation within the major European powers led to the legitimation of both the system and the individual participants. These two trends—of interaction among sovereign states and greater identification of individuals with their respective states—strengthened each other. In doing so they firmly laid the foundations for the dominant tradition in the literature on international relations, in which security became synonymous with the protection from external threats of a state's vital interests and core values. This tradition in international relations, which portrays states as unitary actors responding to external threats or posing such threats to other states, has been stronger in the field of security studies than in the rest of the discipline, which has lately become more open to competing explanations of state behavior in the international arena.[26]

Developments since 1945 strengthened the traditional Western notions about security. In dividing the Western world (i.e., Europe and its offshoots) into two halves, and in stabilizing that division by means of a balance of terror based on mutual assured destruction (MAD) capability, the Cold War (and its later manifestation, détente) froze the predominant Western view of security into a bipolar model. The concept of alliance security was superimposed on the concept of state security, even as its essential externally directed orientation remained unchanged. Moreover, by making the security of NATO, the Warsaw Pact, and the major industrial states of Europe and North America the central focus of the security of the international system as a whole, the dominant strand in Western strategic thinking increasingly obliterated even the distinction between the realist (state-centric) and idealist (system-centric) approaches to the study of international security.

The application of this historically conditioned definition of security to the analysis of Third World situations has, however, created major intellectual and conceptual problems. This has been the case because the three major characteristics of the concept of state security as developed in the Western literature—namely, its external orientation, its strong link with systemic security, and its binding ties with the security of the two major alliance blocs during the Cold War era—have been so thoroughly diluted in the Third World that the explanatory power of the concept has been vastly reduced when applied to Third World contexts.

To take the first and fundamental attribute of the Western concept of security—external directedness—it is clear that despite the rhetoric of many Third World leaders, the sense of insecurity from which these states suffer emanates largely from within their boundaries rather than from outside. Although this does not mean external threats do not exist, it does imply that such threats often attain prominence largely because of the conflicts that abound within Third World states. Furthermore, it can be argued that these internal conflicts are frequently transformed into interstate conflicts because of their spillover effect into neighboring, often similarly domestically insecure states. Outstanding examples of such interconnectedness between domestic and interstate conflicts were the India-Pakistan War over Bangladesh in 1971 and the Iran-Iraq War of 1980 to 1988, which followed on the heels of revolutionary turmoil in Iran.[27]

The Third World's weak link with the systemic security agenda further circumscribes the usefulness of the Western concept of security in explaining the problems of security Third World states face. This situation reflects the remarkable difference between the security concerns of the Third World states and those of the developed countries in relation to the international system as a whole. The Third World's relative unimportance to the strategic balance during the Cold War era was, paradoxically, borne out by the fact that the superpower competition for influence was carried on with the greatest zeal in the Third World. It is no wonder, then, that conflicts proliferated in the Third World while the industrial and strategic heartland of the globe remained free of major interstate conflict after the end of World War II. Systemic security has therefore had an inverse relationship with the security of Third World regions and has often contributed to insecurity in the developing world. It has done so by turning the Third World into a relatively low-cost, low-stakes arena in which the rivalries of the major powers could be played out without affecting those powers' vital interests or posing the threat of general war in the nuclear age.

The close link between alliance security and state security that was such a prominent feature of the postwar political landscape in Europe was conspicuously absent in the Third World. Although several Third World states were allied with one or the other superpower, such alliances were either fluid and temporary (as in the case of Egypt and Somalia), served as inadequate deterrents to regional conflicts involving superpower allies (for example, Vietnam and Iraq), or were unable to prevent the dismemberment of at least one aligned state (Pakistan). Therefore, the nature of alliances and superpower commitments to their allies in the Third World was vastly different from such alliances and commitments in the developed world. In contrast to the postwar situation in Europe, alliance security was not synonymous with the security of even the most overtly aligned states in the Third World. The only exceptions were Israel and South Korea, for reasons that could not be replicated elsewhere.[28]

Regarding the three dimensions of the definition of security that has dominated the Western literature on international relations during the postwar years—its external orientation, positive links with systemic security, and the correspondence of state security with alliance security—the situation in the Third World has been radically different from that at the heart of the global strategic system that includes North America, Europe, and Japan. In light of the disjuncture between the Euro-American and Third World experiences in terms of consolidation of state structures and their relationships with the international security system, it is essential that the concept of security in the context of the Third World be defined differently from the definition generally found in the Western literature on international relations.

Third World Concept of Security

Bearing these differences in mind and remaining sensitive to the connection between domestic and external threats faced by Third World states, I propose the following definition of security for purposes of this volume. I believe this definition conveys the multifaceted nature of the concept, integrates these facets into a conceptual whole, and retains its analytical utility by avoiding undue elasticity.

The definition of security used here purports to be state centered in character, emphasizing the primarily political connotation of the term and the major enterprise in which Third World countries have been engaged since decolonization—state building. However, this emphasis on the primacy of the political realm in the definition of security does not mean the political realm can or should be totally insulated from other realms of human and social activity when it comes to dealing with security issues. Although it retains its primacy in the definition of security, the political realm must be informed by these other areas of human activity. However, the influence of the other realms on matters that affect security must be filtered through the political realm and must be directly relevant to that realm. In other words, when developments in other realms—ranging from the economic to the ecological—threaten to have immediate political consequences or are perceived as being able to threaten state boundaries, political institutions, or governing regimes, these other variables must be taken into account as a part of a state's security calculus. Short of that, the political and security realm must maintain its distinctiveness from other realms. Phenomena such as economic deprivation and environmental degradation should be analyzed as events, occurrences, and variables that may be linked to, but are essentially distinct from, the realm of security as defined for purposes of this book.

The concept of security is, therefore, used here in an explicitly political sense. It is used in the restricted sense of applying to the security of the state—in terms of both its territory and its institutions—and to the security of those who profess to represent the state territorially and institutionally. In other words, security-insecurity is defined in relation to vulnerabilities—*both internal and external*—that threaten or have the potential to bring down or weaken state structures, both territorial and institutional, and governing regimes. According to this definition, the more a state or regime—and often it is difficult to disentangle issues of state security from those of regime security in the Third World—leans toward the invulnerable end of the vulnerable-invulnerable continuum, the more secure it will be. Other types of vulnerability, whether economic or ecological, become integral components of our definition of security only if they become acute enough to acquire political dimensions and threaten state boundaries, state institutions, or regime survival. In other words, debt burdens, rain-forest decimation, or even famine do not become part of the security calculus for our purpose unless they threaten to have political outcomes that either affect the survivability of state boundaries, state institutions, or governing elites or weaken the capacity of states and regimes to act effectively in the realm of both domestic and international politics.[29]

This definition of security has not been propounded with a view to denigrate the brave attempts that have been made by scholars and analysts as diverse as Caroline Thomas and Jessica Mathews to expand the concept of security from its original Western ethnocentric form, which emphasized the military and external dimensions of security, to encompass the global realities of the last decades of the twentieth century. However, whereas definitions such as those propounded by Thomas and Mathews are commendable as attempts to inject greater flexibility into the concept of security, when they are not applied with adequate discrimination they run the risk of rendering the term too elastic, thereby detracting seriously from its utility as an analytical tool.

To take one example, Caroline Thomas has argued that in the context of the Third World, security

> does not simply refer to the military dimension, as is often assumed in Western discussions of the concept, but to the whole range of dimensions of a state's existence which are already taken care of in the more developed states . . . for example, the search for internal security of the state through nation-building, the search for secure systems of food, health, money and trade, as well as the search for security through nuclear weapons.[30]

This rather comprehensive definition of security, although valuable as a counterbalance to the traditional military-oriented definition of the term, provides a good example of how excessive open-endedness can prevent the delimitation of the concept, thereby reducing its analytical utility. Thomas's definition, although it includes explicit political issues such as nation building, also encompasses arenas of food, money, and health without providing explicit links between these arenas and political outcomes. Such conceptual elasticity, when adopted by authors less discriminating than Thomas, can be a recipe for intellectual indiscipline.

Similarly, Jessica Mathews's attempt to portray environmental decline and climate change as major sources of insecurity in the 1990s is valuable in pinpointing important challenges facing the human race as we move into the twenty-first century.[31] But this attempt confuses the issue by wrapping these problems in the security blanket. This is the danger that Daniel Deudney, an author sympathetic to environmental concerns, warned against when he argued,

> National-security-from-violence and environmental habitability have little in common. . . . The rising fashion of linking them risks creating a conceptual muddle rather than a paradigm or worldview shift—a *de-definition* rather than a *re-definition* of security. If we begin to speak about all the forces and events that threaten life, property and well-being (on a large scale) as threats to our national security, we shall soon drain them of any meaning. All large-scale evils will become threats to national security.[32]

Mathews herself demonstrates an understanding of the occasional and diffuse impact of environmental degradation on security issues and the resultingly unclear relationship between the two. She states, "Environmental decline occasionally leads directly to conflict, especially when scarce water resources must be shared. Generally, however, its impact on nations' security is felt in the downward pull on economic performance and, therefore, on political stability."[33] Greater awareness of the indirect nature of this link, and greater discrimination in the use of security rhetoric when dealing with environmental concerns, are, therefore, imperative in order to maintain the analytical usefulness of the concepts of security and of environmental degradation.

It has also become fashionable to equate security with other values some analysts consider intrinsically more important than, and morally superior to, the political-military phenomena and objectives traditionally encompassed by the concept of security. For example, Ken Booth has said that security should be equated with emancipation: "Emancipation is the freeing of people (as individuals and groups) from the physical and human constraints which stop them carrying out what they would freely choose to do. . . . Security and emancipation are two sides of the same coin. Emancipation, not power or order, produces true security. Emancipation, theoretically, is security."[34]

The problem with such semantic juggling is that it totally obfuscates the meanings of both security and emancipation. Booth's definition refuses to acknowledge that a society or group can be emancipated without being secure and vice versa. Moreover, such semantic acrobatics tend to impose on the Third World a model of contemporary Western polities as national states that have largely solved their legitimacy problem and possess representative governments that preside over socially mobile populations that are relatively homogeneous and usually affluent and free from want. This model is far removed from Third World realities. It may therefore be possible to equate emancipation with security in Western Europe (although grave reservations are in order even on that score). But it would be extremely far-fetched and intellectually disingenuous to do the same in the case of the Third World, where basic problems of state legitimacy, political order, and capital accumulation are far from being solved and may even be getting worse. In the context of the Third World—where the legitimacy of states and regimes is constantly challenged, and where demands for economic redistribution and political participation perennially outrun state capacities and create major overloads on political systems—an explicitly political definition of security provides an analytical tool of tremendous value. This tool should not be sacrificed at the altar of utopian thinking, even if Booth would prefer to call it "utopian realism."[35]

If it is to give scholars a viable analytical tool to use in grappling with the dominant concerns of Third World state elites and the major determinants of Third World state behavior, the concept of security must be defined in primarily political terms and in relation to the challenges to the survivability and effectiveness of states and regimes. Given the historical juncture at which Third World states find themselves, this means their security calculus must take into account domestic as well as external threats. Furthermore, given the comparative infancy of most Third World states, a paradigm with sufficient power to explain their security predicament must deal with what Edward Azar and Chung-in Moon called the "software" in addition to the "hardware" aspect of their security problem.[36]

Azar and Moon operationalized the concept of "security software" by breaking it down into three primary components—legitimacy, integration, and policy capacity. They attempted to classify Third World states into a number of clusters based upon the different ways the three dimensions of state security—threats (security environment), hardware (capabilities), and software—interact with one another. Their attempt to introduce software into the security calculus of Third World states is commendable. Furthermore, their operationalization of the concept primarily in terms of political variables adds to the richness of the definition of security and clearly delimits the scope of the term, which makes the concept intellectually manageable and analytically useful. Since most aspects of the software dimension of security are intertwined with the twin processes of state making and nation building in the Third World, I return to a more detailed discussion of this theme in Chapter 2.

To conclude this part of the discussion, let me reiterate that a definition of the concept of security that has adequate explanatory power in the context of the Third World must meet two criteria. First, it must go beyond the traditional Western definition of security and overcome the external orientation and military bias that are contained in the Western definition. Second, it must remain firmly rooted in the political realm while being sensitive to variables in other realms of societal activity that may have an impact on the political realm and may filter through into the security calculus of Third World states because of their potential to influence political outcomes. Armed with such a definition of security and aware of the complexities surrounding the subject, I now define the Third World and, more important, the Third World state.

Defining the Third World

First, the term *Third World*—used to describe the underdeveloped, poor, weak states of Asia, Africa, and Latin America that together make up a substantial numerical majority among the members of the international system—has by now assumed a life of its own independent of the usage of the terms *First World* and *Second World.* These two terms have become redundant in their original sense with the end of bipolarity and the Cold War. One can argue, however, that major socioeconomic and political distinctions remain between the advanced, industrialized countries of Western Europe and North America and the former communist countries of Central and Eastern Europe. These distinctive characteristics can justify the use of the terms First World and Second World to distinguish these two categories of states even today.

Just as certain social, economic, and political characteristics have come to mark the former members of the Warsaw Pact, making them distinct from the NATO countries even after the collapse of the Soviet bloc, several characteristics of Third World countries set them apart even more sharply from the industrialized countries of North America and Western Europe and from Russia and its former European satellites. These characteristics were independent of the dynamics of the Cold War and have been largely unaffected by the end of bipolarity. In fact, even during the heyday of the Cold War, states that were aligned with one bloc or the other (for example, Cuba, Vietnam, Pakistan, the Philippines) were described as Third World states, although in a strict sense they did not belong to the "Third Force," which initially gave the Third World its name. Not only were these aligned states characterized by political analysts as Third World states, but they also participated in Third World forums such as the Group of 77. Some, such as Cuba and Vietnam, were even members of the Non-Aligned Movement, which was specifically conceived in the context of Cold War rivalry in order to represent the interests of states that stood outside the great global contest conducted by the superpowers and their allies.[37]

The emphasis on shared characteristics among Third World states must not blind us to the fact that there is much diversity as well as a host of intramural conflicts among this category of states. It is clear to the most superficial observer that Afghanistan is not India, nor is Haiti Brazil.[38] In turn, however, these differences should not prevent us from attempting to discover the shared characteristics that determine the self-perceptions of the diverse peoples who belong to the Third World. The Third World is in important ways a perceptual category, albeit one that is sufficiently well-grounded in political, economic, and social realities to make it a useful analytical tool in explaining state behavior.

We should not assume, however, that any definition of the term *Third World* would give us foolproof and fixed criteria by which we can classify individual states. Given the relative lack of precision in the social sciences, which is a function of the phenomena they are supposed to describe, the concept of the Third World may suffer from a degree of inexactness and may be surrounded by controversy. This is more true when the concept is applied to cases that fall at the margins of this category, such as the East Asian newly industrialized countries (NICs), or those that are just emerging out of the turmoil generated by the disintegration of the former Soviet Union, the retrenchment of Russian power, and the accompanying upheavals in Eastern and Southeastern Europe—for example, the states of the Caucasus, Central Asia, and the Balkans. As with many other valid concepts in the social sciences that lack meticulously delineated parameters, the concept of the Third World has flexible frontiers rather than rigid boundaries. This flexibility helps the analyst use the term to encompass marginal and recent cases without losing sight of the contested nature of the concept's application to such cases.

Some scholars argue that the Third World (although now fashionably termed the South or the periphery in deference to the end of the Cold War) has become more relevant as a conceptual category in the post–Cold War era than it ever was during the days of the Cold War. The dichotomy between the developed, affluent, and powerful North and the underdeveloped, poor, and weak South is visible in even starker terms now than was true during the Cold War. This is the case because the Second World had allied itself with the Third World on several crucial issues and by its very existence had provided a certain amount of balance to the West-North in the international system, thereby giving the Third World some degree of political and economic leverage vis-à-vis the industrialized democracies. This balancing effect provided greater complexity to the international political and economic scene, thereby rendering the North-South division somewhat fuzzy. A result of the end of the Cold War, as Shahram Chubin has noted, has been that "the South is under siege—from an international community impatient to meddle in its affairs. States of the South are losing their sovereignty, which in many cases was only recently or tentatively acquired."[39]

In a parallel but distinct line of argument, James Goldgeier and

Michael McFaul wrote that the northern core and the southern periphery of the international system will not only go their different ways in managing international political and economic relations within these two categories of states, but their trajectories will further diverge with the end of the Cold War. As a result, it will be

> the tale of two worlds of international politics in the post–cold war era. In the core, economic interdependence, political democracy, and nuclear weapons lessen the security dilemma; the major powers have no pressures for expansion. The result is a relationship consistent with a liberal model of international politics. Conflicts do not disappear, but they are not resolved militarily. In the periphery, however, absolute deterrents that might induce caution do not exist. A variety of political systems ranging from democracies to monarchies coexist side by side, and interdependence between peripheral states is subordinate to dependence on core states. Pressures for expansion are still present, stemming from goals of wealth, population, and protection as well as from internal instabilities. Under these conditions . . . structural realism is inadequate to explain the behavior of states in the core but is relevant for understanding regional security systems in the periphery.[40]

In light of the continuing relevance of the term *Third World* (and its synonyms, South and periphery) we must therefore attempt to define the concept in terms of its fundamental and determining characteristics. Elbaki Hermassi provided one starting point that emphasizes the distinctiveness of the Third World in sociological terms and also portrays the major unifying themes in the Third World experience.

> Sociological analysis of the Third World ought to start with what seems to us the central and crucial problem of its regimes—namely, the stark fact that because of a conjunction of factors—conquest, colonization, domination—as well as previous development policies, Third World societies are split societies in the economic, geographic, social, and political sense. The most obvious evidence is in the separation between the privileged sectors, which are tied to the world system, and the underprivileged and marginal masses.[41]

Other perspectives can be added to this one. For example, S. D. Muni has argued the case for Third World distinctiveness from a developmental perspective.

> It is from this perspective that the Third World is distinct and separate from the other two worlds . . . for the context of development in these countries in the post–Second World War period has been conditioned by their pre-colonial evolution and colonial trauma. It is now becoming increasingly clear to many sensitive social scientists and statesmen that in terms of goals, levels, patterns and strategies, the experience of either capitalist or socialist development may not be fully applicable to Third World countries. . . . Therefore, it is on the basis of the contexts, goals, strategies and outcomes of development that the Third World is a distinct concept and a category by itself.[42]

We can add further that the Third World forms a distinctive category if we use the yardstick of power applied collectively to the postcolonial states. By the criterion of power—defined in terms of economic, technological, and military capabilities—the Third World as a whole (notwithstanding certain important but partial exceptions) appears remarkably inferior to the developed states of the North. This disparity in power and the perception of such disparity give meaning to the concept of the Third World as far as Third World leaders and their politically conscious constituencies are concerned. The disparity also explains the rationale behind collective bargaining strategies adopted by the grouping of Third World states, especially on economic and technological issues.[43]

Two fundamental factors lie at the root of the Third World character and provide much of the explanation for the split nature of Third World societies; for their distinctive developmental problems, needs, and trajectories; and for their feeling of acute vulnerability vis-à-vis the international establishment composed of the advanced, industrialized states of the global North. These are, first, the stage of state making at which Third World states currently find themselves and, second, the timing of their entry into the international system as full, formal members of the system of juridically sovereign states. Taken together, these two factors explain most of the predicaments faced by Third World states today and clarify a great deal about the behavior of Third World states domestically and internationally.

This general assertion does not mean that discrete policies adopted by individual states have no effect on the way issues of development and security are addressed by these states. It does mean, however, that these policies are largely determined by the two fundamental facts of Third World political life described earlier—their infancy as modern states and their late entry into the system of states. The success of governmental policies can be best measured by their capacity to overcome the internal and external impediments imposed by these two interrelated conditions, which greatly circumscribe Third World states' room for political and economic maneuver.

The prototypical Third World state can be seen to possess certain basic characteristics. The most important of these are lack of internal cohesion, in terms of both great economic and social disparities and major ethnic and regional fissures; lack of unconditional legitimacy of state boundaries, state institutions, and governing elites; easy susceptibility to internal and interstate conflicts; distorted and dependent development, both economically and socially; marginalization, especially in relation to the dominant international security and economic concerns; and easy permeability by external actors, be they more developed states, international institutions, or transnational corporations.

Putting these major characteristics together provides a composite, grand characterization of the Third World as weak, vulnerable, and insecure—with these traits being the function of both domestic and external factors. In the real world, individual Third World states exhibit different degrees of vulnerabilities, weaknesses, and insecurities. However, in the final analysis, when added to the developed states of Europe and North America on a security-insecurity continuum, almost all the Third World states will be found bunched close to the insecurity end, whereas the reverse will be true of the industrialized democracies.

Therefore, notwithstanding the occasional rhetoric of Third World leaders to the contrary, insecurity is the defining characteristic of Third World states—even those such as China, India, or Brazil that may boast significant amounts of hardware capability. In the absence of its software counterpart, it is extremely difficult to translate hardware capability into adequate and effective security as defined in this chapter. In the rest of the book I attempt to catalog and analyze the main sources of insecurity in the Third World and to describe as fully as possible the security predicament of the Third World state.

Notes

1. Robert Gilpin, *The Political Economy of International Relations* (Princeton: Princeton University Press, 1987): 10.

2. Immanuel Wallerstein is the leading exponent of world systems theory. For details of this theory see his three major works: *The Modern World-System: Capitalist Agriculture and the Origins of the European World Economy in the Sixteenth Century* (New York: Academic, 1974); *The Modern World-System II: Mercantilism and the Consolidation of the European World Economy, 1600–1750* (New York: Academic, 1980); and *The Modern World-System III: The Second Era of Great Expansion of the Capitalist World Economy, 1730–1840s* (New York: Academic, 1989). For a critique of world systems theory, see Aristide R. Zolberg, "Origins of the Modern World System: A Missing Link," *World Politics* 33, no. 2 (January 1981): 253–281.

3. For example, see Tom J. Farer, "The United States and the Third World: A Basis for Accommodation," *Foreign Affairs* 54, no. 1 (October 1975): 79–97.

4. The neoconservative position has been most elegantly stated in Robert W. Tucker, *The Inequality of Nations* (New York: Basic Books, 1976). For a critique of this position, see Fouad Ajami, "The Global Logic of the Neoconservatives," *World Politics* 30, no. 3 (April 1978): 450–468.

5. Stephen D. Krasner, *Structural Conflict: The Third World Against Global Liberalism* (Berkeley: University of California Press, 1985).

6. For the dependent development argument, see Peter Evans, *Dependent Development: The Alliance of Multinational, State and Local Capital in Brazil* (Princeton: Princeton University Press, 1979).

7. In Atul Kohli (ed.), *The State and Development in the Third World* (Princeton: Princeton University Press, 1986): 16.

8. For a comprehensive analysis of the Gulf crisis and war, see Ibrahim Ibrahim (ed.), *The Gulf Crisis: Background and Consequences* (Washington, D.C.: Georgetown University, Center for Contemporary Arab Studies, 1992).

9. Robert L. Rothstein, "Epitaph for a Monument to a Failed Protest? A North-South Retrospective," *International Organization* 42, no. 4 (Autumn 1988): 725–748.

10. See Mohammed Ayoob, "The Third World in the System of States: Acute Schizophrenia or Growing Pains?" *International Studies Quarterly* 33, no. 1 (March 1989): 67–79.

11. For an incisive analysis of the current disjuncture between Third World and Western perceptions of world order, see Shahram Chubin, "The South and the New World Order," *Washington Quarterly* 16, no. 4 (Autumn 1993): 87–107.

12. The point that the Third World state elites' attachment to the Westphalian formula is largely the product of their weaknesses and vulnerabilities is made convincingly in Robert H. Jackson, *Quasi-States: Sovereignty, International Relations and the Third World* (Cambridge: Cambridge University Press, 1990).

13. Ali Mazrui, "The Triple Heritage of the State in Africa," in Ali Kazancigil (ed.), *The State in Global Perspective* (Aldershot: Gower, 1986): 107.

14. Infrastructural power has been defined by Michael Mann as "the capacity of the state actually to penetrate civil society, and to implement logistically political decisions throughout the realm." Michael Mann, "The Autonomous Power of the State: Its Origins, Mechanisms and Results," in John A. Hall (ed.), *States in History* (Oxford: Basil Blackwell, 1986): 113.

15. For a discussion of unconditional legitimacy of state structures and regimes, see Mohammed Ayoob, "Security in the Third World: The Worm About to Turn?" *International Affairs* 60, no. 1 (Winter 1983–1984): 44.

16. For an elaboration on this theme, see Mohammed Ayoob, "Subnational and Transnational Actors," in Edward A. Kolodziej and Roger E. Kanet (eds.), *Coping with Conflict After the Cold War* (Baltimore: Johns Hopkins University Press, forthcoming).

17. This definition of security is adapted from the discussion in Harold K. Jacobson, *Networks of Interdependence: International Organizations and the Global Political System* (New York: Alfred A. Knopf, 1979): 148.

18. Walter Lippmann, *US Foreign Policy: Shield of the Republic* (Boston: Little, Brown, 1943): 51.

19. Arnold Wolfers, *Discord and Collaboration: Essays on International Politics* (Baltimore: Johns Hopkins University Press, 1962): 150.

20. Morton Berkowitz and P. G. Bock, "National Security," in David L. Sills (ed.), *International Encyclopedia of the Social Sciences* (New York: Macmillan, 1968): 40.

21. Martin Wight, "Western Values in International Relations," in Herbert Butterfield and Martin Wight (eds.), *Diplomatic Investigations* (London: Allen and Unwin, 1966): 103. The implications for international security of Wight's conception of international society, even in the post–Cold War era, are very interesting. Although not spelled out explicitly, some of these are clearly implied in Barry Buzan, "From International System to International Society: Structural Realism and Regime Theory Meet the English School," *International Organization* 47, no. 3 (September 1993): 327–352.

22. For a representative sample of idealist thought, see Norman Angell, *The Great Illusion*, 4th rev. and enlarged ed. (New York: Putnam's, 1913) (first published 1909).

23. For example, see Leonard Beaton, *The Reform of Power: A Proposal for an International Security System* (London: Chatto and Windus, 1972). Also see the writings of Robert Jervis, especially "Cooperation Under the Security Dilemma," *World Politics* 30, no. 2 (1978): 167–214.

24. For example, see Robert O. Keohane and Joseph S. Nye, *Power and Interdependence* (Boston: Little, Brown, 1977).

25. Martin Wight, *Systems of States* (Leicester: Leicester University Press, 1977): 152.

26. For an analysis of the relationship between analysts' perceptions of the nature of the state and their definitions of national security, see Barry Buzan, *People, States and Fear: An Agenda for International Security Studies in the Post–Cold War Era,* 2d ed. (Boulder: Lynne Rienner Publishers, 1991): 57–111.

27. For details of the Bangladesh crisis and war, see Richard Sisson and Leo E. Rose, *War and Secession: Pakistan, India and the Creation of Bangladesh* (Berkeley: University of California Press, 1990). For the Iran-Iraq War, see Shahram Chubin and Charles Tripp, *Iran and Iraq at War* (Boulder: Westview Press, 1988).

28. Israel was, and continues to be, an exception because of the intensity of U.S. commitment to its security as defined largely by Israel itself. This, in turn, is related to the fact that U.S. policy toward Israel is a domestic political issue in the United States and not merely a foreign policy concern. The special circumstances of the Korean War of the period 1950–1953 determined U.S. commitments to South Korea during the entire period of the Cold War.

29. For an earlier attempt to define security in explicitly political and state-centric terms while retaining its multifaceted character and its connections with other realms of societal activity, see Mohammed Ayoob, "The Security Problematic of the Third World," *World Politics* 43, no. 2 (January 1991): 257–283.

30. Caroline Thomas, *In Search of Security: The Third World in International Relations* (Boulder: Lynne Rienner Publishers, 1987): 1.

31. Jessica Tuchman Mathews, "The Environment and International Security," in Michael T. Klare and Daniel C. Thomas (eds.), *World Security: Trends and Challenges at Century's End* (New York: St. Martin's Press, 1991): 362–380.

32. Daniel Deudney, "The Case Against Linking Environmental Degradation and National Security," *Millennium* 19, no. 3 (Winter 1990): 465. Emphasis in the original.

33. Mathews, "Environment and International Security," 366.

34. Ken Booth, "Security and Emancipation," *Review of International Studies* 17, no. 4 (October 1991): 319.

35. Ibid., 317.

36. Edward E. Azar and Chung-in Moon, "Legitimacy, Integration and Policy Capacity: The 'Software' Side of Third World National Security," in Edward E. Azar and Chung-in Moon (eds.), *National Security in the Third World: The Management of Internal and External Threats* (College Park: Center for International Development and Conflict Management, University of Maryland, 1988): 77–101.

37. For an overview of the origins and evolution of the Non-Aligned Movement, see Peter Willetts, *The Non-Aligned Movement: The Origins of a Third World Alliance* (London: Francis Pinter, 1978).

38. One can, of course, argue similarly that the Netherlands is not Canada, nor is the Czech Republic Bulgaria.

39. Shahram Chubin, "The South and the New World Order," *Washington Quarterly* 16, no. 4 (Autumn 1993): 88.

40. James M. Goldgeier and Michael McFaul, "A Tale of Two Worlds: Core and Periphery in the Post–Cold War Era," *International Organization* 46, no. 2 (Spring 1992): 469–470.

41. Elbaki Hermassi, *The Third World Reassessed* (Berkeley: University of California Press, 1980): 172.

42. S. D. Muni, "The Third World: Concept and Controversy," *Third World Quarterly* 1, no. 3 (July 1979): 126–127.

43. For further elaboration on this theme, see Mohammed Ayoob, "The Third World in the System of States: Acute Schizophrenia or Growing Pains?" *International Studies Quarterly* 33, no. 1 (March 1989): 67–79. For a systematic account of Third World attempts from the 1950s through the early 1980s at building coalitions to bargain with the developed countries and the successes and failures of such efforts, see Robert A. Mortimer, *The Third World Coalition in International Politics,* 2d ed. (Boulder: Westview Press, 1984).

■ 2 ■

State Making and Third World Security

We cannot comprehend the complexities of the security predicament of the Third World state without understanding the process of state building underway in the Third World. I have argued elsewhere that the internal dimension of security, which is inextricably intertwined with the process of state making, is the core variable that determines the Third World state's security problematic.[1] I return to a more detailed treatment of this argument later. For the moment, it suffices to say that a solid grasp of the state-building process in the Third World is analogous to the beginning of wisdom for students and scholars of Third World security.

Keith Jaggers offered a good working definition of state building. According to him,

> Conceptually, state-building can be usefully defined as a state's ability to accumulate power. State building is the process by which the state not only grows in economic productivity and government coercion but, also, in political and institutional power. More precisely, in the power of state elites to overcome environmental, social, and political forces which stand in the way of their policy objectives. Given these requirements, I view state power to have three distinct faces: (a) power as national capabilities; (b) power as political capacity; and (c) power as institutional coherence.[2]

The last two dimensions of power in Jaggers's definition mesh well with the concept of "security software" as defined by Edward Azar and Chung-in Moon and discussed in Chapter 1 of this book.[3] We could, in fact, argue that Jaggers's definition of "power as political capacity" is synonymous with the Azar and Moon notions of legitimacy and integration and that "policy capacity" as defined by Azar and Moon is a function of Jaggers's definition of "power as institutional coherence." If we juxtapose these two analyses, it is easy to conclude that the level of security enjoyed by a state has a positive correlation with the degree of stateness achieved by that state—the latter, in turn, being a function of the state elite's relative success in the state-making enterprise.

Writing from a comparative historian's perspective, Charles Tilly provides us with a definition of state making (a term used interchangeably with state building in this book) that in many ways complements but also extends the scope of the definition provided by Jaggers. In answer to the question, "What do states do?" Tilly, drawing upon the historical experiences of state making in Western Europe, concludes that they act as the principal source of "organized violence." He elaborates by stating that

> under the general heading of organized violence, the agents of states characteristically carry on four different activities: 1. War making: Eliminating or neutralizing their own rivals outside the territories in which they have clear and continuous priority as wielders of force 2. State making: Eliminating or neutralizing their rivals inside those territories 3. Protection: Eliminating or neutralizing the enemies of their clients 4. Extraction: Acquiring the means of carrying out the first three activities—war making, state-making and protection.[4]

Both Jaggers and Tilly discern a positive relationship between war and state making, although Jaggers—after a regression analysis incorporating thirty-nine interstate and civil wars in Europe and the Americas between 1815 and 1954—qualifies this conclusion by adding that the "effects of war on the state-building process will not be universal, instead, they will vary with the nature of the war experience."[5] Tilly is more categorical in his assertion that "war makes states."[6] His sample goes back into the European past to the beginning of the making of the modern state, when war as an instrument for state making could be perceived in an undiluted form; therefore, Tilly is able to grasp the essence of the relationship between state making and war in a more dramatic fashion than is Jaggers. According to Tilly, "Major mobilizations for war provided the chief occasions on which states expanded, consolidated, and created new forms of political organizations."[7] However, Tilly also both broadened and qualified this conclusion by adding that "war making, extraction, and capital accumulation interacted to shape European state-making."[8]

Following up on the analyses provided here, we can formulate a composite definition of state making based upon the activities essential to this process. Thus defined, state making must include the following.

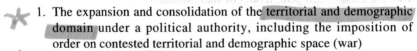

1. The expansion and consolidation of the territorial and demographic domain under a political authority, including the imposition of order on contested territorial and demographic space (war)
2. The maintenance of order in the territory where, and over the population on whom, such order has already been imposed (policing)
3. The extraction of resources from the territory and the population under the control of the state essential to support not only the war-making and policing activities undertaken by the state but also the

maintenance of apparatuses of state necessary to carry on routine administration, deepen the state's penetration of society, and serve symbolic purposes (taxation)

These three broad categories of activities depend, however, on the state's success in monopolizing and concentrating the means of coercion in its own hands within the territory and among the population it controls. That is why the accumulation of power becomes so crucial to the state-making enterprise: The more primitive the stage of state building, the more primitive and, therefore, coercive the strategies employed to accumulate and concentrate power in the hands of the agents of the state. As Youssef Cohen, Brian Brown, and A. F. K. Organski demonstrated in a seminal article published in 1981, "The extent to which an expansion of state power will generate collective violence depends on the *level* of state power prior to that expansion . . . the lower the initial level of state power, the stronger the relationship between the *rate* of state expansion and collective violence."[9]

Building States

Although state building is the quintessential political activity undertaken by all state elites in the early stage of consolidation of political authority, significant differences exist in the process that led to the emergence of Third World states compared with the same process in Western Europe, where the earliest of the modern national states—which came to be perceived as models for national states elsewhere—were established. The inherent similarity in the logic of the state-building process in terms of "primitive central state power accumulation"[10] provides us with explanations for the current replication by Third World states of several dimensions of the early European experience of state making. Simultaneously, the difference in the pace at which state building has to be undertaken in the Third World, plus the dramatically changed international environment in which Third World state making must proceed, explain the divergence in other dimensions from the earlier European model of state building. The similarities and differences are equally important, as is the bearing they have on the security predicament of the Third World state. Most of the rest of this chapter, therefore, is devoted to analyzing these similarities and differences and to evaluating their role in defining the Third World's security problematic.

When we talk about state building we are concerned with the building and consolidation of modern national states, as distinct from the traditional political entities ranging from city-states to agrarian and bureaucratic empires. This distinction has been brought out well by Anthony Giddens, who has characterized traditional premodern states as "essentially segmental in character. The administrative reach of the political center is low, such that the members of the political apparatus do not 'govern' in the modern sense. Traditional states have frontiers, not borders."[11] Modern national states, to which Giddens refers as nation-states, on the other hand, are based on "the concept of sovereignty, linked to the notion of impersonal administrative power. . . . The development of nation-states presumes the dissolution of the city/countryside relations basic to traditional states and involves the emergence of administrative orders of high intensity (associated with borders)." Furthermore, according to Giddens, "Compared with traditional states, nation-states are for the most part internally pacified, such that the monopoly of the means of violence is normally only indirectly the resource whereby those who rule sustain their 'government.'" Finally, "Nation-states only exist in systemic relations with other nation-states. . . . 'International relations' is coeval with the origins of the nation-states."[12]

Although Giddens has used the term *nation-state* to describe the modern national state, it is necessary to point out that there is a clear conceptual as well as a real-world distinction between national states and nation-states. This distinction has been highlighted by Charles Tilly, who has defined the former as "relatively centralized, differentiated, and autonomous organizations successfully claiming priority in the use of force within large, contiguous, and clearly bounded territories." Nation-states, on the other hand, are those "whose peoples share a strong linguistic, religious, and symbolic identity."[13] Nationalism, the necessary condition for the establishment of nation-states—although not of national states—has been defined by Ernest Gellner as "primarily a principle which holds that the political and the national unit should be congruent."[14]

National states that have performed successfully over a long period of time and have, therefore, knit their people together in terms of historical memories, legal codes, language, religion, and similar factors may evolve into nation-states or at least provide the necessary conditions for the emergence of nation-states, but they are not synonymous with nation-states. Furthermore, historically, national states predate the emergence of nation-states; they are the products of the state-making enterprise rather than of nationalism or nation building. This is the reality to which Gellner referred when he pointed out that "nationalism emerges only in milieux in which the existence of the state is already very much taken for granted. The existence of politically centralized units, and of a moral political climate in which such centralized units are taken for granted and are treated as normative, is a necessary though not sufficient condition of nationalism."[15]

Historical evidence has convincingly demonstrated that in almost all cases in Europe, with the exception of the Balkans (an exception that may provide the clue to the current violence and strife in that region), the emergence of the modern national state was the precondition for the formation

Ship To:

Emily Gosselin
2824 MENLO AVE
LOS ANGELES, CA 900072220

Ship From:

TEXTBOOKSNOW-AMAZON
8950 W PALMER ST
RIVER GROVE, IL 60171

Return Information (cut and attach to the outside of return shipment)

TEXTBOOKSNOW-AMAZON
8950 W PALMER ST
RIVER GROVE, IL 60171
(Attn: Returns)

Order #: 058-6809214-8051535

DW44125

Date: 01/15/2009

Order #: 058-6809214-8051535

SKU	Qty	Condition	Title	Price	Total
2823326U	1	Used	Third World Security Predicament 9781555875763	$ 14.96	$ 14.96

Sub Total	$	14.96
Shipping & Handling	$	3.99
Tax	$	0.00
Total	**$**	**18.95**

Order #: 058-6809214-8051535

Refunds: All items must be returned within 30 days of receipt. · Pack your book securely, so it will arrive back to us in its original condition. To avoid delays, please use the return section and label provided with your original packing slip to identify your return. Be sure to include a return reason. · For your protection, we suggest using a traceable, insured shipping service (UPS or Insured Parcel Post). We are not responsible for lost or damaged returns. · Item(s) returned must be received in the original condition as sold and including all additional materials such as CDs, workbooks, etc. · We will initiate a refund of your purchase price including applicable taxes within 5 business days of receipt. Shipping charges will not be refunded unless we have committed an error with your order. · If there is an error with your order or the item is not received in the condition as purchased, please contact us immediately for return assistance.

Reason for Refund/Return:
Condition Incorrect Item Received Incorrect Item Ordered Dropped Class Purchased Elsewhere Other

Contact Us: For customer service, email us at customerservice@textbooksNow.com.

of the nation. The earliest modern states of Europe became states before they became nations. Even in the case of latecomers such as Germany and Italy, core states (Brandenburg-Prussia and Piedmont-Savoy, respectively) preceded the creation of the German and Italian nations (although not necessarily of an embryonic national consciousness among the German and Italian cultural and literary elites) and took the lead, principally by force of arms, in the unification of Germany and Italy into national states. That these states were still some distance away from being nation-states was embodied in Massimo d'Azeglio's famous remark at the first sitting of the Italian parliament: "We have made Italy, now we have to make Italians."[16]

The essential similarity between the German and Italian experiences on the one hand and the French and English experiences on the other has been summed up well by Cornelia Navari:

> When Hegel insisted that it was the state that created the nation, he was looking backwards to the history of France, not forward to the history of Germany. When Germany was unified "from above" in 1870 and the Reich was formed, this way of proceeding did not appear to most Germans to be at variance with the experience of their Western neighbors—a substitution of Union "by force" for the "organic growth" of France and England. It appeared to be a repetition of it, differing only in that it was less bloody. Here, as there, the state was moving outwards into diverse feudal remnants of the old order, dissolving them, making all obedient to the same law.[17]

Liah Greenfeld's impressive research on the evolution and growth of nationalism in England, France, Russia, Germany, and the United States, although undertaken on the assumption that "historically, the emergence of nationalism predated the development of every significant component of modernization," ends up corroborating the chronological order of the national state preceding the nation-state.[18] It does so by placing the emergence of nationalism—the precursor of the idea of the nation-state—in the eighteenth and nineteenth centuries, well after the idea of the national (in the sense of sovereign, differentiated, modern) state had become established in much of Europe and certainly in Western Europe.

Her only exception to this dating is England, where she traces the idea of nationalism back to the sixteenth century. This can be explained by the earlier evolution of the national state and of the concept of popular sovereignty in England. However, we should clearly bear in mind the distinction between English nationalism and the idea of the British nation-state. Whereas English nationalism may have been at the core of the creation of the British national state, it simultaneously fueled feelings of minority ethnonationalisms in other parts of Britain—that is, in Scotland and Wales—a problem that to this day has prevented the emergence of a clear British, as distinct from English, national identity.

According to Greenfeld, in contrast to the "civic" nationalism of

England, which greatly influenced the development of the U.S. idea of nationalism,

> particularistic nationalism reflecting. . . the meaning of the "nation" as a "people" extolled as the bearer of sovereignty . . . and its fusion with geo-political and/or ethnic characteristics of particular populations did not emerge until the eighteenth century. . . . Collectivistic nationalism appeared first, and almost simultaneously, in France and Russia, then, close to the end of the eighteenth century and in the beginning of the nineteenth, in German principalities. While France, from many points of view, represented an ambivalent case (its nationalism was collectivistic and yet civic), Russia and Germany developed clear examples of ethnic nationalism.[19]

The chronological sequence in the Third World as it relates to the establishment of the national state and the evolution of nationalism bears very close resemblance to that of early modern Europe, with the state taking clear historical precedence over the nation. As Anthony Smith has put it very succinctly, "The Western model is essentially a 'state system' rather than a 'nation system'; and this has been its fateful legacy to Africa and Asia." Smith goes on to point out that despite the differences in geopolitical and cultural terms between Europe and the Third World, "The central point . . . of the Western experience for contemporary African and Asian social and political change has been the primacy and dominance of the specialized, territorially defined and coercively monopolistic state, operating within a broader system of similar states bent on fulfilling their dual functions of internal regulation and external defense (or aggression)."[20]

The centrality of this experience and its impact on Third World political formations explain the fact that although leaders of many Third World states today speak in the idioms of nationalism and of nation-states, they are primarily committed to, as well as engaged in, the construction of national states along the lines of the states of Western Europe of the seventeenth to the nineteenth centuries. It further explains the priority given by state elites in the Third World to the primitive accumulation of power in the hands of the state over the creation of popular consensus about the content and parameters of nationalism in fragmented societies. As the European experience has demonstrated, creation of a popular consensus can be both a long process and one that could initially exacerbate divisions in horizontally and vertically divided societies; state makers in a hurry have neither the time, the patience, nor the inclination to sort out the complexities of the process and to wait for its culmination.

However, to assuage their own and, more important, others' late-twentieth-century consciences, they tend to couch their (often coercive) strategies of state building in the rhetoric of nation building. In other words, they justify state making in the guise of the imposition of national consciousness from above, by persuasion if possible and by force if necessary. This justification creates not only semantic but also conceptual confusion by artificially conflating two distinct processes that may sometimes run parallel to each other and may even interact with one another fairly intensely but that have their own separate dynamics and discrete end products, even though in the ideal type the end products merge into a composite creature called the nation-state.

Third World Options Outside the System of States

One possible criticism of my propensity to emphasize the centrality of state making in the political life of Third World states must be addressed before I proceed. This is the fashionable criticism made by certain segments of the intellectual elites in the Third World that this approach is based on the false and deterministic premise that political developments in the Third World must take the same course as those in the developed societies of Western Europe and North America. The criticism is misplaced for two reasons.

First, the rhetoric as well as the policies of Third World governments make it clear that the model they emulate is the developed world. Second, there are certain systemic compulsions for even moderately effective participation in the modern system of states that no member of that system can afford to deny, except at great cost to itself. Among them, the most fundamental compulsion is that of adequate stateness, defined as demonstrated centralized control over territory and population, monopoly over the means of violence within the state's boundaries, and the capacity to significantly permeate the society encompassed by the state. Without the demonstration of adequate stateness, the participation of Third World states in the international system will remain heavily qualified and will occur at the sufferance of the established members of the system.

The option of changing the international system in such a way as to eliminate the centrality of the state and, therefore, of stateness is not viable for the Third World for a number of reasons. These reasons include the Third World political elites' genuine commitment to the maintenance of the state system because, among other things, it gives these elites and the states they rule a greater degree of autonomy from external pressures than any alternative mode of global political organization would provide. As Ali Kazancigil has written, "The Third World state is a crucial factor in the dialectic of dependence and autonomy in which it is simultaneously and to changing degrees a relay in the dependence-domination process, as well as a space within which the objectives of freedom and sovereignty can possibly be achieved."[21] Even if this commitment were to change, bringing about such a radical transformation of the world political system would require capabilities far beyond the collective capacity of the Third World.

Theoretically, Third World countries are free to not adopt the same route as that of the West, to strike out on their own different path or paths, and, as a drastic last resort, even to opt out of the system of states altogether. But if they decide to adopt any of these strategies, they cannot complain that they are relegated to secondary status in the system or are completely left out of consideration. As long as effective participation in the system of states remains the goal for these countries as articulated by their political elites, including those elements of these elites that seem to be consciously searching for alternatives to the present international order,[22] the acquisition of adequate stateness will be demanded of them and will remain a precondition for their effective participation in the international system.

Time and State Building

Having demonstrated the centrality of state building to the political life of Third World states and hinted at the similarities to and differences from the early European experience in state making, I now establish specific links between the process of state building and the security problems facing Third World states. These connections can be established with little difficulty if we scrutinize the roots of insecurity within Third World states. These roots include the lack of unconditional legitimacy for state boundaries, state institutions, and regimes; inadequate societal cohesion; and the absence of societal consensus on fundamental issues of social, economic, and political organization. These problems typically arise during the early stages of state building, when state makers attempt to impose order, monopolize instruments of violence, and demand the exclusive loyalties of their populations.

European state makers had to overcome these same problems in their efforts to extract resources, build institutions, acquire political legitimacy, and deepen and broaden the state's penetration of society—that is, to make their states' existence secure territorially and institutionally. This process was painfully slow and extraordinarily violent. As Tilly observed:

> The building of states in Western Europe cost tremendously in death, suffering, loss of rights, and unwilling surrender of land, goods, or labor. . . . The fundamental reason for the high cost of European state-building was its beginning in the midst of a decentralized, largely peasant social structure. Building differentiated, autonomous, centralized organizations with effective control of territories entailed eliminating or subordinating thousands of semiautonomous authorities. . . . Most of the European population resisted each phase of the creation of strong states.[23]

Tilly's description of conditions in Europe at the birth of national states has an uncanny resemblance to present conditions in many Third World societies. This helps to explain why, if we arrange the current state-building strategies in the Third World on a continuum ranging from coercion to persuasion, even states such as India that fall relatively close to the persuasion end are forced to rely on significant amounts of coercion—as witnessed in Punjab, Kashmir, and the Northeastern region—to consolidate the authority of the state in regions in which it has faced major challenges.

To replicate the process by which modern national states are created, Third World state makers need two things above all—lots of time and a relatively free hand to persuade and coerce the disparate populations under their nominal rule to accept the legitimacy of state boundaries and institutions, to accept the right of the state to extract resources from them, and to let the state regulate important aspects of their lives. Unfortunately for Third World state elites, neither of these two commodities is available in adequate measure.

My point regarding the availability of time becomes clear if we take a closer look at the amount of time it took for the states of Western Europe to emerge as full-fledged national states enjoying the habitual obedience of their populations, secure in the legitimacy of their borders and institutions (although borders were never entirely free from challenge), and, therefore, positioned to respond to societal demands since those demands no longer ran counter to the accumulation of power in the hands of the state. It was not until the beginning of the twentieth century that the states of West Europe and their offshoots in North America emerged as the responsive and representative national states of today—the end products of the state-making process of at least four hundred years' duration. It is instructive to note that Joseph Strayer traced the origins of the modern European state to the Investiture Conflict of the last quarter of the eleventh century. However, he has argued that even two hundred years later the existence of the European state was still very tentative. According to Strayer, "While the sovereign state of 1300 was stronger than any competing political form, it was still not very strong. . . . It took four to five centuries for European states to overcome their weaknesses, to remedy their administrative deficiencies, and to bring lukewarm loyalty up to the white heat of nationalism."[24]

Charles Tilly has located the appearance of the modern national state as the preeminent political form in Europe in the early part of the sixteenth century—"after 1500" is the phrase he uses. He criticized Strayer's test for determining whether a political entity is a state in the modern sense as "relatively soft." According to Tilly, between 1300 and 1500 several alternative routes—including theocratic federation, empire, perpetuation of feudalism—if taken by political entities in Europe, would have precluded the emergence of the national state or would have made the picture extremely mixed. It was only after 1500, Tilly argued, that the national state "won out . . . [as a result of] territorial consolidation, centralization, differentiation of the instruments of government from other sorts of organization, and monopolization (plus concentration) of the means of coercion."[25] But, according to Tilly, even in the seventeenth and eighteenth centuries "both the primacy and the ultimate form of the state were much in doubt. . . . As seen from 1600 or so, the development of the state was very contingent; many aspiring states crumpled and fell along the way."[26]

Whether one accepts Strayer's chronology or Tilly's argument regarding the evolution of modern states in Europe, one thing is clear: The national state in Europe as we know it today had a long and painful gestation period that took anywhere from four (Tilly) to seven (Strayer) centuries to reach its culminating stage. Unfortunately for Third World state makers, their states cannot afford the luxury of prolonging the traumatic and costly experience of state making over hundreds of years, as was done in Western Europe. The demands of competition with established modern states and the demonstrated effectiveness of socially cohesive, politically responsive, and administratively effective states in the industrialized world make it almost obligatory for Third World states to reach their goal within the shortest time possible or risk international ridicule and permanent marginalization within the system of states. The pioneers of European state making (although not the latecomers such as Germany and Italy) were remarkably free from such systemic pressures and demonstration effects because all the leading contenders for statehood—England, France, Spain, Holland—were essentially in the same boat trying to navigate the same uncharted sea.

As a result, the early modern states of Europe had adequate time at their disposal to complete the process of state making and to do so in three phases:

1. The establishment of the centralized, "absolutist" state at the expense of a feudal order that had begun to lose much of its economic and political utility.[27]
2. The merging of the subjects of the centralized monarchy into a people with a common history, legal system, language, and often religion (in the sense of Christian schisms), thus leading to the evolution of a national identity and the transformation of the centralized monarchical state into a nation-state.
3. The gradual extension of representative institutions (dictated by the need to co-opt into the power structure new and powerful social forces that emerged as a result of the industrial revolution) over the decades, if not centuries. Above all, as Stein Rokkan has pointed out, "What is important is that the Western nation-states were given a chance to solve some of the worst problems of state-building before they had to face the ordeals of mass politics."[28]

When European states did not have this chance and had to telescope some of these sequential phases into each other, they suffered from a "cumulation of crises."[29] This condition applied particularly to the important states of Germany and Italy, which emerged as unified national states only in the closing decades of the nineteenth century and were immediately faced with the pressures of mass politics. In fact, it can be argued that the emergence of Italian fascism and German nazism was a result of the Italian and German state elites' inability in the first two decades of the twentieth century to successfully respond, in a context of mass politics, to the accumulated crises threatening their respective states.[30]

If this could be the case, especially with Germany, which was centered upon Prussia—a strong state with a very respectable record of state building that contained about two-thirds of the population of the German Reich and more than two-thirds of its industrial resources—we can well imagine the enormity of the challenge faced by the postcolonial states of the Third World. The problem for those states has been compounded by the fact that they are under pressure to demonstrate adequate stateness quickly and to perform the task of state making in a humane, civilized, and consensual fashion—all in an era of mass politics. The inadequacy of the time element and the fact that several sequential phases involved in the state-making process have had to be collapsed or telescoped together into one mammoth state-building enterprise go a long way in explaining the security predicament of the Third World state. Furthermore, the demand for humane treatment of subject populations during the early stages of state building has made that task enormously difficult and complicated in the Third World. This is a theme to which I return later.

At this point it is worth reflecting upon Charles Tilly's conclusions about the findings of his major edited work, *The Formation of National States in Western Europe,* to dispel the notion that European state making was a well-thought-out idea that was implemented by successive generations of state makers according to a preconceived plan.

> Our study of the European experience suggests that most of the transformations European states accomplished until late in their histories were by-products of the consolidation of central control. . . . For the most part, that experience does not show us modernizing elites articulating the demands and needs of the masses, and fighting off traditional holders of power in order to meet those needs and demands. Far from it. We discover a world in which small groups of power-hungry men fought off numerous rivals and great popular resistance in pursuit of their own ends, and inadvertently promoted the formation of national states and widespread popular involvement in them.[31]

This conclusion, based on the evidence provided by some of the foremost historians of state making in Europe, demonstrates that state making and its corollary, nation building, especially among the earliest European national states such as England and France, were not the result of a deliberate scheme that had to be implemented within a certain period of time in order to reach a certain set of predetermined objectives. The earliest national states were the products of a long period of uncoordinated, although often simultaneous, political acts undertaken by princes and statesmen in different parts of Western Europe. This development also happened to coincide and interact with important social and economic factors, such as changes in the mode of production, and the consequent emergence of powerful new social forces and economic and political interest groups.

Difficulties of Imposing Deadlines

The Third World is attempting to replicate this largely unpremeditated and uncoordinated evolutionary process but on a ridiculously short timetable and with a predetermined set of goals. The existence of a model to emulate, and the pressures generated by international and domestic elites' demands that postcolonial states translate their juridical statehood into effective statehood within the shortest possible time, make the task of state makers in the Third World so difficult as to border on the impossible.[32] Fitting an evolutionary historical process into a series of deadlines is a difficult and dangerous exercise. It distorts the process of natural evolution and raises hopes for and fears of the final goal, thereby increasing the load on affected political systems to such a degree that they are threatened with serious disequilibrium.

This disequilibrium lies at the root of the chronic political instability that we witness in most Third World states today. Instability, in turn, engenders violence and insecurity, as state-making strategies adopted by state elites to broaden and deepen the reach of the state clash with the interests of counterelites and segments of the population that perceive the extension of state authority as posing a direct danger to their social, economic, or political interests. Given adequate time, these conflicts of interest could be overcome peacefully through prolonged negotiations. Alternatively, the state could adopt a strategy of piecemeal incorporation and could overcome opposition gradually by dividing its opponents, eroding their support base, and neutralizing different segments of the opposition one at a time—even if this meant using force against them. When spread over a period of time and essentially localized regionally and socially, state-induced violence and counterviolence could give the appearance of a succession of manageable crises in the drawn-out process of state building.

However, given the short amount of time at the disposal of state makers in the Third World and the consequent acceleration in their state-making efforts, crises erupt simultaneously, become unmanageable as they overload the political and military capabilities of the state, and lead to a cumulation of crises that further erodes the legitimacy of the fragile postcolonial state. Furthermore, international norms that do not permit states established by the process of decolonization to alienate their juridical sovereignty can require even the least viable states—whether they be Lebanon, Liberia, or Somalia—to maintain the fiction of sovereign status. By denying unviable states an honorable exit, these norms turn their existential dilemma into a security predicament. This is a theme to which I return in Chapters 4 and 8.

The comparison with the West European experience in terms of the length of time available to state makers and the possibility for unviable states to leave the system by absorption or disintegration helps highlight the fact that the lack of adequate time to sequentially complete the phases of state making and nation building and the impossibility of alienating juridical statehood explain the high levels of insecurity and violence in the Third World. In this chapter I am principally concerned with the dimension of time, and I return in a later chapter to the issue of international norms and their role in the exacerbation of the Third World states' security problems.

The Latin American case appears superficially to be somewhat different from that of the rest of the Third World, because the former colonies of Spain and Portugal in South America acquired political independence during the first half of the nineteenth century. This gave them a lead of more than a century over the colonies of Asia and Africa. However, for a host of reasons—the main one being the importation of the economic and political cultures of preindustrial Iberia and Iberian settlers who formed the majority of the elites in the former Spanish and Portuguese colonies—Latin American political development, including its traditions of state making and nation building, remained fossilized well into the twentieth century. The era of industrial society (in terms of its demonstration effect rather than its realization), with its model of a socially mobile population encompassed within a strong state structure presided over by a representative government, caught up with Latin America around the same time it did with much of Asia, if not Africa. Although the intervening century may have given major Latin American states the time to consolidate and legitimate state boundaries, their preindustrial social structures retarded other aspects of state making, above all those of societal penetration and societal cohesion.

There is also the notion that in Latin America the discontinuities introduced by colonial rule were even more severe than elsewhere, because they included the implantation by force of arms of alien European populations and an alien religion on a scale not witnessed in any other part of the Third World, with the partial exception of South Africa. Furthermore, the importation of slave labor from Africa into parts of South America, especially Brazil, and the Caribbean, introduced additional racial-cum-social fissures into a continent already sharply divided among the natives, the mestizos (people of mixed European and native Indian ancestry), and the descendants of European settlers. Thus the relatively early acquisition of political independence gave Latin American states only a marginal advantage over their Asian and African counterparts in terms of accomplishing the twin tasks of state making and nation building and, therefore, of mitigating, if not solving, their security predicament. In any event, a Latin American lead over Asia and Africa of a little over a century was not much in relation to the length of time it took for European states to complete their process of state making.[33]

Distortions of Colonialism

As the Latin American case demonstrates, Third World attempts at rapid state making have been made immeasurably more difficult, and the security predicament of the postcolonial state has been made more acute, by the distortions introduced by colonialism into the process of state formation. The colonial experience did provide many Third World countries with proto-states that could be used as jumping-off points for the creation of a post-colonial political order. Further, without the colonial interlude non-European elites might not have become familiar with the notion of the modern national state to the extent that they are now; nor would these states have been integrated so easily into the system of states that expanded out of its original European home.

However, the discontinuities introduced by the colonial process were equally, if not more, important to the future political evolution of Third World countries and peoples and to the generation of challenges to the security of their states and regimes. The first of these discontinuities was the creation of colonial administrative units by the imperial powers in near-total disregard for the populations' precolonial affinities and loyalties. Political boundaries drawn for purposes of administrative convenience or as a result of territorial trade-offs among imperial powers arbitrarily cut across ethnic, tribal, religious, and linguistic ties; dismembered established political units; and linked more than one precolonial political entity in uneasy administrative unions. Africa is the outstanding example of the arbitrary carving up of an entire continent by the European powers. As Robert Jackson pointed out, "The political map of Africa is devoid by and large of indigenous determination in its origins. All but a very few traditional political systems were subordinated or submerged by the colonialists. Decolonization rarely resulted in their elevation. . . . Political Africa is an intrinsically imperial cum international construct."[34] Asia and the Middle East were also not immune to such arbitrariness. In fact, the arbitrary division of the Arab portions of the Ottoman Empire after World War I and their assignment to Britain and France ranks on par with the partition of Africa in the closing decades of the nineteenth century.[35]

As a result of such cavalier construction of colonial borders, imperial powers bequeathed to their postcolonial successor regimes territorial entities that were composed of distinct and sometimes hostile ethnic groups or that divided previously homogeneous ethnic communities into two or more states. Most new Third World states, therefore, found themselves facing challenges of either a secessionist or an irredentist character soon after emerging into independent statehood. In some cases, postcolonial states got the worst of both worlds when they were left simultaneously facing problems created by both these predilections of their former masters.

Colonial rule also delayed the transformation of several major colonies from backward to modern economies through what should have been natural processes of economic development. Such rule thus stunted the growth of the social classes—especially the commercial and industrial bourgeoisie—whose commitment to a centralized, effective state had made a major difference between success and failure in the state-building process in Europe. Colonial rule derailed the evolutionary process of economic development in many colonial societies by introducing major discontinuities in the economic sphere in order to extract maximum benefit from the resources of those societies for the metropolitan economies and to turn them into captive markets for metropolitan manufactured products. Colonial rule disrupted or destroyed flourishing agricultural economies by switching them from food to cash crops meant for export. It also decimated traditional handicraft industries. This latter process has been termed the deindustrialization of colonial economies "in the sense that the proportion of national income generated by, and the percentage of population dependent on, industry of various kinds declined."[36]

Colonial policies also decimated the class of large-scale native traders and financiers that had dominated the monetized sector of the more sophisticated precolonial economies such as that of India. In other words, colonial rule led to the fossilization, indeed, the retardation, of the colonies' economic structures, because "commercialization [was] forced on many third world countries by using non-market coercion, and . . . the process of commercialization has often resulted in an economic structure which has acted as a brake on economic development; further, the process of commercialization generally led to the removal of surpluses from third world countries. . . . There was in fact a massive net transfer of surplus from the third world countries to the metropolitan heartland."[37]

Another major distortion introduced by colonial rule came about because of the colonial powers' proclivity to use multiple "traditional" structures of authority in the colonies as instruments of rule that mediated between the colonial power and the colonized populace. This strategy was used primarily by the British in Nigeria, India, Malaya, and elsewhere to employ traditional wielders of authority as conduits for the exercise of colonial power. This colonial policy not only checked but even reversed the normal process of political development in most colonial territories by establishing major impediments to the creation of modern authority structures based on rational principles of legitimacy. Both the Nigerian and Malaysian states must still compete with these traditional authority structures for the loyalty of their populations; the Indian attempt at state building was severely hampered in its early days by disputes revolving around the fate of so-called native rulers in key princely states such as Hyderabad and Kashmir. As Ali Mazrui noted, this form of indirect rule, especially in the African colonies, "aggravated the problems of creating a modern nation-state after independence. The different groups in the country maintained their separate ethnic identities by being ruled in part through their own native institutions . . . different sections of the population perceived each other as strangers, sometimes as aliens, increasingly as rivals, and ominously as potential enemies."[38]

This was, however, only part of the story. Many of these so-called traditional authority structures that were used to mediate between the colonizer and the colonized were themselves the products of colonial rule, either through the revival and augmentation of precolonial political institutions that often had lost their authority and fallen into near disuse or through the creation of what were essentially new institutions that were given traditional nomenclatures to provide them with a semblance of traditional legitimacy.[39] Furthermore, new ethnic solidarities were formed during colonial rule largely as a result of the workings of the colonial process, which introduced new definitions of communal identity. These solidarities were determined by various factors, including migration from rural to urban areas, links between Western education and upward social mobility, a change from subsistence farming to cash-crop production, and increasing concentration of populations around areas of labor-intensive extractive and manufacturing enterprises. These new ethnic solidarities were also crucially influenced by the piecemeal introduction of representative government based on colonially devised formulas of communal representation that tended to consolidate tribal, religious, and linguistic solidarities and to sharpen ethnic divisions.

This situation has been particularly true in the case of Africa where, as Jeffrey Herbst has written,

> in many cases, what are today viewed as long-standing tribal differences only became apparent just before and after an independent African nation was created, at which time it suddenly became necessary for groups to organize on a broader basis in order to gain enough of a political presence to pressure for resources being allocated in the newly created capital city. The Ibo, for example, did not mobilize as Ibo until they were grouped together with others within

> the political framework of a colony and were suddenly faced with the prospect of losing out in all types of allocation decisions in a distant capital unless they organized as a distinct group. Certainly, it can be argued that in some cases in which there were preexisting loyalties, the establishment of European frontiers divided a coherent group. However, in most cases (such as that of the Ibo), it was the creation of well-defined national boundaries that forged ties among competing ethnic groups.[40]

Even in India, where religious-communal identities (but not antagonisms) at the local level had crystallized before the advent of the British Raj, it was during the colonial period that these identities were augmented, consolidated, and pitted against each other—often as a result of a deliberate colonial policy of "divide and rule"—at the "national" level, finally leading to the partition of the country in 1947.[41]

Modernization as a Destabilizer

The process of modernization—including urbanization, literacy, industrialization, internal migration, and similar factors—which continued and in many cases accelerated after decolonization, augmented the destabilizing consequences of the colonial legacy of politicized ethnic and communal identities. This, as Robert Melson and Howard Wolpe have pointed out, is characteristic of the early phase of modernization, which "far from destroying communalism, in time both reinforces communal conflict and creates the conditions for the formation of entirely new communal groups."[42] Ernest Gellner has similarly argued,

> In its early stages, industrial society . . . engenders very sharp and painful and conspicuous inequality, all the more painful because [it is] accompanied by great disturbance, and because those less advantageously placed, in that period, tend to be not only relatively, but also absolutely miserable. In that situation—egalitarian expectation, non-egalitarian reality, misery, and cultural homogeneity already desired but not yet implemented—latent political tension is acute, and becomes actual if it can seize on good symbols, good diacritical marks to separate ruler and ruled, privileged and underprivileged.[43]

The conclusion that early stages of modernization heighten ethnic and communal tensions has been corroborated by, among others, Susanne Rudolph and Lloyd Rudolph, who have drawn upon the case of communal conflict between Hindus and Muslims in India. While analyzing the Hindu fanatics' successful attempt in December 1992 at tearing down a 450-year-old mosque in Ayodhya, the Rudolphs have argued that the most enthusiastic participants in the attack on the mosque came from urban, lower-middle-class families. According to the Rudolphs, "They are the educated unemployed, not the poor and illiterate. Frustrated by the lack of good jobs and opportunities, they are victims of modernization, seeking to victimize others. . . . In an India where, despite its problems, the numbers of persons under the poverty line has been declining and entrepreneurship expanding exponentially, their expectations have run well ahead of available opportunities." The Rudolphs concluded, "Which identities become relevant for politics is not predetermined by some primordial ancientness. . . . The hatred is modern, and may be closer than we think."[44]

The aggravation of ethnic and communal fissures by the coupling of the colonial inheritance and the process of modernization, which themselves have rewarded different ethnic and communal groups unevenly, has led in several cases to the outbreak of separatist insurgencies demanding secession from the postcolonial state. This situation poses the ultimate internal security threat to the structures of a number of Third World states. It should be pointed out that the character of many Third World states encourages ethnic separatism. Most separatist movements arise from the fact that whereas Third World societies are overwhelmingly multiethnic in their composition, many Third World state elites deny this reality and attempt to construct monoethnic states (in terms of control of power structures and allocation of resources) that are dominated by a single ethno-linguistic or ethno-religious group—for example, the Sinhalese in Sri Lanka, the Thais in Thailand, the Burmans in Myanmar, and the Turks in Turkey.

This situation has led Myron Weiner to conclude, "Hegemonic rather than accommodative ethnic politics characterize the new states. In country after country, a single ethnic group has taken control over the state and used its powers to exercise control over others. . . . In retrospect, there has been far less 'nation-building' than many analysts had expected or hoped, for the process of state-building has rendered many ethnic groups devoid of power and influence."[45] As a result of the gross inequalities in the sharing of political and economic power within most multiethnic states—inequalities that are frequently perpetuated by deliberate state policy—ethnicity invariably becomes politicized, which frequently poses serious threats to the security of Third World states.[46]

This conclusion is borne out by Ted Gurr's recent study on minorities at risk for the United States Institute of Peace. Gurr defined minorities at risk as those groups that "have suffered from economic or political discrimination or were alienated enough from the state to seek greater autonomy." According to his study, "Seventy-three of the 98 largest Third World countries have one or more significant minorities at risk; . . . in 14, more than half the population is at risk." Furthermore, Gurr estimated that "more than 60 percent (108 of 179) of the Third World minorities . . . took some kind of violent political action against authorities between 1945 and 1989. Forty-five of them supported serious insurgencies."[47]

As these figures demonstrate, attempts at secession—that is, separation from, or the breakup of, an established state—in the Third World, although rarely successful for a number of reasons I discuss later in the book, pose continuing threats to the legitimacy of state boundaries, state institutions, and political regimes in many postcolonial societies. According to the data compiled for 1990 by the Stockholm International Peace Research Institute (SIPRI), of the thirty-one major armed conflicts—almost all of them in the Third World—during that year, only one was of an interstate character. The rest were divided almost equally between conflicts to control government (where the legitimacy of regimes was challenged) and state-formation conflicts (where the legitimacy of existing states was challenged, meaning where secession was the goal).[48] These figures demonstrate both the great importance of the internal dimension of security in the security problematic of the Third World and the considerable role played by secessionist conflicts within the internal security arena in the Third World.[49]

Popular Demands Complicate State Making

The problems of state making and of state and regime security in the Third World are further complicated by two other factors now at work in the developing countries that were either absent or very weak during the analogous stage of state making in Western Europe. These factors are the demand for political participation by increasing numbers of politically mobilized people, who account for a substantial proportion of the population, and the demand for a more equal distribution of the economic cake, again by substantial segments of the general public.

Claims for political participation and social and economic justice complicate the task of Third World state makers by tremendously increasing the demands upon them and upon the states they are trying to build. This contrasts with the situation of early state makers in Europe, who could single-mindedly pursue their goals of accumulating power and extracting resources without being distracted by demands for economic redistribution and political participation, except by small segments of the privileged strata of society. As Charles Tilly has pointed out, "The European state-makers constructed, then imposed, strong national governments before mass politics began. In new states, these two processes tend to occur together. That is the 'cumulation of crises' already anticipated by the experiences of Germany and Italy."[50] Despite the apparently easier task the European state makers had in crafting their states, Tilly noted that in every instance this task was attended by "immense conflict, uncertainty and failure" and involved great pain and cost in both human and material terms.[51]

In short, state making in Europe, particularly during its early crucial stages, was not an enterprise conducted by political liberals or by advocates of the welfare state. But in the later twentieth century, the model of an ideal democratic welfare state that all states must try to achieve, coupled with the communications revolution, which makes Third World populations aware of both their human and political rights, makes the task of Third World state makers immensely difficult. Satisfying popular demands can frequently run counter to the imperatives of state making, because state making, as the European experience has demonstrated, is a rather unsavory task and often involves levels of coercion that are bound to be unacceptable to populations that have been influenced by notions of human rights (for both groups and individuals), political participation, and social justice. I return to this theme in Chapter 8.

The demand for political participation also raises the fundamental issue of regime legitimacy in the Third World. It is no wonder that, as the SIPRI data for 1990 demonstrated, there are as many conflicts in the Third World over challenges to the legitimacy of regimes and demands for regime change as there are over demands for state breaking and state making. Since many, if not most, regimes in the Third World are narrowly based and authoritarian in character, and even those that are representative in the formal sense of the term are only quasi-democratic in the way they function, they are often perceived as less than legitimate by sizable segments of their populations—partly because people use the Western yardstick of political legitimacy to measure the functioning and performance of their own states.

The reality regarding political legitimacy in the Third World is, however, starkly different. Political legitimacy has been aptly described by Charles Anderson as a "characteristic of a society which enables men to disagree vigorously over the policies that government should pursue or the personnel that should occupy the decision-making posts, yet to support common notions of the locus of decision-making authority, the technique by which decisions are to be made, and the means by which rulers are to be empowered."[52] Since the last three factors, which are so essential for underwriting the legitimacy of political systems and regimes—namely, societal consensus on the locus of decisionmaking authority, on the technique by which decisions are to be made, and on the means by which rulers are to be empowered—are conspicuously absent in many parts of the Third World, electoral contests are often perceived as the continuation of ethnic, communal, class, or personal strife by other means. This situation explains the fragility of democratic experiments in much of the Third World. It also explains the ever-present fear that "democratic waves" may be followed by social, economic, and political chaos and may be summarily reversed by military strongmen acting either in their own interests or in collusion with powerful social, economic, and ethnic groups that feel their interests are threatened by the rhetoric or policies of elected governments. Examples of such reversals can be seen from Haiti to Burundi. Even in a relatively well-established Third World democracy such as India, representative institutions and liberal-constitutionalist principles of governance are being powerfully challenged and increasingly threatened by groups that can only be characterized as neofascist in character.[53]

If the Indian case demonstrates the erosion and decay of established political institutions that for four decades had performed the crucial function of peacefully arbitrating conflicting societal interests, the majority of African and Middle Eastern countries demonstrate the failure on the part of their state elites to establish such institutions in the first place. This failure has been both the cause and the consequence of the legitimacy crisis they face today. Most regimes in Africa and the Middle East do not meet the test of political legitimacy by a long measure because they preside over artificial colonial constructs that are very vulnerable to internal challenges. These regimes, therefore, tend to be extremely repressive in their reactions to the first murmurings of political dissent. Moreover, since these regimes perceive themselves as besieged, they also tend to rely on kinship ties or the secret police or both to keep themselves in power, thus combining the worst features of the patrimonial state and the police state. The Iraqi and Syrian regimes are leading examples of this phenomenon in the Middle East, based as they are on the support of minority ethnic groups buttressed by the unchecked power of the omnipresent *mukhabarat* (intelligence service).[54] Such regimes also engender violent opposition because they do not allow the political space necessary for legitimate opposition activity. Thus, we find a vicious circle of violence and counterviolence feeding upon each other and exacerbating the already high levels of insecurity in many Third World states.

Summary

The political capacities of Third World states are overloaded by the conjunction of many of the factors and forces discussed in this chapter. These factors include the lack of adequate time required for state building; the near impossibility until recently of alienating juridical sovereignty once it is achieved; the highly disruptive colonial inheritance; the accentuation of ethnic fissures in the early stages of modernization, leading to frequent attempts at secession; the demands for political participation, economic redistribution, and social justice at a very early stage in the state-making process; and the unrepresentative and authoritarian character of many regimes, which spawns a vicious circle of violence and counterviolence as regimes are challenged and react with brutal force. The political overload that comes about from the combination of all or many of these factors lies at the root of the high degree of insecurity witnessed in most Third World countries. This overload also provides the basic logic for the argument made at the beginning of this chapter: that the internal dimension of security is of paramount importance in the totality of the Third World state's security calculus. In other words, internal insecurities fundamentally determine the security predicament of the Third World state. These insecurities, in turn, are intimately related to the ongoing process of state building in postcolonial societies. They are manifested through the state's attempts to impose its version of political order, often by force, and through the equally frequent violent resistance to such imposition by substantial segments of the Third World's population.

However, Third World state making is not conducted in an international vacuum; external variables have tremendous influence in determining the outcome of specific attempts at state building. These external pressures emanate from both the regional and the global environments in which Third World states operate. It is to these external variables that I turn my attention in the next few chapters.

Notes

1. Mohammed Ayoob, "Security in the Third World: Searching for the Core Variable," in Norman Graham (ed.), *Seeking Security and Development: The Impact of Military Spending and Arms Transfers* (Boulder: Lynne Rienner Publishers, 1994: 15–28). Also, Mohammed Ayoob, "The Security Predicament of the Third World State: Reflections on State-Making in a Comparative Perspective," in Brian Job (ed.), *The Insecurity Dilemma: National Security of Third World States* (Boulder: Lynne Rienner Publishers, 1992): 63–80.

2. Keith Jaggers, "War and the Three Faces of Power: War Making and State Making in Europe and the Americas," *Comparative Political Studies* 25, no. 1 (April 1992): 29.

3. Edward E. Azar and Chung-in Moon, "Legitimacy, Integration and Policy Capacity: The 'Software' Side of Third World National Security," in Edward E. Azar and Chung-in Moon (eds.), *National Security in the Third World: The Management of Internal and External Threats* (College Park: University of Maryland, Center for International Development and Conflict Management, 1988): 77–101.

4. Charles Tilly, "War Making and State Making as Organized Crime," in Peter B. Evans, Dietrich Rueschemeyer, and Theda Skocpol (eds.), *Bringing the State Back In* (New York: Cambridge University Press, 1985): 181.

5. Jaggers, "War and the Three Faces of Power," 59.

6. Tilly, "War Making and State Making," 170.

7. Charles Tilly, *Coercion, Capital, and European States, AD 990–1990* (Cambridge: Basil Blackwell, 1990): 70.

8. Tilly, "War Making and State Making," 172. For a more extensive treatment of the subject by Tilly, see the first and last chapters in Charles Tilly (ed.), *The Formation of National States in Western Europe* (Princeton: Princeton University Press, 1975).

9. Youssef Cohen, Brian R. Brown, and A. F. K. Organski, "The Paradoxical Nature of State Making: The Violent Creation of Order," *American Political Science Review* 75, no. 4 (1981): 905. Emphasis in the original.

10. Ibid., 902.

11. Anthony Giddens, *The Nation-State and Violence* (Berkeley: University of

California Press, 1987): 3–4. Although Giddens's characterization of city-states as segmental and as having low political reach may surprise some readers, he argues convincingly that "city-state organization precluded the existence, within the relevant territorial areas, of centralized political authority of a broad kind. It might be thought that the city-state, being small and confined, can achieve a more comparable degree of concentration of authoritative resources to the modern state. However, such is not the case. . . . Small though it is, the city-state typically only develops a low level of direct administrative control over its subjects. . . . The small size of the administrative organizations of the city-state, together with the restricted nature of its military power, ensures that the level of control over most of its population is normally no greater than that of the large-scale bureaucratic empire" (39–40).

12. Ibid., 4.

13. Tilly, *Coercion, Capital, and European States,* 43, 3.

14. Ernest Gellner, *Nations and Nationalism* (Ithaca: Cornell University Press, 1983): 1.

15. Ibid., 4.

16. Quoted in E. J. Hobsbawm, *Nations and Nationalism Since 1780: Programme, Myth, Reality* (Cambridge: Cambridge University Press, 1990): 44.

17. Cornelia Navari, "The Origins of the Nation-State," in Leonard Tivey (ed.), *The Nation-State: The Formation of Modern Politics* (Oxford: Martin Robertson, 1981): 34.

18. Liah Greenfeld, *Nationalism: Five Roads to Modernity* (Cambridge: Harvard University Press, 1992): 21.

19. Ibid., 14.

20. Anthony D. Smith, *State and Nation in the Third World* (New York: St. Martin's Press, 1983): 11, 17.

21. Ali Kazancigil, "Introduction," in Ali Kazancigil (ed.), *The State in Global Perspective* (Aldershot: Gower, 1986): xvi.

22. Probably the most prominent and intelligently articulate author writing from this alternative perspective is the Indian political scientist Rajni Kothari. For a sampling of his views, see Rajni Kothari, *State Against Democracy, Transformation and Survival,* and *Rethinking Development,* all (Delhi: Ajanta Publications, 1988).

23. Charles Tilly, "Reflections on the History of European State-Making," in Tilly (ed.), *Formation of National States in Western Europe,* 71.

24. Joseph R. Strayer, *On the Medieval Origins of the Modern State* (Princeton: Princeton University Press, 1970): 23, 57.

25. Tilly, "Reflections on the History of European State-Making," 26–27.

26. Ibid., 7.

27. For details, see Perry Anderson, *Lineages of the Absolutist State* (London: New Left Books, 1974).

28. Stein Rokkan, "Dimensions of State Formation and Nation-Building: A Possible Paradigm for Research on Variations Within Europe," in Tilly (ed.), *Formation of National States in Western Europe,* 598.

29. Ibid., 586.

30. For theoretically informed accounts of the "cumulation of crises" in Italy and Germany, see the chapters on Italy and Germany by Raymond Grew and John R. Gillis, respectively, in Raymond Grew (ed.), *Crises of Political Development in Europe and the United States* (Princeton: Princeton University Press, 1978).

31. Charles Tilly, "Western State-Making and Theories of Political Transformation," in Tilly (ed.), *Formation of National States in Western Europe,* 633, 635.

32. For a discussion of the difference between juridical and effective (or

empirical) statehood, see Robert H. Jackson, *Quasi-States: Sovereignty, International Relations and the Third World* (Cambridge: Cambridge University Press, 1990): Chapters 1 and 2.

33. For details of the Latin American case, see Howard J. Wiarda, "Social Change, Political Development and the Latin American Tradition," in Howard J. Wiarda (ed.), *Politics and Social Change in Latin America,* 2d rev. ed. (Amherst: University of Massachusetts Press, 1982): 3–26.

34. Robert H. Jackson, "Quasi States, Dual Regimes, and Neoclassical Theory: International Jurisprudence and the Third World," *International Organization* 41, no. 4 (Autumn 1987): 525. For a perceptive analysis of the colonial legacy of the African state, see Crawford Young, "The African Colonial State and Its Political Legacy," in Donald Rothchild and Naomi Chazan (eds.), *The Precarious Balance: State and Society in Africa* (Boulder: Westview Press, 1988): 25–66.

35. For a concise description of the carving up of the Ottoman Empire's Arab territories by Britain and France, see William R. Polk, *The Arab World,* 4th ed. (Cambridge: Harvard University Press, 1980): 93–112. For more detailed analyses, see Elizabeth Monroe, *Britain's Moment in the Middle East* (Baltimore: Johns Hopkins University Press, 1963); and David Fromkin, *A Peace to End All Peace: Creating the Modern Middle East 1914–1922* (New York: Henry Holt, 1989).

36. Amiya Kumar Bagchi, *The Political Economy of Underdevelopment* (Cambridge: Cambridge University Press, 1982): 34.

37. Ibid., 18, 33. For a detailed analysis of the retardation of colonial economies under European rule, see Chapter 2, "Methods of Exploitation and the Phenomenon of Economic Retardation," 20–40.

38. Ali Mazrui, "The Triple Heritage of the State in Africa," in Kazancigil (ed.), *The State in Global Perspective,* 112.

39. For further analysis and examples of the creation of "traditional" authority structures during colonial rule, see Joel S. Migdal, *Strong Societies and Weak States: State-Society Relations and State Capabilities in the Third World* (Princeton: Princeton University Press, 1988): 97–141; and Ulf Himmelstrand, "Tribalism, Regionalism, Nationalism, and Secession in Nigeria," in S. N. Eisenstadt and Stein Rokkan (eds.), *Building States and Nations* (Beverly Hills: Sage Publications, 1973): 427–467.

40. Jeffrey Herbst, "The Creation and Maintenance of National Boundaries in Africa," *International Organization* 43, no. 4 (Autumn 1989): 680.

41. For details, see Mushirul Hassan, *Nationalism and Communal Politics in India, 1916–1928* (Delhi: Manohar, 1979); and David Page, *Prelude to Partition: The Indian Muslims and the System of Control, 1920–1932* (Delhi: Oxford University Press, 1982).

42. Robert Melson and Howard Wolpe, "Modernization and the Politics of Communalism: A Theoretical Perspective," *American Political Science Review* 64, no. 4 (December 1970): 1113.

43. Gellner, *Nations and Nationalism,* 73–74.

44. Susanne Hoeber Rudolph and Lloyd I. Rudolph, "Modern Hate: How Ancient Animosities Get Invented," *New Republic* (March 22, 1993): 28, 29.

45. Myron Weiner, "Political Change: Asia, Africa, and the Middle East," in Myron Weiner and Samuel P. Huntington (eds.), *Understanding Political Development* (Boston: Little, Brown, 1987): 35–36.

46. For strong statements and details of this argument, see David Brown, "From Peripheral Communities to Ethnic Nations: Separatism in Southeast Asia," *Pacific Affairs* 61, no. 1 (Spring 1988): 51–77; and David Brown, "Ethnic Revival:

Perspectives on State and Society," *Third World Quarterly* 11, no. 4 (October 1989): 1–17.

47. Ted Robert Gurr, "Third World Minorities at Risk Since 1945," in Sheryl J. Brown and Kimber M. Schraub (eds.), *Resolving Third World Conflict: Challenges for a New Era* (Washington, D.C.: United States Institute of Peace Press, 1992): 53, 57. For more complete data and fuller explanations, see Ted Robert Gurr, *Minorities at Risk: Origins and Outcomes of Ethnopolitical Conflicts* (Washington, D.C.: United States Institute of Peace Press, 1993).

48. Karin Lindgren, Birger Heldt, Kjell-Ake Nordquist, and Peter Wallensteen, "Major Armed Conflicts in 1990," *SIPRI Yearbook 1991* (Oxford: Oxford University Press, 1991): 345.

49. For a comprehensive treatment of ethnic conflict, including secessionism, see Donald L. Horowitz, *Ethnic Groups in Conflict* (Berkeley: University of California Press, 1985).

50. Tilly, "Reflections on the History of European State-Making," in Tilly (ed.), *Formation of National States,* 69.

51. Tilly, "Western State-Making," in Tilly (ed.), *Formation of National States,* 610.

52. Charles W. Anderson, "Toward a Theory of Latin American Politics," in Wiarda (ed.), *Politics and Social Change in Latin America,* 310.

53. For an analysis of these challenges to the Indian political system, see Mohammed Ayoob, "Dateline India: The Deepening Crisis," *Foreign Policy,* no. 85 (Winter 1991–1992): 166–184. Also see Amartya Sen, "The Threats to Secular India," *New York Review* (April 8, 1993): 26–32.

54. For the Iraqi regime, see Samir al-Khalil, *Republic of Fear: The Politics of Modern Iraq* (Berkeley: University of California Press, 1989). For the Syrian regime, see Raymond A. Hinnebusch, *Authoritarian Power and State Formation in Ba'thist Syria: Army, Party and Peasant* (Boulder: Westview Press, 1990). For a perceptive review of the literature on authoritarian regimes in the Middle East, see Jill Crystal, "Authoritarianism and Its Adversaries in the Arab World," *World Politics* 46, no. 2 (January 1994): 262–289.

■ 3 ■

Interstate Conflict and Regional Insecurity

There are two major sources of interstate conflict and insecurity in the Third World: (1) the intermeshing of domestic insecurities with interstate antagonisms, and (2) the autonomous dynamic of regional conflict, which is often centered on the aspirations of preeminent regional powers. In some instances, as in South Asia, these aspirations have been vigorously opposed by a smaller power, usually with the help of great powers from outside the region. In other instances, as in the Gulf, the existence of more than one regional power center has led to interstate tensions and conflicts as the ambitions of the different centers have clashed with each other.

I begin my analysis by concentrating on the intertwining of intrastate conflicts with interstate conflicts. Intrastate conflicts, as Chapter 2 pointed out, are closely linked to the state-making process in individual Third World states. However, state building in the Third World is not conducted in a regional vacuum. Third World states impinge upon the state-making process of other states in their neighborhood, especially those contiguous to them. This is a mutual and reciprocal process and is a function of arbitrarily drawn colonial boundaries and the inadequate stateness of Third World states. Both of these factors lead to the proliferation of contested demographic and territorial space and to frequent interstate conflicts in postcolonial territories. Since such contests involve not only neighboring states but also populations within states that reluctantly accept or actively deny the legitimacy of postcolonial state boundaries and that have ethno-linguistic or ethno-religious links with peoples in neighboring states, interstate conflicts in the Third World frequently become enmeshed with secessionist and irredentist challenges to postcolonial states.

It is clear to any discerning observer that many interstate conflicts in the Third World are the legacies of the colonial era, particularly of the process through which colonial proto-states were established and the way in which power was transferred from the colonial authority to the successor native elites. For example, the unfinished business of the transfer of power from British to indigenous hands in the Indian subcontinent has continued to haunt the successor states, India and Pakistan, for the past forty-five years in the form of the Kashmir dispute.[1] Similarly, Indonesia's policy of "confrontation" with Malaysia in the early and mid-1960s was largely a response to the political strategy devised by the British to divest themselves of their Southeast Asian possessions while keeping much of their strategic presence intact.[2] Finally, the most prominent example of conflicts that fall into this category—the Arab-Israeli dispute over Palestine—owes its origins to the conflicting promises made by Great Britain to Zionist and Arab leaders during World War I, the vacillation in British policy during the British mandate in Palestine, and London's inability or unwillingness to devise a formula for the transfer of power to a successor government in a territory it was mandated to groom for self-government.[3]

Colonially imposed artificial boundaries and the arbitrary allocation of peoples to states, especially in Africa but also in Asia and the Middle East, also laid the foundations for many interstate conflicts born out of irredentism. This has been defined by Naomi Chazan as "any political effort to unite ethnically, historically, or geographically related segments of a population in adjacent countries within a common political framework."[4] Conflicts spawned by irredentist claims have included those between Pakistan and India over Kashmir, between Afghanistan and Pakistan over Pakistan's North-West Frontier Province (NWFP), between Ethiopia and Somalia over the Ogaden, and between Morocco and Algeria, Mauritania, and the Polisario over the Western Sahara. It is surprising, given the arbitrary character of African boundaries and the ethnically patchwork nature of the African states' populations, that there have not been many more irredentist wars on that continent. One possible explanation lies in the fact that almost all African states are vulnerable to the irredentist challenge and, therefore, are wary of undertaking or encouraging such ventures against neighboring states.

The Iraqi invasion of Kuwait in 1990 also had its roots in Iraqi irredentism toward the oil-rich emirate. This, in turn, had its origins in London's machinations to ensure the independence of its protectorate, Kuwait, under British auspices from the British-mandated territory, Iraq, thereby thwarting the ambitions of the larger state.[5] Boundaries mediated and, therefore, determined by the countries' colonial powers also contributed to the war between Iraq and Iran from 1980 to 1988 and to the 1962 border conflict between India and China.[6]

The events of the past few years in the Balkans also attest to the validity of this proposition. Both secessionism and irredentism in the Balkans—which possess great potential for interstate conflict and, therefore, pose grave threats to regional security—can be explained largely by the fact that political boundaries in the Balkans, as with those in the Third World, did not evolve out of indigenous processes of state making but were imposed by outside great powers. More than two decades ago, in a prescient article on the Balkans, Najdan Pasic noted:

> From the Holy Alliance and the Congress of Berlin to the Yalta Conference, where spheres of influence in the Balkans were calculated in percentages, the Balkan peoples had their destinies carved by others. The parceling out of political and national structures in the Balkans was in a substantial part the product of such external forces. In this respect, the historical circumstances surrounding nation-building in the Balkans bear a close resemblance to those in which nations and independent national states have taken shape in other parts of the economically underdeveloped world.[7]

Recent events have confirmed the similarity between the Balkans' security problems and those of the Third World and also the Balkan states' status as members of the Third World. This status is thrown into bold relief if we use the stage of state making and the time of the states' full entry into the international system as the defining criteria for membership in the Third World. Furthermore, most of the other defining characteristics of Third World states spelled out in Chapter 1 apply in good measure to the Balkan states. I return to this subject later in the book.

Intrastate Aspects of Regional Conflict

The argument that most conflicts in the Third World have their roots in the domestic or intrastate arena has been made forcefully in Chapter 2. I do not want to belabor that assertion here except to point out that according to Kalevi J. Holsti's conservative estimate of wars and major armed interventions during the 1945–1989 period (only two of fifty-eight, according to Holsti, occurred outside the Third World), the large majority of such conflicts—forty-seven—were the product of one or more of three factors: national liberation from colonial rule, state creation, and regime legitimacy. These factors are all firmly rooted in the domestic arena of political activity.[8] As Holsti has observed elsewhere, the overwhelming majority of conflicts in the international system since 1945 have been "a ubiquitous corollary of the birth, formation, and fracturing of Third World states."[9]

Many, probably most, of these conflicts have also had an interstate dimension, thereby making them genuinely regional in character. However, this dimension has usually been inextricably intertwined with domestic issues of state making, state breaking, and regime legitimacy involving one or more participants in a conflict. The outstanding example of intermeshing of the domestic and interstate dimensions of conflict was the internal crisis in Pakistan in 1971 and the subsequent India-Pakistan War, which led to the separation of Bangladesh from the rump state of Pakistan in December of that year. The internal crisis had its roots in regional disparities, interethnic tensions, and the repeated denial of democratic rights to Pakistan's Bengali majority. But the interstate dimension was provided by (1) the movement of approximately 10 million refugees from East Pakistan into the neighboring regions of India, (2) the ethnic affinities of the Bengali population of the Indian state of West Bengal with the population of East Pakistan, and (3) the Indian decisionmakers' perception that Pakistan's truncation would radically improve India's security environment by reducing Pakistan's ability to wage war against India over the disputed state of Jammu and Kashmir.[10]

The latest phase of the India-Pakistan dispute over Kashmir is a further dramatic manifestation of the intertwining of intrastate and interstate dimensions of conflict. The struggle for the Valley of Kashmir has taken on the character of a three-way contest among India, Pakistan, and the various armed insurgent groups battling Indian security forces, with varying degrees of Pakistani support.[11]

The interconnections between domestic and interstate conflict in the Third World should not lead us to ignore the genuinely interstate dimension of regional conflict—that is, the element of conflict between neighboring, usually contiguous, states over disputed territories and populations. There is undeniably an autonomous regional dynamic that also affects the security of developing states and regions and is related to the regional balance of power, especially to the preeminent regional power's attempt to preserve a favorable status quo and that of its principal challenger or challengers to change the prevailing balance in their favor.

It should be noted, however, that the regional dimension of conflict is often determined by the process of state making undertaken concurrently by contiguous states in the Third World. The simultaneous nature of this process, which frequently includes the assertion of political and military control over demographic and territorial space contested by neighboring states, underlies many of the conflicts among developing countries that appear to the outside observer to be instances of regional conflict tied to regional balance-of-power issues. However, there is a major and obvious link between the state-making process and the regional balance of power: The more that balance is tilted in a particular state's favor, the easier it is for that state to enhance its state-building goals by successfully asserting its control over contested territories and populations at the expense of neighboring states.

Internal and External Factors: Symbiotic Relationship

If we accept the argument that most regional conflicts are related to issues of state making and state breaking, as well as those of regime legitimacy (a conclusion that is augmented by the events of the past few years in the Balkans and in the successor states of the former Soviet Union), we would logically conclude that domestic factors play a much more important role in the origins of these conflicts. However, this relatively simple conclusion about the basic domestic roots of most Third World conflicts becomes difficult to establish clearly in many instances. In many conflicts that have originated as intrastate conflicts, the relationship between internal and external factors is symbiotic in character, in the sense that one set of factors cannot thrive without the presence of the other and vice versa.

This situation is aptly summarized in Donald Horowitz's celebrated statement, "Secession lies squarely at the juncture of internal and international conflict."[12] The relevance of this statement goes beyond the issue of secession and covers almost all types of conflict in the Third World, including those that have resulted from the opposite side of the secessionist coin—namely, irredentism. The Kurdish case provides an interesting example of the conjuncture between secessionism and irredentism. Since the Kurds form substantial minorities in the currently constituted states of Turkey, Iraq, and Iran, their individual demands vis-à-vis these states are pitched in autonomist or secessionist terms. However, strong segments of Kurdish political opinion also aspire to unite the Kurds inhabiting Turkey, Iran, and Iraq into a single Kurdish state. This aspiration is an expression of Kurdish irredentism, but the absence of a Kurdish parent state makes these irredentist ambitions difficult to achieve politically and to classify analytically.[13] The Kurdish case provides excellent evidence for Horowitz's statement that "secessions and irredentas are near neighbors that can be pulled apart for analysis but with points of contact and even, at times, a degree of interchangeability that might permit groups to choose one or the other and that also makes it necessary to treat the two phenomena together, in order to have a full view of each."[14]

Secessionist Conflicts

Since the symbiotic relationship between domestic and external—especially regional—factors is demonstrated most clearly in the case of conflicts revolving around secessionist demands, which form a sizable proportion of conflicts in the Third World, it is worthwhile to analyze further the dynamics of secessionist conflicts and to clearly discern the interactions between internal and external factors and forces affecting these conflicts. This is necessary in order to decipher the conditions that determine the outcome of secessionist attempts. It is also necessary in order to be able to apply the terms of interaction between internal and external forces to other cases of Third World conflicts that do not necessarily involve the issue of secession or state breaking but that are centered largely on challenges to incumbent elites and that have as their goal change of regimes rather than the alteration of state boundaries.

Horowitz has elaborated upon his point about the interconnection between domestic and international factors in the case of secession by stating, "Whether and when a secessionist movement will emerge is determined mainly by domestic politics, by the relations of groups and regions within the state. Whether a secessionist movement will achieve its aims, however, is determined largely by international politics, by the balance of interests and forces that extend beyond the state."[15]

A close look at secessionist attempts makes it very clear that external linkages are crucial to the attainment of the objectives secessionist movements set for themselves, and the nature of such linkages often demarcates the difference between success and failure for secessionist endeavors. This assertion is borne out by Alexis Heraclides's comparison of seven cases of attempted secessionism, which has led him to conclude:

> In armed struggles for separatism, the posture of the international system (primarily states and IGOs [intergovernmental organizations]) is salient to conflict resolution. The role of states is the crucial intermediate variable for the conflict's violent or peaceful resolution or nonresolution. If a secessionist movement is unable to win a military victory and is not prepared to compromise on independence, it can only be "saved" if there is high-level external state intervention and diplomatic recognition. If a movement is willing to settle for less than complete independence, external state involvement can be crucial for raising the costs of the conflict and creating a stalemate, thereby "convincing" the incumbent government and secessionists to negotiate and agree on some form of meaningful devolution. Alternatively, lack of external state support can lead either to the defeat and abandonment of the separatist bid or to the lengthy continuation of the armed conflict.[16]

In light of Heraclides's conclusion, it is not surprising that in many instances of attempted secession, the very formulation of the objectives of secessionist groups are greatly influenced, and sometimes determined, by the nature and strength of the groups' links to external actors and their perception of the degree of support for and opposition to their demands by important foreign actors—be they states or international organizations—that are crucial to their cause. The best example of this phenomenon is the reluctance on the part of the major Kurdish nationalist movements in Iraq to openly couch Kurdish demands in the vocabulary of independent statehood. This reluctance was especially evident in the wake of the Iraqi defeat in the 1991 Gulf War, when prospects for an independent Kurdish state in Iraqi Kurdistan appeared to be brighter than they had been since the Ottoman defeat in World War I. However, given the Iraqi Kurds' dependence on several foreign backers—especially the contiguous regional powers Turkey and Iran, which are faced with their own problems of Kurdish secessionism—the Iraqi Kurdish leadership, itself divided into competing factions, steadfastly stuck to its demand, at least in public, for autonomy within rather than secession from the Iraqi state, so as not to alienate these crucial regional supporters.[17]

The Role of Regional Powers

On the basis of the available data about successful secessions from postcolonial states, it can be argued that in order to succeed, a Third World secessionist movement needs strong external military support from the preeminent regional military power. In this context, three things seem to be crucial: (1) The external supporter must be willing to fight and be able to win a war against the parent state from which the secessionist movement wants to separate; (2) the external supporter's military capabilities in the region and its political influence internationally should be sufficient to deter other external powers, whether regional or extra-regional, from intervening militarily on behalf of the parent state in order to prevent secession; and (3) the external supporter's objectives must coincide with those of the secessionist movement in terms of breaking the parent state, for otherwise the external supporter could come to a compromise settlement with the parent state even in the midst of a war, thus leaving the secessionist movement out in the cold and probably much worse off than if it had not attempted a secessionist war.

The two major successful attempts at secession from postcolonial states, Bangladesh and Northern Cyprus, attest to the validity of these propositions. In both cases the external supporters, India and Turkey, were militarily preeminent regional powers that could also deter counterintervention by external powers. The objectives of both India in 1971 and Turkey in 1974 coincided with those of the separatist movements in East Pakistan and Northern Cyprus in terms of breaking up Pakistan and Cyprus. In both cases the parent states, Pakistan and Cyprus, could not offer India and Turkey blueprints for compromise settlements that would have been acceptable to the latter and, therefore, could not convince New Delhi and Ankara to scale down their support to the secessionist forces in Pakistan and Cyprus.

Such a combination of internal and external circumstances is extremely difficult to replicate. This assertion is borne out by the fact that although there have been many secessionist attempts in the Third World, only Bangladesh and Northern Cyprus (and now Eritrea, discussed later) have been successful. The failure of the Biafran attempt to secede from Nigeria in the 1967–1970 civil war provides evidence of the crucial role of external supporters. The absence of a preeminent regional power—in fact, the only candidate for that honor in West Africa was, and is, Nigeria itself—that was committed to the Biafran struggle, and the ambivalence, if not hostility, of major nonregional powers toward the Biafran secession attempt, were crucially responsible for the attempt's failure.[18]

Similarly, the inability of the Tamil secessionists to carve out a homeland in northern and eastern Sri Lanka, despite a decade-long bloody war against Colombo and the presence of 60 million sympathetic Tamils across the Palk Strait in India's southern state of Tamil Nadu, further demonstrates the crucial role of the preeminent regional power—India, in this case—in bringing the insurgency to a successful conclusion. Caught between domestic Tamil pressures for a Tamil homeland in Sri Lanka and New Delhi's regional grand strategy, which rules out the dismemberment of Sri Lanka, India vacillated between putting pressure on Colombo to grant the Tamils substantial autonomy and fighting the major Tamil insurgent group, the Liberation Tigers of Tamil Elam (LTTE), to protect the territorial integrity of the Sri Lankan state. This vacillation in Indian strategy antagonized both the Sri Lankan government and the LTTE. It also prevented India from successfully playing the honest broker, despite its commitment of around 50,000 peacekeeping troops and a drawn-out military campaign against the LTTE between 1987 and 1990 in an effort to implement the 1987 India–Sri Lanka Accord. This accord had guaranteed Tamil autonomy without sacrificing the political unity of the Sri Lankan state. It is clear that although the Tamil secessionists have the ability to continue to harass the Sri Lankan government from their strongholds in the Jaffna Peninsula, they cannot attain their goal of independent statehood in the absence of Indian military and political support.[19]

The more recent Eritrean success in achieving formal separation from Ethiopia falls into a separate category from the examples of Bangladesh and Northern Cyprus. A good case can be made that Eritrean independence from Ethiopia after three decades of bloody fighting was only the reemergence of the postcolonial Eritrean state, which, freed from Italian rule by the British in 1941, was federated with Ethiopia in 1952 under a scheme imposed by the United Nations and then was annexed by Addis Ababa in 1962 with the connivance of the major powers. Only in 1993 did Eritrea belatedly emerge as an independent postcolonial state, a status it had been denied since the dawn of the decolonization era. Eritrea, in fact, represented a major exception to the operation of the new norms of the international system, which guaranteed juridical sovereignty and territorial integrity to the former colonies of European powers.[20]

Russian Role in Central Asia and the Caucasus

The breakup of the Soviet Union and the emergence of several states in Central Asia and the Caucasus region that can be classified as belonging to the Third World also present us with interesting case studies of overt or latent intrastate conflicts with great potential for regional involvement and consequent transformation into interstate conflicts. Almost all of the Soviet successor states in the Caucasus and in Central Asia are deeply riven by ethnic fissures and regional disparities that provide a great deal of potential for internal strife based on secessionist demands and on challenges to the legitimacy of incumbent regimes.[21] At the same time, there is considerable overlap in the ethnic composition of the populations of neighboring states in these regions. This overlap provides much raw material for interstate conflict arising out of irredentist and secessionist demands.

Azerbaijan and Georgia in the Caucasus are already faced with severe secessionist challenges that have turned into full-fledged wars. Here again, the role of Russia—the militarily preeminent regional power with the political clout and military capacity to deter external intervention in the Soviet successor states—in extending or withholding military support to the secessionist elements appears to be the crucial variable likely to determine the fate of Abkhazian and Armenian secessionist movements in Georgia and Azerbaijan, respectively.[22] In Tajikistan the Russian-backed regime composed of former communists is locked in fierce combat with Islamic and democratic forces supported by sympathetic Tajik elements from across the border in Afghanistan. Again, Russia's military role is crucial in maintaining the Tajik regime in power, however repressive its rule and however shaky its control over the country may be.[23] The Russian role is likely to become increasingly important in shoring up pro-Moscow regimes in Central Asia and in preventing them from succumbing under the pressure of democratic and Islamic forces. As a perceptive journalist noted, the current situation in Central Asia "is replete with echoes of the domino theory once invoked for communism. Central Asia is, in effect, Russia's Central America."[24]

Regional Powers and Regime Change

All of the cases of conflict mentioned here, although primarily domestic in their origins, demonstrate the close—indeed, symbiotic—relationship between internal and external dimensions of state and regional security in the Third World. In the case of successful instances of secession, they also demonstrate the crucial role of preeminent regional powers with interests that coincide with those of secessionist elements vis-à-vis the parent or incumbent state. But the role of regional powers is not limited to cases of attempted secession. Challenges to incumbent political elites and movements for regime change also often depend for their success upon external support and encouragement, once again from neighboring, and preferably militarily and politically preeminent, states in the region. The forces that in 1958 overthrew the pro-Western Hashemite monarchy in Iraq, almost toppled King Hussein of Jordan, and forcefully challenged the Maronite establishment in Lebanon, thus starting Lebanon's first civil war, drew their inspiration as well as considerable support from Nasser's Egypt, the preeminent power in the Arab world that was pursuing its own regional and pan-Arab agenda.[25]

More recently, the success of the democratic movement in Nepal in April 1990 owed much to Indian support, some of it offered crucially but inadvertently by New Delhi's decision in 1989 to close off landlocked Nepal's trade routes, all of which—with the exception of one sparsely used mountainous highway through the Himalayas to Tibet—run through India to the sea. The Indian decision to blockade Nepal was made ostensibly because of a breakdown in India-Nepal trade and tariff talks. In actuality, it was made to show India's displeasure at Nepal's acquisition of some arms, especially antiaircraft guns, from China. The Indian embargo threatened Nepal with economic strangulation and discredited the monarchy, both for its inept handling of Nepal's relations with its most important neighbor and predominant trade partner and for the dramatic worsening of the Nepalese people's economic plight following the imposition of restrictions by India. By detracting from the legitimacy of monarchical rule, this last factor provided a major boost in terms of popular support to the democratic movement and may have made the difference between success and failure in the movement's attempt to install a parliamentary system and impose effective curbs on the power of the Nepalese monarchy.[26]

Defining Region

So far, in my discussion of intermeshing domestic and regional dimensions of conflict and security in the Third World, I have taken the term *region* for granted, without defining its meaning and explicating its relevance to the security predicament of the Third World state. It is important at this stage to attempt to define the term *region* to put my analysis into proper conceptual perspective.

A relatively comprehensive working definition of a regional subsystem, a synonym for region, was provided by William Thompson two decades ago. He wrote that attributes used to identify regional subsystems are geographic proximity, regularity and intensity of interaction between actors to the extent that a change at one point in the subsystem affects other points, internal and external recognition of a group of states as a distinctive area, and a size consisting of at least two and probably more actors.[27] Building on Thompson's insight, Raimo Vayrynen contended that "a regional subsystem is characterized by a certain *distinctiveness* and *proximity,* not only in the geographical but also in the economic and political sense. Proximity is institutionalized by means of mutual interaction and common organizations."[28] Writing in a similar vein, Louis Cantori and Steven Spiegel argued that "all subordinate systems [that is, regions] are delineated—at least in part—by reference to geographical considerations, but social, economic, political and organizational factors are also relevant. Consequently, members of subordinate systems are proximate, but they need not be contiguous."[29]

If we combine these definitions, it becomes clear that geographic propinquity and intensity of interaction form the core variables that define a region. It is crucial to point out, however, that any valid measurement of intensity of interaction must include cooperation, competition, and conflict. The inclusion of competition and conflict, in addition to cooperation, distinguishes the concept of region from the notion of security community as defined by Karl Deutsch and applied to North America and Western Europe.[30]

One can argue that in the case of the Third World the intensity of conflict might be a better yardstick than that of cooperation to judge whether a group of states comprises a region. This argument is based on the logic that holds that states that share cultural traits and historical memories have a greater tendency to be locked into conflict with each other than those that have maintained cultural and historical distance from each other. Moreover, this assertion is borne out by the intensity of conflict in the Indian subcontinent, as well as that of the internecine disputes in the Arab world. The current state of affairs in the Balkans further reinforces this conclusion. Given the infancy of Third World states, the simultaneity of their state-making process, their artificial, colonially imposed boundaries, and the consequent overlap in the affinities of significant segments of their populations across state boundaries, these states constitute regional subsystems based more on overt or latent conflict than on cooperation.

Third World economies within discrete regions generally tend to be similar and mutually competitive rather than complementary; consequently, cooperative and mostly economic interactions are less important than competitive and conflictual ones. Third World states also tend to be at similar stages of technological development and, therefore, do not possess the advanced technology that would make them attractive as exporters of technology to other Third World states. These two factors preclude much economic and technological cooperation among these states. Third World patterns of economic, military, and technological cooperation tend to run on a North-South rather than a South-South axis. This situation is a function of the economic, technological, and military dependence of Third World states on the developed states of North America, Europe, and Japan—a result of the imposition of an international division of labor devised during the colonial era and perpetuated by the economic, military, and technological superiority of the North over the South.[31]

It is the importance of conflict and the consequent preoccupation of Third World state elites with security and insecurity issues vis-à-vis neighboring states that originally led Barry Buzan to use the term *security complexes* to characterize what I have been describing as regions or regional subsystems. Since security complexes were seen by Buzan as revolving around major conflictual dyads, such as that of India and Pakistan in South Asia, his initial formulation appeared to describe "insecurity complexes," despite his assertion that he attempted to define "regional security subsystems in terms of patterns of amity and enmity that are substantially confined within some particular geographical area." Buzan admitted during his early formulation that "unlike most other attempts to define regional subsystems, security complexes rest, for the most part, on the interdependence of rivalry rather than on the interdependence of shared interests."[32]

However, he later refined his formulation to take into account shared interests and the intensity of cooperative interaction as well as the intensity of conflictual relations: "A security complex is defined as a group of states whose primary security concerns link together sufficiently closely that their national securities cannot realistically be considered apart from one another. . . . Security complexes emphasize the interdependence of rivalry as well as that of shared interests."[33]

The greatest advantage of Buzan's definition is that by focusing on regions in terms of security interdependence, it avoids many of the problems contained in earlier attempts at defining regions such as those by Michael Brecher, Bruce Russett, and Cantori and Spiegel.[34] These earlier efforts, as Buzan noted, were hamstrung by "their attempt to tackle region across the whole agenda of international relations, and to set up a detailed comparative politics framework. Consequently, none of these approaches resulted in any widely accepted definition of region."[35]

A further benefit of the adoption of Buzan's definition is that it helps us to interpose an intermediate level between the highest and lowest levels of security analysis—namely, international security and state security. By doing so, it allows us to concentrate on the autonomous regional dynamics of conflict and security, not to the exclusion of the security dynamics discernible at the levels of the international system and the individual state but without being overwhelmed by those dynamics. Therefore, we can begin to talk about regional security in terms of the pattern of relations among members of the security complex. We can also talk about the relationship of the entire complex with the overarching system of international security that is dominated by the security relationship and the balance of power among the great powers.

Defining a region by emphasizing the autonomy of regional dynamics of conflict and security also permits analysts to note that most security issues in Third World regions have a life of their own independent of great power relationships. However, great power intrusions into regional conflicts are able to exacerbate or mitigate such conflicts. Highlighting the autonomy of regional dynamics also helps us to understand that regional actors in the Third World are not susceptible to total or even substantial control by great powers, even if one of these powers may appear to be the patron of a regional protagonist in a conflict. This has been most clear in the case of the U.S.-Israeli relationship during the past quarter century, when the Israeli client has often determined the contours of the U.S. patron's policy in the Middle East rather than the reverse.[36] Pakistan's attempt in the 1950s and 1960s to mold U.S. policy in South Asia to suit its own security interests vis-à-vis India, although less successful than that of Israel in the Middle East, nevertheless put severe strains on Indo-American relations. Moreover, it pushed U.S. policy in South Asia in directions that were deleterious to long-term U.S. political and strategic interests.[37]

It was not only the U.S. superpower whose policies became hostage to the interests and policies of its Third World friends and clients. Soviet policies toward South Asia from the late 1960s to the end of the 1980s were often critically influenced by Indian assessments of Indian security rather than being the outcome of a Soviet grand design imposed on Moscow's so-called Indian ally.[38] This situation has been equally true of Soviet "clients" in the Middle East, a fact demonstrated most dramatically by Iraq's decision to launch a war against Iran in September 1980, in total disregard of Soviet attempts to establish good relations with revolutionary Iran.[39] Therefore, during the Cold War era the paradoxical situation existed in which Third World actors were easily permeable by the superpowers but also retained their autonomy of initiative in conflicts and on issues that were central to regional security concerns.

Regional Power Centers and Regional Security

In many instances, the major evidence of the existence of a security complex—a region defined primarily in conflict and security terms—is the presence of a preeminent power in a geographic area with latent or overt claims to the status of security manager of that area. As Vayrynen wrote, "Usually such [regional] power centers sit at the top of the hierarchy of an identifiable regional subsystem; Indonesia, India, pre-revolutionary Iran and Nigeria may serve as examples of this tendency. Regional subsystems dominated by one power centre are unipolar, while in the bipolar alternative two dominant centres have to arrange their mutual relations."[40]

Regional power centers can give coherence to regions by arranging the security concerns of discrete geographic areas around their own ambitions and capabilities. However, the capacity to provide coherence also means that regional powers have the potential to increase the conflict level in their regions if their claims for primacy are either disputed by other regional actors or are not accepted as legitimate by most members of a regional subsystem. Where, as in the case of Israel in the Middle East, the preeminent military power is a state whose inherent resources do not match its military capabilities and political ambitions, the region it inhabits is a leading candidate for political and military instability. The Middle East security complex has demonstrated that this is the case, because the political aspirations and military superiority of a claimant such as Israel are perceived as totally illegitimate by other members of the regional subsystem and are constantly challenged politically and militarily.[41] As the Israeli case has shown, one method by which such an aspirant to regional predominance can hope to preserve its superiority is by exercising a nuclear weapons monopoly in its region and by maintaining this monopoly at all costs, thereby making the regional security complex even more unstable and unpredictable.[42]

Perhaps the most clear-cut example of a power in a discrete Third World region that possesses inherent capabilities that create preeminence is that of India. It is no wonder that regional security issues in South Asia revolve around India. But even in this case, "the overwhelming predominance of India [is] constrained by the presence of a Pakistan that is too strong to be dominated by India."[43] The existence of Pakistan as challenger and regional spoiler has detracted from both the efficacy and the legitimacy of India's role as security manager of the South Asian region.[44] However, as W. Howard Wriggins has commented, "Though suggestive, the security dilemma is not an exact paradigm for Indo-Pakistani relations, because the disparity between India and Pakistan was so great [that] the anxiety of the much larger India often appeared to reflect regional ambitions more than genuine fears."[45]

The Gulf, strategically and economically the most valuable piece of real estate in the Third World because it contains approximately 60 percent of the world's proven oil reserves, depicts a tripolar situation, with Iran, Iraq, and Saudi Arabia vying with each other for regional dominance. The situation in the Gulf is further complicated by its close links to the larger Middle East regional security complex. The Gulf, one can argue, is simultaneously a security complex in its own right and a subcomplex of the Middle Eastern security complex, which explains the inability and unwillingness of the Saudi and Iraqi regimes to clearly demarcate their ambitions and goals in the Gulf from their similar concerns in the wider Arab world.[46]

The Southeast Asian case is remarkably different from the examples of South Asia and the Middle East for several reasons. First, since the mid-1960s Indonesia, the preeminent power in Southeast Asia in terms of population and resources, has deliberately downplayed the overt assertion of its demographic and political preeminence. It has also attempted to work through a consensus established within the Association of Southeast Asian Nations (ASEAN) while at the same time expecting the other members of ASEAN to respect its views. Thus the other ASEAN states—Malaysia, Singapore, Thailand, the Philippines, and Brunei—have found it unnecessary to demonstrate overtly their latent fear of Indonesian domination. In other words, there has been a basic consensus among the members of ASEAN about the role of the pivotal power in the ASEAN subregion, a consensus to which that pivotal power—Indonesia—has subscribed. For a lack of more precise terminology, this consensus falls somewhere between "first among equals" and "center of gravity" but possesses enough elasticity to fit either of these descriptions, depending upon the circumstances and issue areas under discussion.[47]

Until recently, a second pole of regional power in Southeast Asia had been Vietnam, which had not only dominated the Indochina subregion but also confronted ASEAN over Cambodia. Whereas Vietnamese power has been eroded greatly by the disintegration of its former Soviet superpower ally, Hanoi, with its military capabilities, continues to be an important player in the Southeast Asian regional security arena and is a potential challenger to overt assertions of Indonesian hegemony.

However, what has made the Southeast Asian regional security complex unique is not the existence of Indonesia and Vietnam as two rival centers of power but the proximity of Southeast Asia to China and Japan, the two major Asian powers. Both countries have traditionally, and at different times, considered Southeast Asia their backyard and their natural sphere of influence. During the Cold War, the Japanese maintained a low political profile, and Chinese ambitions were thwarted by the direct or surrogate presence of the United States and the Soviet Union in the region. However, in the post–Cold War era the Southeast Asian security complex is bound to be profoundly influenced by the future relationship between China and Japan, as Japan emerges as an autonomous political actor and China finds many Cold War restraints removed as a result of Russian retrenchment and U.S. introversion.

In the final analysis, Southeast Asia will have little autonomy from the overarching Asia-Pacific regional balance, which, given its geographic configuration, will include Russia and the United States in addition to China and Japan.[48] This is a situation the leaders of most Southeast Asian, especially ASEAN, states desperately want to avoid. However, given the history of Chinese and Japanese involvement in Southeast Asia and their current political and economic interests in the region, it will be extremely difficult to prevent this scenario if Sino-Japanese relations become adversarial.[49] A realistic conclusion is that the two rival powers likely to contend for predominance in Southeast Asia in the post–Cold War era will be China and Japan, not Indonesia and Vietnam, and that the future of the Southeast Asian security complex will revolve around the rivalry between the former two nations.

Regional Organizations and Regional Conflicts

There have been several attempts at managing or at least easing regional conflicts in the Third World through regional or subregional organizations such as ASEAN and the Gulf Cooperation Council (GCC).[50] However, the role of such organizations has been very limited and sometimes even counterproductive in the management of regional conflict. Arguably, both ASEAN and GCC contributed to the exacerbation of regional conflicts by institutionalizing regional cleavages—the former between anti-communist ASEAN and Communist Indochina and the latter between the Saudi-led monarchies of the Arab littoral of the Gulf and revolutionary Iran. In the cases of ASEAN and GCC, neither the Southeast Asian nor the Gulf regions became more secure by bridging the major intraregional divides than they were before the advent of these organizations.[51]

This does not mean the two organizations were unsuccessful in ameliorating intramural conflicts among the members of GCC and ASEAN. GCC accomplished this amelioration largely by institutionalizing Saudi predominance in the Arab littoral of the Gulf. In the case of ASEAN, overt and latent bilateral antagonisms between Malaysia on the one side and Indonesia, the Philippines, Thailand, and Singapore on the other were significantly muted, if not fully resolved. These antagonisms were related to the disputes generated by the simultaneous state-building enterprises conducted by the state elites in these countries after the withdrawal of colonial empires.

The fundamental rationale for ASEAN's founding was characterized by Michael Leifer as "collective internal security." According to him, "Regional partnership was intended to control conflict, to ease the management of fragile political systems and so to mitigate vulnerability." This meant that "external adventurism [against each other] would be discouraged" and also that "the contagion of internal political disorder would be prevented from spreading from an infected state to contaminate the body politic of regional partners, and from providing a point of entry to South-East Asia for competing external powers."[52] Leifer's description of ASEAN's central task highlights the importance of the internal dimension of security, especially regime security, in the construction of regional or subregional security structures.

This aspect of ASEAN's regional cooperation for security has been analyzed in detail by Amitav Acharya, whose conclusion, he has argued convincingly, is applicable in equal, if not greater, measure to GCC: "In the perception of the regional actors in the context of their individual security predicament as well as their outlook on regionalism, the notion of national and regional security has in essence been a concern with regime security."[53] Similarly, Osama Harb has contended that the main motivation for forming GCC in 1981 was "co-operation and co-ordination between member states to preserve security within their territorial borders. In other words, this meant the maintenance of public order as defined by the regimes in these countries."[54]

Regionalism, or, rather, subregionalism, has come full circle in the case of both ASEAN and GCC, providing evidence for the thesis that successful regional cooperation is based primarily on the convergence of regime interests relating to internal security, especially the shared perceptions of internally generated threats to the security of states and the stability of regimes. Regimes that share similar perceptions of internal threats are likely to have similar ideological orientations and links with extra-regional power centers. Symmetry in strategic perceptions has usually gone hand in hand with shared regime security concerns. With their pro-Western orientations, ASEAN and GCC provide good examples of the connection between regime security concerns and external strategic and political orientations.[55]

The ineffectiveness of the South Asian Association for Regional Cooperation (SAARC) as a regional organization can be explained by the lack of congruence in regime security concerns and basic asymmetries in the external orientations of regional states in South Asia.[56] Coupled with this lack of congruence is the absence of a regional consensus on the role of the pivotal power in South Asia—India. As with ASEAN in its initial phase, SAARC was ostensibly organized as an organization to deal with economic, technical, and cultural cooperation and as one that eschewed security issues and high politics. In fact, Article 10 of the SAARC Charter lays down clearly that "bilateral and contentious issues shall be excluded from the deliberations." However, in practice, political and security concerns—primarily bilateral issues between India and its neighbors—have continued to form the not-so-hidden agendas of SAARC summits and meetings of foreign ministers.

Furthermore, the idea of SAARC, as originally floated by Bangladesh in the early 1980s, was to constrain India's freedom of action in dealing bilaterally with its smaller neighbors by enmeshing the regional giant in a web of multilateral relationships. It is no wonder that political and security issues have been the center of discussion in bilateral, informal meetings of heads of government held during SAARC summits; have led to constant maneuverings by Pakistan and India at SAARC meetings to paint the other in a bad light; and have even led to the cancellation of at least one summit because it coincided with a particularly tense moment in India–Sri Lanka relations.

A major difference between SAARC and ASEAN and GCC is the pan-regional nature of SAARC compared with the subregional nature of both ASEAN and GCC. Whereas SAARC was established as a regionally inclusive organization to contain India and to multilaterally manage the relationships of the smaller countries in the region with the regional big power, ASEAN and GCC were exclusive in their nature and were limited to states and regimes with similar threat perceptions, regime interests, and strategic orientations.

ASEAN and GCC resulted from regional polarization and its reinforcement in the 1960s between North Vietnam and the noncommunist regimes of Southeast Asia and in the 1980s between revolutionary Iran and the Arab monarchies of the Gulf. In this sense, participating nations formed "defence communities" rather than "security communities."[57] Moreover, ASEAN and GCC were founded as a result not only of interstate polarization but also of the fear among the ruling elites of Southeast Asia and the Gulf that the communist and Islamic revolutionary contagions could spread throughout non-Communist Southeast Asia and the conservative Arab monarchies of the Gulf. This was the chief concern that united these states under regional groupings such as ASEAN and GCC in an effort to provide themselves with collective regime security. Given the distribution of power in Southeast Asia and the Gulf, as well as the interest of major external powers in the two regions, the noncommunist countries of Southeast Asia and the Gulf monarchies could reasonably assume that they could balance Vietnamese and Iranian power, respectively, with a generous amount of external help that seemed to be forthcoming from the West, especially from the United States.

In contrast, South Asia combined huge disparity in power with the centrality of India's geographic location and the economic dependence of several of the smaller regional states on India for trade and transit. This meant that India's neighbors, except for Pakistan, were in no position to balance or even alienate India beyond a point that could bring economic and political retribution from New Delhi either in the form of trade embargoes or support for antiregime movements. It was no wonder that the initiative for a pan-regional organization in South Asia came from the smaller states of the region, led by Bangladesh, whose interests would have been adversely affected by regional polarization—a logical outcome had they openly joined Pakistan against India to curb Indian power and ambitions.

After some initial hesitation, India and Pakistan agreed to join the regional association, as neither wanted the other to dominate the organization because of its own absence. Consequently, SAARC is somewhat of a paradox. Not only has it come into existence despite the rivalry between India and Pakistan; it has also come to encompass that rivalry within the organization. But the institutionalization of regional polarization has been avoided at the cost of organizational effectiveness and has led to collective immobilism within SAARC on issues that dominate the security landscape of the South Asian region, including those of Kashmir and the Tamil insurgency in Sri Lanka.

Finally, another major difference between ASEAN and GCC and SAARC is that whereas the first two groups had the blessings and the active encouragement of a power bloc led by a superpower, SAARC was established by an autonomous initiative within its region, largely independent of great power interests and in the face of great power skepticism. Both the involvement of great powers and the lack of such involvement can be double-edged swords. Involvement may smooth the way for regional security groups by providing them with crucial external political support and the military hardware necessary to enhance the security of their members collectively. It can also generate counterinvolvement by a rival great power or powers, can escalate regional arms races, and can lead to the convergence of regional and global polarizations, thus making the security dilemma of regional states more acute. Noninvolvement by great powers has its own negative and positive effects. On the one hand, it reduces the stimulus to build effective security organizations and to find solutions to intramural disputes because of the absence of crucial external catalysts interested in regional or subregional harmony; on the other, it separates regional security issues from global antagonisms, thereby insulating regional rivalries—however imperfectly—from great power interference and exacerbation.

It is difficult to say which of the two models is preferable for the management of regional security issues. Although ASEAN and GCC have enhanced subregional security (especially the security of regimes), they have tended to reinforce and exacerbate regional polarization. SAARC, although preventing formal polarization in the region, remains marginal to the region's central security concerns. Regional security is not assured—except in very limited ways—by the existence and functioning of regional or subregional organizations such as SAARC, ASEAN, and GCC, because regional security structures are, in the final analysis, hostages to the nature of the relationships among their members and between their members and other regional states. They are also profoundly influenced by the way in which issues of systemic security, as represented by the policies of the great powers, impinge upon regional security concerns.

This reference to the great powers is a good way to remind us that regions do not function in a global vacuum and that the international dimension of security, fashioned largely by the political and security relationships of the great powers, impinges upon state and regional security issues—often rather dramatically. It is to this dimension, in all its multifaceted complexities, that I turn in the following chapters.

Notes

1. For the seminal work on the origins and evolution of the Kashmir dispute, see Sisir Gupta, *Kashmir: A Study in India-Pakistan Relations* (Bombay: Asia Publishing House, 1966). For a diverse but interesting collection of more recent analyses of the issue, see Raju G.C. Thomas (ed.), *Perspectives on Kashmir: The Roots of Conflict in South Asia* (Boulder: Westview Press, 1992).

2. For various explanatory theories of Indonesian behavior during its "confrontation" with Malaysia, see J. A. C. Mackie, *Konfrontasi: The Indonesian-Malaysian Dispute 1963–1966* (Kuala Lumpur: Oxford University Press, 1974).

3. For two very readable accounts of the origins and evolution of the conflict over Palestine, see Elizabeth Monroe, *Britain's Moment in the Middle East, 1914–1956* (Baltimore: Johns Hopkins University Press, 1963); and David Gilmour, *The Dispossessed* (London: Sphere Books, 1983).

4. Naomi Chazan, "Introduction: Approaches to the Study of Irredentism," in Naomi Chazan (ed.), *Irredentism and International Politics* (Boulder: Lynne Rienner Publishers, 1991): 1.

5. For details, see David H. Finnie, *Shifting Lines in the Sand: Kuwait's Elusive Frontier with Iraq* (Cambridge: Harvard University Press, 1992).

6. For the origins of the Iraq-Iran conflict, see Tareq Ismail, *Iraq and Iran:*

The Roots of Conflict (Syracuse: Syracuse University Press, 1982); for the roots of the Sino-Indian border war, see Neville Maxwell, *India's China War* (London: Jonathan Cape, 1970).

7. Najdan Pasic, "Varieties of Nation-Building in the Balkans and Among the Southern Slavs," in S. N. Eisenstadt and Stein Rokkan (eds.), *Building States and Nations,* Vol. 2 (Beverly Hills: Sage, 1973): 130.

8. Kalevi J. Holsti, *Peace and War: Armed Conflicts and International Order, 1648–1989* (Cambridge: Cambridge University Press, 1991): Table 11.1, 274–278. The only two cases in Holsti's tabulation that fell outside the Third World were the Soviet interventions in Hungary (1956) and Czechoslovakia (1968). Holsti's estimate is termed conservative because he used stringent criteria to determine whether outbreaks of armed violence fell under his definition of wars and major armed interventions. Other observers have put the figure for conflicts in the post-1945 period much higher. For example, Evan Luard estimated that between 1945 and 1986, there were 127 "significant wars." Of these, Europe accounted for 2, Latin America for 26, Africa for 31, the Middle East for 24, and Asia for 44. According to Luard's estimate, more than 98 percent of all international conflicts during that period took place in the Third World. Evan Luard, *War in International Society* (London: I. B. Tauris, 1986): Appendix 5, 442–447.

9. K. J. Holsti, "International Theory and War in the Third World," in Brian L. Job (ed.), *The Insecurity Dilemma: National Security of Third World States* (Boulder: Lynne Rienner Publishers, 1992): 38.

10. For an excellent study of the Bangladesh crisis that highlights the mutually reinforcing nature of domestic and international factors in a regional conflict, see Richard Sisson and Leo E. Rose, *War and Secession: Pakistan, India, and the Creation of Bangladesh* (Berkeley: University of California Press, 1990).

11. For a perceptive account of the roots of the current insurrection in the Kashmir Valley and its linkage and interaction with the stakes, interests, and policies of the Indian and Pakistani states, see Ashutosh Varshney, "India, Pakistan and Kashmir: Antinomies of Nationalism," *Asian Survey* 31, no. 11 (November 1991): 997–1019.

12. Donald L. Horowitz, *Ethnic Groups in Conflict* (Berkeley: University of California Press, 1985): 230.

13. For details of the emergence and the tortuous course of Kurdish ethnonationalism in Iran, Iraq, and Turkey, see Nader Entessar, *Kurdish Ethnonationalism* (Boulder: Lynne Rienner Publishers, 1992).

14. Donald L. Horowitz, "Irredentas and Secessions: Adjacent Phenomena, Neglected Connections," in Chazan (ed.), *Irredentism and International Politics,* 9.

15. Horowitz, *Ethnic Groups in Conflict,* 230.

16. Alexis Heraclides, "Secessionist Minorities and External Involvement," *International Organization* 44, no. 3 (Summer 1990): 378. For a more elaborate statement of this thesis, see Alexis Heraclides, *The Self-Determination of Minorities in International Politics* (London: Frank Cass, 1991).

17. For the complexities of the Kurdish issue after the Gulf War, see Robert Olson, "The Kurdish Question in the Aftermath of the Gulf War: Geopolitical and Geostrategic Changes in the Middle East," *Third World Quarterly* 13, no. 3 (1992): 475–499. Also see John Darnton, "Kurds Rebuilding Shattered Land, Winning a Precarious Autonomy," *New York Times* (January 21, 1994): A1, A8.

18. For a comprehensive account of external involvement in the Nigerian civil war, see John J. Stremlau, *The International Politics of the Nigerian Civil War, 1967–1970* (Princeton: Princeton University Press, 1977).

19. For the multiplicity of India's roles in the Tamil–Sri Lanka conflict and the vacillation in its policy, see K. M. de Silva, "Indo–Sri Lankan Relations,

1975–1989: A Study in the Internationalization of Ethnic Conflict," in K. M. de Silva and R. J. May (eds.), *Internationalization of Ethnic Conflict* (New York: St. Martin's Press, 1991): 76–106. Also see P. Venkateshwar Rao, "Ethnic Conflict in Sri Lanka: India's Role and Perception," *Asian Survey* 28, no. 4 (April 1988): 419–436; and Sankaran Krishna, "A Fatal Convergence: India and Sri Lanka," *Studies in Conflict and Terrorism* 15, no. 4 (Winter 1992): 267–282.

20. For details of the Eritrean struggle for independence from Ethiopia, see Lionel Cliffe, "Forging a Nation: The Eritrean Experience," *Third World Quarterly* 11, no. 4 (October 1989): 131–147.

21. For a comprehensive analysis of politics, including analyses of ethnicity and secession, in the former Soviet republics, see Ian Bremmer and Ray Taras (eds.), *Nations and Politics in the Soviet Successor States* (Cambridge: Cambridge University Press, 1993). For a perceptive analysis of the post-Soviet situation in Central Asia, see Shireen T. Hunter, "The Muslim Republics of the Former Soviet Union: Policy Challenges for the United States," *Washington Quarterly* 15, no. 3 (Summer 1992): 57–71.

22. For a convincing analysis of the Russian role in the secessionist movements in the former Soviet republics, see Thomas Goltz, "Letter from Eurasia: The Hidden Russian Hand," *Foreign Policy* 92 (Fall 1993): 92–116. According to Goltz, "The Russian policy appears to be based on the tacit threat of dismemberment of those states that wish to leave Moscow's orbit" (92). For corroborating analyses, see John P. Hannah, "The (Russian) Empire Strikes Back," Melor Sturua, "Yeltsin's Newest Proconsul," and Mark A. Uhlig, "The Endless War," all in *New York Times* (October 27, 1993): A23.

23. For a good assessment of the situation in Tajikistan in fall 1993, see Raymond Bonner, "Asian Republic Still Caught in the Web of Communism," *New York Times* (October 13, 1993): A3.

24. Raymond Bonner, "Playing Dominoes in Central Asia: Why All Eyes Are on a Place Called Tajikistan," *New York Times* (November 7, 1993): section 4, 4.

25. For details of Nasser's, and, therefore, Egypt's, preeminent role in inter-Arab politics, see Malcolm H. Kerr, *The Arab Cold War: Gamal 'Abd al-Nasir and His Rivals, 1958–1970,* 3d ed. (New York: Oxford University Press, 1971). Egypt under Nasser came to represent the force of Arab nationalism that, in terms of its pristine ideology, assumed the illegitimacy and transitory nature of Arab states, creatures of imperialism that were destined to be welded into a single pan-Arab state. Although Nasser himself was initially reluctant to embrace pan-Arabism, after the 1956 Suez crisis he realized its instrumental value in enhancing the interests of the Egyptian state and of his own regime and used it for these ends. Nasser's success, which was also responsible for his ultimate failure because he allowed Egypt's commitments to outrun its capabilities, nonetheless demonstrated the fragile and limited legitimacy of both states and regimes in the Arab world. For a thorough and incisive analysis of the problem of political legitimacy in the Arab world, see Michael C. Hudson, *Arab Politics: The Search for Legitimacy* (New Haven: Yale University Press, 1977).

26. For an analysis of the interaction between India's regional security concerns vis-à-vis Nepal and China and domestic political developments in Nepal in 1990 leading to the establishment of a democratic government in that country, see John W. Garver, "China-India Rivalry in Nepal: The Clash over Chinese Arms Sales," *Asian Survey* 31, no. 10 (October 1991): 956–975, especially 969–973.

27. William R. Thompson, "The Regional Subsystem: A Conceptual Explication and a Propositional Inventory," *International Studies Quarterly* 17, no. 1 (March 1973): 101.

28. Raimo Vayrynen, "Regional Conflict Formations: An Intractable Problem

of International Relations," *Journal of Peace Research* 21, no. 4 (1984): 340. Emphasis in the original.

29. Louis J. Cantori and Steven L. Spiegel, "The International Relations of Regions," in Richard A. Falk and Saul H. Mendlovitz (eds.), *Regional Politics and World Order* (San Francisco: W. H. Freeman, 1973): 340.

30. For an explication of the concept of security community, see Karl Deutsch et. al., *Political Community and the North Atlantic Area* (Princeton: Princeton University Press, 1957).

31. For a valuable analysis of the military dimension of this dependent relationship that is at the same time informed by the wider dynamic of the South's dependence on the North, see Michael Barnett and Alexander Wendt, "The Systemic Sources of Dependent Militarization," in Job (ed.), *The Insecurity Dilemma,* 97–119.

32. For Buzan's original formulation, see Barry Buzan, "A Framework for Regional Security Analysis," in Barry Buzan, Gowher Rizvi, et. al., *South Asian Insecurity and the Great Powers* (London: Macmillan, 1986): 3–32. The quotes are from pages 7 and 8.

33. Barry Buzan, *People, States and Fear: An Agenda for International Security Studies in the Post–Cold War Era,* 2d ed. (Boulder: Lynne Rienner Publishers, 1991): 190.

34. Michael Brecher, "International Relations and Asian Studies," *World Politics* 15, no. 2 (1963): 213–235; Bruce M. Russett, *International Regions and the International System* (Chicago: University of Chicago Press, 1967); Louis J. Cantori and Steven L. Spiegel, *The International Politics of Regions: A Comparative Approach* (Englewood Cliffs: Prentice-Hall, 1970).

35. Buzan, *People, States and Fear,* 189.

36. For two very different views of the Israeli-U.S. relationship, see Nadav Safran, *Israel: The Embattled Ally* (Cambridge: Belknap Press, 1981); and Stephen Green, *Taking Sides: America's Secret Relations with a Militant Israel* (New York: William Morrow, 1984).

37. For details of Pakistan-U.S. relations, see Shirin Tahir-Kheli, *The United States and Pakistan: The Evolution of an Influence Relationship* (New York: Praeger, 1982); for Indo-U.S. relations, see Harold A. Gould and Sumit Ganguly, *The Hope and the Reality: U.S.-Indian Relations from Roosevelt to Reagan* (Boulder: Westview Press, 1992).

38. For the Indo-Soviet relationship, see Ramesh Thakur, "India and the Soviet Union: Conjunctions and Disjunctions of Interests," *Asian Survey* 31, no. 9 (September 1991): 826–846.

39. For the Iraqi-Soviet relationship during the course of the Iran-Iraq War, see Saharam Chubin and Charles Tripp, *Iran and Iraq at War* (Boulder: Westview Press, 1988): Chapter 10. Also see Oles M. Smolansky, with Bettie M. Smolansky, *The USSR and Iraq: The Soviet Quest for Influence* (Durham: Duke University Press, 1991): Chapter 7.

40. Vayrynen, "Regional Conflict Formations," 340.

41. For a perceptive analysis of Israel's role as a regional great power, see Nils A. Butenschon, "Israel as a Regional Great Power: Paradoxes of Regional Alienation," in Iver B. Neumann (ed.), *Regional Great Powers in International Politics* (London: Macmillan, 1992): 95–119.

42. For a more detailed statement of this argument, see Mohammed Ayoob, "Unravelling the Concept: 'National Security' in the Third World," in Bahgat Korany, Paul Noble, and Rex Brynen (eds.), *The Many Faces of National Security in the Arab World* (London: Macmillan, 1993): 45–48.

43. Thomas Perry Thornton, "Regional Organizations in Conflict Management," *Annals of the American Academy of Political and Social Science* 518 (November 1991): 136.

44. For details of this argument, see Mohammed Ayoob, "India in South Asia: The Quest for Regional Predominance," *World Policy Journal* 7, no. 1 (Winter 1989–1990): 107–133.

45. W. Howard Wriggins, "South Asian Regional Politics: Asymmetrical Balance or One-State Dominance?" in W. Howard Wriggins (ed.), *Dynamics of Regional Politics: Four Systems on the Indian Ocean Rim* (New York: Columbia University Press, 1992): 98.

46. For an incisive article that, among other things, demonstrates the inextricable intermeshing of the regional dynamic of security in the Gulf with that of the larger Middle East, see Richard K. Herrmann, "The Middle East and the New World Order: Rethinking U.S. Political Strategy After the Gulf War," *International Security* 16, no. 2 (Fall 1991): 42–75.

47. For a more detailed discussion of the Indonesian position in Southeast Asia, see Arnfinn Jorgensen-Dahl, "Indonesia as a Regional Great Power," in Iver B. Neumann (ed.), *Regional Great Powers in International Politics* (London: Macmillan, 1992): 70–94.

48. For an assessment of the future of the Southeast Asian security complex that reaches similar conclusions, see Amitav Acharya, *A New Regional Order in South-East Asia: ASEAN in the Post–Cold War Era,* Adelphi Paper 279 (London: International Institute for Strategic Studies, 1993): especially 74–78.

49. For what might turn out to be a prescient analysis of Sino-Japanese relations in the not-too-distant future, see Gerald Segal, "The Coming Confrontation Between China and Japan?" *World Policy Journal* 10, no. 2 (Summer 1993): 27–32.

50. Pan-continental organizations such as the Organization of American States (OAS) and the Organization of African Unity (OAU) have been left out of this discussion—OAU because of the numerically unwieldy and highly disparate nature of its membership and OAS because of the membership of a superpower, the United States, in the organization, which has eroded OAS autonomy in matters relating to regional security and, during the Cold War era, which led to the imposition of the logic of great power rivalry on regional concerns. Nowhere was this more clear than in the treatment meted out to Cuba by the OAS after the Castro revolution. The Arab League has also been left out of consideration because of its relative incoherence as a regional organization and its increasing marginality in the politics of the Arab world. In any case, the examples presented in this chapter are meant to be illustrative and not exhaustive in nature.

51. This conclusion independently corroborates Joseph Nye's argument about the "conflict creation" potential of regional organizations. See Joseph S. Nye, Jr., *Peace in Parts: Integration and Conflict in Regional Organization* (Boston: Little, Brown, 1971).

52. Michael Leifer, *ASEAN and the Security of South-East Asia* (London: Routledge, 1989): 1, 3.

53. Amitav Acharya, "Regionalism and Regime Security in the Third World: Comparing the Origins of the ASEAN and the GCC," in Job (ed.), *Insecurity Dilemma,* 163.

54. Osama Al Ghazaly Harb, "The Gulf Co-operation Council and Regional Security in the Gulf," in Mohammed Ayoob (ed.), *Regional Security in the Third World* (Boulder: Westview Press, 1986): 235–236.

55. I have argued this point in Mohammed Ayoob, "Regional Security and the Third World," in Ayoob (ed.), *Regional Security in the Third World,* 20. Also see

Mohammed Ayoob, "Perspectives from the Gulf: Regime Security or Regional Security," in Donald H. McMillen (ed.), *Asian Perspectives on International Security* (London: Macmillan, 1984): 92–116.

56. For details of this argument, see Mohammed Ayoob, "The Primacy of the Political: South Asian Regional Cooperation in Comparative Perspective," *Asian Survey* 25, no. 4 (April 1985): 443–457.

57. For an analysis of the difference between the two conceptions of regional security, with special reference to Southeast Asia, see Amitav Acharya, "The Association of Southeast Asian Nations: 'Security Community' or 'Defence Community,'" *Pacific Affairs* 62, no. 2 (Summer 1991): 159–178.

■ 4 ■

The Third World and the System of States

The politics and international relations and, consequently, the security predicament of Third World states cannot be analyzed in isolation from the role of the Third World in the international system for several reasons. The most prominent reason is that Third World states owe their origins to the expansion of the modern system of states from its original European home. This expansion was mediated by the twin processes of colonialism and decolonization. The globalization of European power and of its attendant norms of international political intercourse introduced colonized territories—later to become Third World states—to the notion of state sovereignty, which is the fundamental defining characteristic of the modern system of states. Along with the notion of state sovereignty came its corollaries: rigidly demarcated and sacrosanct boundaries, mutual recognition of sovereign political entities, and nonintervention in the internal affairs of other states.[1] Third World state elites have internalized these values to an astonishing degree.

The expansion of the international system also introduced the colonies to the idea of national self-determination, an idea that gained in popularity following its application to the European possessions of the defeated Ottoman and Hapsburg Empires after World War I. The ideology of national self-determination played an important role in mobilizing native elites (and, in some instances, larger segments of society) against colonial rule and in legitimizing anticolonial movements, both domestically and internationally.[2]

The second reason for the close connection between what goes on in the international system and what transpires in the domestic arena of Third World states is the special relationship the Third World has with the international system as the weak, intruder majority in the system of states. Third World states constitute about three-quarters of the membership of the international system, although their actual power within that system is not close to their numerical strength. A large number of independent states emerged in the Third World because of the rapid decolonization following World War II. This development posed more than just a problem of quantitative adjustment for the system of states: It posed a much greater qualitative problem. For the first time since the establishment of the system of sovereign states, the newcomers far outnumbered the established membership, which had previously shared a certain similarity in the areas of civilization, religion, political philosophy, and even racial prejudice.

Newcomers such as Russia, Turkey, and Japan had joined the modern system of states at various junctures in its earlier history, but these intruders had always been fewer in number than the established members at the time they were accepted as members. It had, therefore, been relatively easy for the system to accommodate the intruders with little trauma and dislocation. At worst, established members of the system could deal with a recalcitrant newcomer by marginalizing it almost totally, as they did to Ottoman Turkey for much of the time it was a nominal member of the European states system.

The unprecedented expansion of the system of states in such a short time following World War II coincided with the creation of the first truly universal international organization, the United Nations. The nominal equality of its universal membership was qualified by the creation of a category of permanent members of the Security Council, who had the right to veto. But enough egalitarian thrust survived in the General Assembly (and in the proliferation of UN specialized agencies) to have an impact on the norms of state behavior, especially on issues of decolonization, racial equality, and sharing world resources.[3] This change in the norms of political discourse within the international system has tended to increase the collective visibility of the Third World newcomers in that system, particularly on issues of political morality and reallocation of global resources. This transformation has been all the more striking because the high profile of Third World states has borne little relationship to the political, military, economic, and technological capabilities—the traditional indexes of power—at their command.

The disjuncture in the political visibility and capabilities of the Third World has been thrown into sharper relief because the collective interests of the new entrants into the club of sovereign states have often been at odds with those of the powerful international establishment—that is, the industrialized states of Europe and North America. This situation has frequently created tensions between the older, more powerful, but fewer established members and the weak, intruder majority.[4] These tensions have been particularly manifested in the arena of international political economy and have been centered on issues of redistribution of resources and wealth, control over common global resources, and transfer of technology considered essential for Third World development.

Some Western observers such as Stephen Krasner have perceived these tensions between the Third World and the industrialized countries as irreconcilable, or as a case of "structural conflict" between the South and the North in the international system. Krasner has gone to the extent of advising the North to disengage as much as possible from the South, because continuing engagement is likely only to promote greater conflict and increased demands from the poor countries of the South on the rich countries of the North.[5] Similarly, some Third World analysts such as Jayantanuja Bandyopadhyaya have argued that "the South must . . . perceive the North-South conflict as a zero-sum game, involving an acute confrontation with the North."[6] Paradoxically, neo-Marxist dependency theorists have prescribed a similar strategy of disengagement for the South as an essential prerequisite for the attainment of their cherished goal of economic and political autonomy for the Third World.[7]

The third reason the workings of the international system are so important to the intrastate and interstate dimensions of security of Third World states is that many Third World states depend for their security upon the military, political, and economic aid they can extract from the powerful members of the international system. This situation is a function of the insecurities and conflicts that abound within Third World regions and that pit neighbors against one another, a subject I discussed in earlier chapters. Many Third World states, including many that professed nonalignment during the Cold War era, have been forced to search for great power patrons (or at least suppliers of military hardware and long-term credits) to bolster their capabilities against regional adversaries and domestic insurgents.

The proliferation during the Cold War years of mutual security agreements, peace and friendship treaties, and informal security arrangements between Third World states and one or the other superpower bore adequate testimony to this phenomenon. Such security links gave Third World ruling elites the assurance that a major power would come to their aid if they were threatened by domestic or external opponents, although, as the cases of Pakistan in 1971 and of Iran in 1978–1979 demonstrated, this did not always happen. In turn, these security links provided the superpowers with the opportunity to extend their influence within the Third World and to acquire bases and facilities as part of their continuing global competition for power and influence. Even Third World states that during the Cold War were genuinely nonaligned in a military and security sense were, and are, linked to the centers of international power because of their dependence upon the advanced industrial countries for trade, aid, investment, and technology. As Richard Feinberg pointed out, "As long as the one-world economy functions, political nonalignment occurs within a larger framework of shared interests."[8]

Contradictory Third World Approaches Toward the Global North

This dependence by individual Third World states on the major centers of economic and military power in the global North at the same time these states have been trying as a group to erode the control powerful Northern states hold over the international political economy appears to be a major—nearly schizophrenic—contradiction in their international behavior.[9] Third World state elites appear doubly schizophrenic because of a further, even more fundamental contradiction in their approach to the international system. As intruders and have-nots in that system, Third World states generally favor structural changes in global economic and political systems to encourage a more equitable distribution of the world's resources.[10] However, their enthusiasm for change, which can often have destabilizing consequences, is neutralized by their role as weak and vulnerable states with a vested interest in preserving predictable norms of state behavior.

Their weakness as states, which is largely a function of the lack of unconditional legitimacy for state structures and governing regimes, gives them a greater stake in the maintenance of order within the international system than the stake held by the developed states of the North, which face few, if any, major challenges to their legitimacy. This becomes clear if we define order as a guarantee of (1) the existence of states once they are established, (2) the stability of the territorial possessions of states, and (3) the sanctity of contracts among states, which provides a reasonable predictability in interstate relations.

The Third World states' favorable predisposition toward the maintenance of international order, and the security and economic dependence of many of these states on the developed countries of the North, reinforce their commitment to the global status quo. This means that most Third World states act as collaborators with the international establishment in preserving an international order that at the same time and at a different level they consider inequitable.

This contradiction within the dispositions of Third World state elites means that whereas one set of concerns reinforces the Third World states' dependence on the developed states, the other set pushes them toward demanding greater autonomy from the major powers that act as managers of the international system. However, if a fundamental conflict arises between the two sets of objectives, the decisionmakers in Third World states are likely to favor their state and regime interests over the more diffuse interests of the collective Third World. This is the logic the state-centered nature of the international system demands of them. But in the absence of such fundamental conflicts of interest in the coming decades over issues likely to figure in the global agenda (for example, global resource reallocation, transfer of technology, global ecological management), most Third World states can be expected to continue espousing both sets of objectives, because both sets enhance their capacity to act as rightful members of the system of states.

It is a mistake to dismiss Third World states' collective aspirations for greater economic and political autonomy as hypocritical verbiage. In terms of day-to-day foreign policy decisions, these aspirations are often buried under the more weighty immediate concerns of "reasons of state." Nevertheless, aspirations for autonomy are the products of a historical process of unequal interaction—in military, economic, political, cultural, and technological terms—between the populations and the elites of these countries and their former colonial masters, and they continue to have great resonance within the countries.

The collective sense of insecurity in the Third World regarding the developed states is based on the perception of deprivation and impotence in both the colonial past and current interaction between the North and the South, interaction that is heavily weighted in favor of the North. This perception was augmented during the Cold War by the presence of two visible tendencies in the international system in the aftermath of World War II. First, the stratification within the international system between the developed and developing worlds allowed the developed world's military and political rivalry to be exported to the Third World. Second, despite such exportation, the same stratification in the global hierarchy insulated the core of the international system—the two superpowers and their respective alliance systems—from the conflicts and instabilities prevalent in the Third World, which drastically curtailed the impact of the Third World's security concerns on the international system's security agenda. I return to this point in Chapter 5.

Reconcilable Contradiction

The perception of dual impotence during the days of bipolarity reinforced the feeling among Third World intellectual and political elites that there are two types of actors in the international system. The primary actors consist of the superpowers, their European allies, and Japan. The secondary actors comprise the Third World of Asia, Africa, and Latin America. The sparsely populated and affluent oil-exporting countries of the Gulf form a part of the Third World, despite their high per capita incomes. They have almost all of the characteristics that define Third World states. Their one-product economies, which are almost totally dependent upon the industrialized countries' demand, technologies, and financial markets; their security dependence on the major centers of global power; and the problems of legitimacy in terms of their regimes and state structures make them almost typical Third World states, even though they temporarily control vast amounts of oil dollars.[11]

The one striking exception to this category of secondary actors is China, which was able to break the power barrier between the two sets of actors by achieving nuclear weapons capability and inheriting a veto-wielding permanent seat in the UN Security Council. However, in light of

China's domestic economic and political contradictions, Beijing's membership in the category of primary international actors remains rather tenuous. During the Cold War era, China's inclusion in the club of great powers was based largely upon the sufferance of the two superpowers and on their calculations of China's importance in their respective global strategies, rather than on the country's inherent importance within the international system.

This dichotomy between primary and secondary actors in the international system does not mean, however, that unmitigated confrontation exists or will exist between the Third World and the more established members of the system of states. The relationship between the Third World states and the developed world is too complex to be determined by any single dimension of that relationship.

This is why it is absurd to deplore, as Eli Kedourie has done, the emergence of "the so-called Third World" whose supposed turbulence and radicalism has brought about a state of "new international disorder." According to Kedourie, "Turbulence can be held at bay or, better still, tamed. But you cannot sit down and smoke the pipe of peace with it, neither can you embrace it in friendship."[12] Arguing from a cultural-legal perspective, Adda Bozeman has come to conclusions similar to Kedourie's, although they are stated less abrasively. According to her, "Loosened from the context of Euro-American jurisprudence, history, and ethic, and associated instead with a new free-wheeling ideology that proclaims unsubstantiated human rights for everyone, the law of nations is now conscripted to serve the cause of political rhetoric and tactics." The present situation, with its massive intrusion of non-European states as actors in the international system, reminds Bozeman of the period before the nineteenth century in the sense that it is "a world that has no common culture and no overarching political order, and that it is no longer prepared to abide by *Western* standards of international conduct."[13]

Hedley Bull and Adam Watson have countered such views by strongly arguing:

> It would be wrong to conclude that as a consequence of the challenge to European dominance in the present century, the international society of the present time is in a state of disintegration. For one thing, it is important not to exaggerate the degree of cohesion that existed in the old, European-dominated system, which in the first half of this century gave rise to war and human catastrophe on a scale far exceeding anything that has taken place since it went into demise. . . . For another thing, we have to remember that the anarchy or disorder that plays so large a role in the global international system of the present time is by no means to be ascribed solely, or perhaps even mainly, to the presence within it of new Asian and African states, or to their attempts to change the rules by which it operates in their favor. The source of the anarchy and disorder is in large measure to be found in factors that would be having their effect on the Western, industrialized world, even if it had not to cope with the problem of adjusting itself to a resurgent Third World: the ideological divi-

> sions arising out of the Russian Revolution, the terrible legacy of the two World Wars, the tensions arising out of rapid technological, economic, and social change, the impact of nuclear weapons.[14]

Statements such as those by Kedourie and Bozeman show both a lack of appreciation of the historical process that encompassed both colonialism and decolonization and an assumption that the Third World is doomed to remain in a state of contradiction with the established "civilized" states in the international system. Furthermore, they assume that there is no scope for mutual accommodation by reforming or even tinkering with the established international order. Whereas a certain degree of tension between the new entrants and established members is to be expected in any institution, elevating this tension to the level of an irreconcilable contradiction is absurd, particularly when we recall that the new entrants to the international system are trying desperately to mold themselves in the image of the established members by internalizing the fundamental, state-centered values on which the system is based—those of sovereignty, nonintervention, hierarchy, and the balance of power. As Bull and Watson have stated, "Third World governments do not want to replace the society of sovereign states but rather to improve their own position within that society. This attachment to juridically equal sovereignty is encouraging to those who welcome continuity with the European system, and disappointing to those who hoped that functional or other pressures would lead to the obsolescence of the sovereign state as the basic unit of international society."[15]

Additionally, the security and developmental concerns of individual Third World states make most, if not all, of those states dependent upon the major industrialized states for arms, political support, capital, and technology. These ties are strong enough in most cases to neutralize—for all practical purposes, except for the occasional rhetoric—the confrontational tendencies of Third World ruling elites toward the industrialized states of Europe and North America. Moreover, given the socioeconomic character of most Third World state elites, it would not be wrong to conclude that their class interests propel them toward accommodation with the industrialized states since they depend on the goodwill of influential social and economic groups in the developed states for their economic welfare and regime security.[16]

Finally, the distinction between the Third World states' individual foreign policy concerns in the international system and their collective concerns about improving their position within that system is more apparent than real. This proposition may not be evident upon cursory examination, but it is based on the premise that issues of status and security cannot be treated in isolation from each other. Given the inequality of power within the international system, issues of status readily turn into issues of security in the view of Third World elites. Therefore, the two sets of concerns are in essence the two sides of the same coin for these new members of the system of states. Issues of status and security may find different manifestations at different times and in connection with different problems, but they result from the same preoccupation with state and regime security by Third World ruling elites. This is especially true because the international system in the post–World War II era has done little to mitigate the security predicament of the Third World.

Juridical Sovereignty and Third World Security

The hierarchical nature of the international system and the division of the world between primary and secondary actors have hampered Third World security. Additionally, certain international norms that have crystallized relatively recently have also had adverse, or at best mixed, effects on the security of Third World states. International norms can be defined as those principles that

> although occasionally subject to circumstantial exceptions . . . are regarded as the starting points in the formulation of a State's external conduct and . . . operate as a touchstone against which the international community can measure the legal acceptability of the actions of its members. . . . Such principles are born when a significant number of States are willing publicly to announce the importance of norms (and their correlative principles) in structuring their international policies or when they show an implicit acceptance of such principles as normative constraints on the State's freedom of action in the international sphere.[17]

In other words, international norms "specify general standards of behavior" on the part of states that are members of the international system.[18] Paradoxically, some new norms that have accentuated the security predicament of the Third World were adopted because of the entry of the postcolonial states into the international system and because of pressure generated by the Third World majority in international forums such as the UN General Assembly.

The United Nations and Territorial Integrity

The first of these norms relates to the fixed nature of juridical sovereignty or statehood once it is conferred by international law and symbolized by membership in the United Nations. The logical corollary of this norm is the sanctity of the borders of postcolonial states. Paradoxically, the international community's commitment to the validity of postcolonial borders was iterated most forcefully in UN General Assembly Resolution 1514, passed December 14, 1960, which codified the right of peoples to self-determination. This resolution, under the title Declaration on the Granting of

Independence to Colonial Territories and Countries, stated that "all peoples have the right to self-determination; by virtue of that right they freely determine their political status and freely pursue their economic, social, and cultural development." At the same time, the resolution stressed the territorial integrity of postcolonial states by declaring, "Any attempt aimed at the partial or total disruption of the national unity and the territorial integrity of a country is incompatible with the purposes and the principles of the Charter of the United Nations."

Soon thereafter, the UN General Assembly passed Resolution 1541 to clarify that the right to self-determination applied only to peoples of the overseas colonies of European empires, not to the various components of the populations of postcolonial states. According to this resolution, a territory was to be considered nonself-governing and its population entitled to self-determination only if it were both "geographically separate" and "distinct ethnically and/or culturally from the country administering it." The combination of these two requirements ruled out the right of self-determination for ethnic minorities in Third World states or within any states that were members of the United Nations. Thereafter, the right of colonial peoples to self-determination was reaffirmed almost annually by the UN General Assembly.[19]

The actions undertaken by the United Nations regarding the attempted secession of Katanga from the Congo (1960–1963) confirmed the view that the right of self-determination applied only to peoples under colonial rule and not to the different ethnic or regional components of postcolonial states.[20] This interpretation was reaffirmed by India's reservation during the adoption of two international human rights covenants in 1966; both began by asserting that "all peoples have the right to self-determination." The Indian reservation made it clear that the right to self-determination applied "only to the peoples under foreign domination" and not to "sovereign independent States or to a section of a people or nation—which is the essence of national integrity."[21]

The twin principles that commit the international community to upholding both the juridical statehood and the boundaries of Third World states are very dear to Third World state elites. Most of these elites preside over states whose geographic contours were designed during the colonial period. They, therefore, have a vested interest in preserving the sanctity of the juridical sovereignty of these states and of their territorial integrity within colonially constructed borders. This objective of Third World state elites receives crucial support from international norms that bestow nearly permanent juridical sovereignty on them and that legally sanction their postcolonial borders.

The fact that the international community bestows juridical sovereignty on postcolonial Third World political entities, even when these entities do not necessarily perform the tasks of statehood effectively, has prompted

Robert Jackson to term the sovereignty of Third World states "negative sovereignty," as opposed to the "positive sovereignty" of the European states. The sovereignty of European states is tied to their efficacy as states and, therefore, is capable of empirical determination. Negative sovereignty, according to Jackson, is sovereign statehood conferred on the former colonies by international law despite the fact that "they lack many of the marks and merits of empirical statehood postulated by positive sovereignty. . . . In short, they often appear to be juridical more than empirical entities: hence quasi-states."[22]

The Third World's tenacious attachment to the norm that postcolonial juridical sovereignty cannot be alienated from even part of a state's territory helps explain the overwhelming 104 to 11 vote in the UN General Assembly on December 7, 1971, against the Indian military intervention in the civil conflict in Pakistan that led to the independence of Bangladesh. This huge margin was all the more surprising since it came at a time when the separation of the two wings of Pakistan appeared inevitable.[23] This same attachment to the principles of territorial integrity and the inalienability of juridical statehood has prevented the de facto separation of the two parts of Cyprus from being translated into a de jure partition of the island.[24]

Comparisons with Europe

Although this set of norms has helped preserve several Third World states that may otherwise have collapsed, it has also added to the security predicament of the Third World state. This point can be understood only by comparison with the European situation at a corresponding stage in its own history of state making. From the early modern period to the end of World War I, the creation of viable states in Europe was accompanied by the relegation of many others to the dustbin of history. Even a cursory reading of European history shows that many states, including Burgundy, Bohemia, Bavaria, and Aragon, to name a few, could not complete the task of state building. Many others, such as Poland and the Baltic states, led precarious lives, losing and regaining their independence several times. The elimination of states that were considered inviable, either because of their internal contradictions or because their existence did not suit great power aspirations, was perfectly acceptable to the European international community virtually until the end of World War I. It is instructive to remember in this context that "the Europe of 1500 included some five hundred more or less independent political units, the Europe of 1900 about twenty-five."[25]

The international consensus on the alienability of juridical statehood began to change during the interwar period and crystallized after World War II in the context of the decolonization of Asia and Africa. Once granted independence, colonies acquired the right to exist as sovereign entities even if many, especially in Africa, did not possess "much in the way of empirical statehood, disclosed by a capacity for effective and civil government."[26] This change in international norms has meant that many political entities in the Third World that in an earlier time would have been considered inviable have continued to exist in a condition of juridical statehood and have received full formal membership in the international system.

This newly crystallized international norm has protected the legal existence of postcolonial states without regard to their internal cohesiveness, but it has not been able to solve or even mitigate the security problems that such states face because of the contradictions that exist within their boundaries and that are inherent in the state-making process. In fact, this international norm may have made the security problems of some states more acute by preventing the legal demise of even the most inviable of these entities, such as Lebanon, Somalia, Angola, Afghanistan, and Liberia. In other words, the crystallization of this norm has transformed what in an earlier age would have been the existential dilemma of such states—"to be or not to be!"—into their perpetual security predicament. Since states, once established, had an open-ended guarantee from the international system that their legal existence was assured, the traumas they suffered and that were, in turn, inflicted on their populations in the process of translating juridical statehood into empirical statehood took on the garb of challenges to their security rather than threats to their existence. It is worth noting parenthetically that this guarantee has begun to weaken in the post–Cold War era. (The effects of this incipient change on the Third World's security predicament are discussed in considerable detail in Chapter 8.) However, this change in international norms, if consolidated, is unlikely to alleviate the Third World's security predicament. In fact, it may considerably worsen the situation and add to the prevalent instability in the Third World. It appears, therefore, that the Third World is caught in a no-win situation in regard to this set of international norms.

A fundamental difference between the European experience and that of the Third World states relates to the consolidation of rules, defined as "specific prescriptions for behavior in clearly defined areas,"[27] governing the system of states. Rules are discrete products of general international norms; they act as vehicles for the application of general norms to specific areas. The established rules of the international system pertaining to sovereignty, territorial integrity, and nonintervention have thus far enhanced and constrained the process of state making in the Third World. The rules have prevented the unrestrained interplay of the internal dynamics of particular states in the making; they have also ruled out interstate war as an instrument of change in the boundaries of states (with limited exceptions, which prove the rule). They have succeeded until recently in underwriting the juridical existence of even the most inviable states in the international system.

External Intervention and Territorial Integrity

Whereas external great powers and stronger Third World states have intervened in the affairs of the weaker states, this intervention has normally stopped short of eliminating or dismembering target states. Moreover, external intervention has usually tended to shore up, rather than alter, the territorial status quo.[28] This has been most evident in the case of Africa, whether in relation to the Nigerian civil war, the Ethiopian-Somalian War, or the Libya-Chad conflict. The Indian intervention in Sri Lanka was aimed as much at preserving the territorial integrity of that country as at ensuring Tamil autonomy. The Syrian military intervention in Lebanon also had as one of its main objectives the maintenance of Lebanon's territorial integrity, even if under Syrian tutelage. Until recently, the only two major cases in which external intervention led to the alteration of postcolonial boundaries were the breakup of Pakistan in 1971 and the de facto division of Cyprus in 1974, the first aided by Indian arms and the second brought about by Turkish military intervention. The fate of a third similar attempt, the incorporation of Kuwait by Iraq in 1990, was foiled by massive international counterintervention led by the United States. Moreover, the division of Pakistan and Cyprus, as I argued earlier, was achieved as a result of a unique conjuncture of factors and forces that would be extremely difficult, if not impossible, to replicate elsewhere in the Third World.

Third World states have to conduct their state-building enterprise within an international framework that encompasses established norms and rules. In contrast, the European states and the modern system of states evolved simultaneously over a period of time. Therefore, during the early years of state making, European state makers worked relatively unhindered by the rules of the system, which had not crystallized fully. The one major exception to this observation was the balance-of-power principle. Although it was employed deliberately at times by the great powers to prevent the domination of the system by a single hegemon, at most other times the balance-of-power principle tended to operate without any conscious effort from the great powers.[29] The principle, however, allowed the expansion and contraction of states, the disappearance of existing states, and the creation of new political entities principally by means of war but also through international deals struck by the strong at the expense of the weak.[30]

Until recently, this process of change in the membership of the system of states seemed no longer possible—especially in the Third World—because international personality, once acquired by postcolonial states, had become virtually impossible to alienate, repudiate, or discard. Gabriel Ben-Dor, writing about the Middle East, pointed out this reality very sharply.

> Countries still may—and do—fail in state building. The cost of failure, however, is not disappearance, but incoherent, uncontrollable conflict. The extreme case in the Middle East is undoubtedly Lebanon: its failures and weaknesses in

> state building have turned it into a dumping ground for revolutionary and ideological forces that the stateness of other countries is unable to tolerate any longer within their own boundaries. But even this process is not irreversible; the price of failure is no longer absolute.[31]

Lebanon has not been an exclusive member of the failed states' club; in fact, recent developments show it may have begun to move out of its failed status. More recent instances in Africa, Central Asia (including Afghanistan), the Caucasus, and the Balkans, however, point to a notable increase in the number of failed and semifailed states. This increase is the result of the paradoxical situation created by an international norm that was conceived to provide legal protection to fragile and vulnerable postcolonial states. This norm, however, has become the source of major internal security problems for some of these states by forcing them to adhere to their internationally bestowed legal status even when they clearly lack the will and the capacity to do so. In Chapter 8 I return to the question of whether the dismemberment of failed states, as a result of the relaxation of this norm in the post–Cold War era, will lead to an improvement or a worsening of the Third World's security predicament.

Impact of Human Rights

A second set of international norms that has affected the security problematic of the Third World is related to human rights, which include civil and political rights as well as economic, social, and cultural rights. The modern conception of human rights can be traced to the natural-law approach as developed in eighteenth-century Europe.[32] But the recent popularity of the cause of human rights in the international arena has come about because of the acceptance by most states of the validity of such rights for all human beings regardless of their citizenship in particular states.

This acceptance was demonstrated soon after the end of World War II when the Preamble of the Charter of the newly established UN declared the organization's determination "to reaffirm faith in fundamental human rights, in the dignity and worth of the human person, [and] in the equal rights of men and women." Article 1 of the Charter listed as one of the fundamental purposes of the United Nations "to achieve international cooperation in . . . promoting and encouraging respect for human rights and for fundamental freedoms for all without distinction as to race, sex, language, or religion."[33] The changing attitude toward human rights as a legitimate concern of the international community that needed to be brought within the ambit of international law led to their codification in the Universal Declaration of Human Rights, adopted in 1948, and the two International Covenants on Human Rights, which were opened for signature and ratification in 1966 and became operative in 1976.

This change in the international consensus regarding human rights was a major development in the evolution of norms that govern the international system. It acknowledged more clearly than ever before that individuals as well as states could be considered subjects of international law. It also signified the international acceptance of the principle that individuals and groups had certain rights independent of their membership in individual states and that these rights did not derive from citizenship but from individuals' status as members of the human species. Furthermore, beginning with the establishment of the UN Commission on Human Rights in the 1970s, several human rights monitoring agencies—both official and nonofficial—have been set up to report on human rights violations and to make habitual violators targets of public condemnation. Amnesty International, founded in 1961, is the most prominent human rights nongovernmental organization (NGO) but is no longer the only one of its kind. Several national, regional, and international NGOs now monitor the performance of, and protest human rights violations by, states around the globe.

Most of the states condemned for human rights violations belong to the Third World majority in the system of states, and many are signatories to the Universal Declaration of Human Rights. Such violations demonstrate that paying obeisance to the ideal of human rights is one thing, but the willingness or ability of states to tolerate the unhindered exercise of those rights by their populations is quite another. Although the existence of human rights monitoring agencies may have made some difference in the way states treat their citizens, more weighty concerns of state and regime security in the Third World have usually taken precedence over human rights in the policies of these states.

The major problem with implementing human rights in the Third World is the fact that the concept of human rights owes its empirical validity to the successful functioning of the industrialized, representative, and responsive states of Western Europe and North America. These states set the standards for effective statehood and for the humane and civilized treatment of citizens by their demonstrated success in meeting the basic needs of their populations, protecting their citizens' human rights, and promoting and guaranteeing political participation. But these states have generally successfully completed their state-building process; they are politically satiated, economically affluent, and unconditionally legitimate in the eyes of their populations. They can, therefore, afford to adopt liberal standards of state behavior because they are reasonably secure in the knowledge that societal demands will not run counter to state interests and will not put state structures and institutions in any grave jeopardy.

It is no wonder, therefore, that the only human rights regime that has some teeth is the regional enforcement regime covering the mainly West European membership of the Council of Europe. This regime includes the European Commission of Human Rights, which has the power to investigate complaints from individuals and states, and the European Court of Human Rights, which has the authority to issue legal judgments that are binding on the member states. But even in this case, as one study has pointed out, 95 percent of all petitions are screened out during the petitioning process, and "statist imperatives [still] tend to outweigh the values of human dignity."[34]

Western notions of civilized state behavior, including those pertaining to human rights, often contradict Third World imperatives of state making, which sanction and frequently require the use of violence against recalcitrant domestic groups and individual citizens. Furthermore, the international norm upholding human rights runs directly counter to the norm that prescribes the inalienability of juridical statehood for Third World states.[35] The norm of juridical statehood upholds the legal existence of Third World states within their colonially constructed boundaries. But the norm of human rights undermines the political legitimacy of these same states by prescribing standards of political behavior that most Third World states, struggling to maintain political order, will not be able to meet for many decades. Moreover, the simultaneous but contradictory operation of the two norms contributes to the internal discontent within Third World states by forcing all of the diverse and dissatisfied elements within those states to remain within their postcolonial boundaries while at the same time encouraging those elements to make political, administrative, and economic demands the states cannot begin to satisfy, either because they lack the capabilities or because doing so could jeopardize their territorial integrity.

A corollary of the international norm that considers human rights to be inalienable is the demand made on the Third World state by the international community that it treat political opponents in a humane manner even when these opponents are openly engaged in political and sometimes military activities aimed at undermining effective statehood and even the territorial integrity of established states. Such a demand pits international human rights concerns directly against the imperatives of state making and state consolidation. It does so not only in the case of predatory states such as Zaire or Sudan but also in the case of democratic members of the international system such as India, a state that finds itself in the dock for using repressive powers against avowedly secessionist elements in Punjab and Kashmir.

We can argue on behalf of Third World states that are still struggling to translate their juridical statehood into empirical statehood that the case for human rights and against the states' use of violence to impose order is not as morally unassailable as it may first appear. This point can be made most effectively in the context of the failed states phenomenon, where state structures have completely collapsed.[36] In the absence of even rudimentarily effective states to provide a minimum degree of political order—as in Lebanon during its civil war or as in Somalia, Afghanistan, Angola,

Burundi, Rwanda, and Liberia today—the concept of human rights remains nothing more than a pure abstraction. In such contexts the human rights ideal is incapable of implementation because in the absence of the sovereign, a truly Hobbesian state of nature prevails, and the physical survival of large segments of populations cannot be assured.

Regardless of the nature of their regimes and the predatory or developmental character of the states themselves, Third World states at this juncture in their development will almost inevitably resort to violent means to pursue their objectives of state making, state consolidation, and regime survival.[37] In the process, human rights of groups and individuals are likely to be violated. However, most of these instances of violation of human rights by states, although deplorable, turn out to be less serious compared with the violence that usually accompanies the failure of the state as in Lebanon, Afghanistan, or Somalia.

These comments should not be taken as an apologia for authoritarian regimes in the Third World that emphasize order at the expense of both justice and political participation. Authoritarian regimes and predatory states (the two must be distinguished, because authoritarian regimes can exist in developmental, intermediate, and predatory states) can contribute a great deal to the creation and augmentation of disorder in Third World states even though they pay lip service to the objective of promoting order. Iran under the shah, the Philippines under Marcos, Zaire under Mobutu, and Nicaragua under Somoza all provide good examples of this tendency. I return to this issue in Chapter 8 to analyze more fully the complex relationship between the nature of regimes and the prevalence of conflict and disorder in the Third World.

Most regimes in the Third World, especially authoritarian ones, attempt to portray threats to their regimes as threats to the state. In some cases, as in Pakistan in 1970 to 1971, this turns out to be a self-fulfilling prophecy.[38] Discerning analysts must, therefore, carefully distinguish between issues of regime security and those of state security. However, given the lack of unconditional legitimacy of regimes and state structures in the Third World and the close perceptual connection between regime and state made by most of the state's population, the line between regime security and state security in many cases becomes so thin and the interplay between the two so dense that it is virtually impossible to disentangle one from the other. As one perceptive scholar pointed out in connection with the Middle East, "Those who rule must attempt to encourage loyalty to the state, of which they hope themselves to be the chief beneficiaries, while at the same time seeking to disguise the fact that their system of power, and thus the identity of the political structure itself, frequently owes more to the old ties of sectarian and tribal loyalty."[39] Currently, Iraq, Jordan, Saudi Arabia, and Kuwait in the Middle East and Sudan, Angola, and Mozambique in Africa provide classic examples of the fusion between state and regime security. In many of these countries the fall of the regime is likely to signal the failure of the state as well. Any student of Tudor England or Bourbon France will find this phenomenon to be very familiar.

One last point needs to be touched upon here in connection with the human rights issue. This relates to the highly positive response advocating human rights can draw from diverse constituencies when used as the normative basis to justify group rights. As a result, human rights rhetoric and justifications for political action when applied to groups, especially ethnic groups, can help transform attempts by such groups to gain recognition of their ethnic identities within existing states into a quest for national self-determination.

Given the multiethnic nature of most Third World states, if human rights are interpreted to include the right to ethnonational self-determination, they are likely to pose grave threats to the territorial integrity and juridical statehood of postcolonial states, once more pitting one set of international norms against another. The demonstration effect of the renewed popularity of national self-determination, interpreted as ethnonational self-determination in the aftermath of the breakup of the Soviet Union and the dismemberment of Yugoslavia, is likely to further accentuate internal challenges to the security of Third World states in the post–Cold War era. I return to this theme for more detailed treatment in Chapter 8.

Summary

To sum up this discussion regarding international norms, the Third World state has increasingly become caught between norms that assume the impending arrival of a global society and those that presuppose the continued functioning of a system of sovereign states even if the sovereignty of states is weakened by unequal capabilities, economic interdependence, and technological breakthroughs of revolutionary proportions.[40] The evolving international norm that prescribes universal human rights is a major indicator of the presumed trend toward a global society. The normative emphasis on the sanctity of political boundaries and the demand that the new states demonstrate their capacity for effective statehood are strong reminders that states have two overriding obligations: one, to protect their juridical statehood, and two, to translate that statehood into empirical statehood.

Third World states are, therefore, caught between two stools. On the one hand, they are expected to approximate human rights standards as measured by the performance yardstick of the industrialized democracies. On the other hand, they are expected to enhance their stateness by extending their dominion over often reluctant populations in the shortest possible time in order to approximate the standards of effective statehood set by the industrialized democracies of Europe and North America. The contradiction between these two sets of normative goals has made the security predicament of the Third World state increasingly acute as efforts by state authorities to extend their control have collided with the requirements for humane treatment of groups and individuals who resist such control.

The tension between the two sets of norms is exacerbated by the increasing concern on the part of the industrialized states of Europe and North America that the human rights of states' opponents in the Third World be adequately protected. This stance is adopted by the industrialized democracies with little regard for the task of state making, which Third World state elites perceive to be their primary political objective at this time. State making, however, has a logic of its own and requires the exercise of coercion even by postcolonial states, such as India, that have traditionally adopted primarily persuasive and consensual strategies for state building.[41]

As a result of these contradictory pressures, most Third World states can neither abdicate their responsibility for, nor fulfill their mission of, state building; they seem to be in a perpetual state of schizophrenia. This condition is accentuated by the workings of the global balance of power, which has done little to ameliorate the insecurity of Third World states and regions. I turn to this subject in the next chapter.

Notes

1. Although the principle of nonintervention has often been flouted in practice and, of late, its centrality to international order has been questioned, R. J. Vincent has argued convincingly that "so long as international society is primarily composed of sovereign states, observance of a general rule of nonintervention can be regarded as a minimum condition for their orderly existence. . . . The principle of nonintervention placed at the frontiers of state sovereignty fulfills an analogous function to that of a 'No Trespassing' sign standing at the perimeter of a piece of property held under domestic law." R. J. Vincent, *Nonintervention and International Order* (Princeton: Princeton University Press, 1974): 331.

2. For excellent analyses of various aspects of the origins and expansion of the modern system of states and the dissemination of its core values, see Martin Wight, *Systems of States* (Leicester: Leicester University Press, 1977); Hedley Bull, *The Anarchical Society: A Study of Order in World Politics* (New York: Columbia University Press, 1977); Hedley Bull and Adam Watson (eds.), *The Expansion of International Society* (Oxford: Clarendon Press, 1984); James Mayall, *Nationalism and International Society* (Cambridge: Cambridge University Press, 1990); Alfred Cobban, *National Self-Determination* (Chicago: University of Chicago Press, 1948); Vincent, *Nonintervention;* and Robert H. Jackson, *Quasi-States: Sovereignty, International Relations and the Third World* (Cambridge: Cambridge University Press, 1990).

3. However, according to Robert W. Tucker, this egalitarian thrust was basically a distortion of the United Nations' original purpose. Writing in 1977, Tucker declared, "If today we are to find in the United Nations the principal institutional expression of the demand for greater equality, we must do so in terms of what the

organization has become and not in terms of what it was initially intended to be." Tucker traced this change, which transformed the United Nations "from an instrument of the great powers to a forum in which the new states could press their claims," to the proliferation of its membership beginning in the late 1950s and to the postwar bipolar structure that allowed the new states far greater leverage to play one bloc against the other than would have been possible if the power structure had been more diffuse. Robert W. Tucker, *The Inequality of Nations* (London: Martin Robertson, 1977): 34.

4. For details of this argument, see Mohammed Ayoob, "The Third World in the System of States: Acute Schizophrenia or Growing Pains?" *International Studies Quarterly* 33, no. 1 (March 1989): 67–79, especially pp. 68–70.

5. For Krasner's thesis of structural conflict and his recommendations to the industrialized countries on how to deal with this conflict, see Stephen Krasner, *Structural Conflict: The Third World Against Global Liberalism* (Berkeley: University of California Press, 1985): Chapters 1 and 10.

6. Jayantanuja Bandyopadhyaya, *North over South: A Non-Western Perspective of International Relations* (New Delhi: South Asian Publishers, 1982): 6.

7. For example, see Andre Gundar Frank, *Capitalism and Underdevelopment in Latin America* (New York: Monthly Review Press, 1967).

8. Richard E. Feinberg, *The Intemperate Zone: The Third World Challenge to U.S. Foreign Policy* (New York: W. W. Norton, 1983): 247.

9. The term *schizophrenia* is used here as an analytical device to describe the dilemma faced by most Third World states in the realm of international relations. My intention is not to refer to the psychological states of mind of Third World leaders but to highlight the contradictory practical dispositions that are chronically encountered in Third World historical situations.

10. It should be acknowledged that Robert Tucker was basically right when he argued that the demands for justice and equality made by Third World states collectively and, therefore, "the challenge to the global status quo of wealth and power is a challenge by states made on behalf of states. The subjects of the new egalitarianism are states and states alone. . . . As such, there is no warrant for seeing in it the necessary precursor of growing equality within states." Tucker, *Inequality of Nations,* 61.

11. For an excellent analysis that corroborates this conclusion, see Khaldoun al-Naqeeb, *Society and State in the Gulf and Arab Peninsula: A Different Perspective* (London: Routledge, 1990).

12. Eli Kedourie, "A New International Disorder," in Bull and Watson (eds.), *Expansion,* 355.

13. Adda Bozeman, "The International Order in a Multicultural World," in Bull and Watson (eds.), *Expansion,* 406. Emphasis added.

14. Hedley Bull and Adam Watson, "Conclusion," in Bull and Watson (eds.), *Expansion,* 433.

15. Ibid., 434.

16. For a sophisticated analysis of the link between Third World elites who dominate the state and powerful socioeconomic groups in the developed countries, see F. H. Cardoso and E. Faletto, *Dependency and Development in Latin America* (Berkeley: University of California Press, 1979).

17. Lee C. Buchheit, *Secession: The Legitimacy of Self-Determination* (New Haven: Yale University Press, 1978): 31.

18. Stephen Krasner, *Structural Conflict: The Third World Against Global Liberalism* (Berkeley: University of California Press, 1985): 4.

19. This analysis of UN General Assembly Resolutions 1514 and 1541 is based on the discussion in Morton H. Halperin and David J. Scheffer, with Patricia L. Small, *Self-Determination in the New World Order* (Washington, D.C.: Carnegie Endowment for International Peace, 1992): 21–22.

20. For a discussion of the UN involvement in the Congo, see Buchheit, *Secession,* 141–153. Buchheit concluded that "in retrospect, the United Nations action in the Congo stands as a major precedent against an international recognition of secessionist legitimacy in circumstances similar to those surrounding the Congo at independence" (151).

21. Quoted in Halperin and Scheffer, with Small, *Self-Determination,* 22.

22. Jackson, *Quasi-States,* 1, 4.

23. For the debate in the UN General Assembly and the General Assembly resolution, see UN General Assembly, *Official Records,* 26th session, in particular plenary meetings 2,002 and 2,003, December 7, 1971.

24. For the background on the Greek-Turkish conflict in Cyprus, the de facto division of the island in 1974, and events thereafter, see Robert McDonald, *The Problem of Cyprus,* Adelphi Paper no. 234 (London: International Institute for Strategic Studies, Winter 1988–1989).

25. Charles Tilly, "Reflections on the History of European State-Making," in Charles Tilly (ed.), *The Formation of National States in Western Europe* (Princeton: Princeton University Press, 1975): 15.

26. Robert H. Jackson, "Quasi-States, Dual Regimes, and Neoclassical Theory: International Jurisprudence and the Third World," *International Organization* 41, no. 4 (Autumn 1987): 529.

27. Krasner, *Structural Conflict,* 4.

28. For one analysis that demonstrates the validity of this assertion, see Mohammed Ayoob, "The Superpowers and Regional 'Stability': Parallel Responses to the Gulf and the Horn," *World Today* 35, no. 5 (May 1979): 197–205.

29. For a discussion of fortuitous versus contrived (or deliberate) balance of power, see Bull, *Anarchical Society,* 104–106.

30. For the operation of the balance-of-power principle, see Ludwig Dehio, *The Precarious Balance* (New York: Vintage, 1965); and Edward Gulick, *Europe's Classical Balance of Power* (Westport, Conn.: Greenwood Press, 1982).

31. Gabriel Ben-Dor, *State and Conflict in the Middle East: Emergence of the Post-Colonial State* (New York: Praeger, 1983): 233.

32. R. J. Vincent, *Human Rights and International Relations* (Cambridge: Cambridge University Press, 1986): 19–36.

33. *UN Charter,* Preamble and Article 1.

34. Burn H. Weston, Robin Ann Lukes, and Kelley M. Hnatt, "Regional Human Rights Regimes: A Comparison and Appraisal," in Richard Pierre Claude and Burns H. Weston (eds.), *Human Rights in the World Community: Issues and Action* (Philadelphia: University of Pennsylvania Press, 1989): 209–211. Quoted in Seyom Brown, *International Relations in a Changing Global System: Toward a Theory of the World Polity* (Boulder: Westview Press, 1992): 112.

35. As Seyom Brown has pointed out, the intellectual position that "servicing . . . basic human rights is the principal task of human polities, and that the worth of any polity is a function of how well it performs this task, has put the legitimacy of all extant polities up for grabs, so to speak. Whether particular nation-states, and the prevailing territorial demarcations, do indeed merit the badge of political legitimacy is, according to this view, subject to continuing assessment; accordingly, neither today's governments nor today's borders are sacrosanct." Brown, *International Relations,* 126.

36. For a discussion of failed states, see Gerald B. Helman and Steven R. Ratner, "Saving Failed States," *Foreign Policy* 89 (Winter 1992–1993): 3–20.

37. For a valuable analysis of different types of states—predatory, developmental, and intermediate—in the Third World, see Peter B. Evans, "Predatory, Developmental, and Other Apparatuses: A Comparative Political Economy Perspective on the Third World State," *Sociological Forum* 4, no. 4 (1989): 561–587. According to Evans, "We can imagine a range of states defined in terms of the way in which they affect development. Some states may extract such large amounts of otherwise investable surplus and provide so little in the way of 'collective goods' in return that they do indeed impede economic transformation. It seems reasonable to call these states 'predatory.' . . . Those who control the state apparatus seem to plunder without any more regard for the welfare of the citizenry than a predator has for the welfare of its prey. Other states, however, are able to foster long-term entrepreneurial perspectives among private elites by increasing incentives to engage in transformative investments and lowering the risks involved in such investments. They may not be immune to 'rent seeking' or to using some of the social surplus for the ends of incumbents and their friends rather than those of the citizenry as a whole, but on balance the consequences of their actions promote rather than impeding transformation. They are legitimately considered 'developmental states.' . . . Most Third World countries have 'other apparatuses.' The balance between predatory and developmental activities is not clear-cut but varies over time, and depends on what kind of activities are attempted" (562–563).

38. For details of the Pakistani crisis of 1970–1971, see Richard Sisson and Leo E. Rose, *War and Secession: Pakistan, India, and the Creation of Bangladesh* (Berkeley: University of California Press, 1990).

39. Charles Tripp, "Near East," in Robert S. Litwak and Samuel F. Wells, Jr. (eds.), *Superpower Competition and Security in the Third World* (Cambridge: Ballinger, 1988): 113.

40. For two studies that best capture the tension between the evolving norms of global society and the continuing imperatives of a state-centric international system, see Stanley Hoffmann, *Duties Beyond Borders: On the Limits and Possibilities of Ethical International Politics* (Syracuse: Syracuse University Press, 1981); and Vincent, *Human Rights.*

41. For several perceptive analyses of the multiple dimensions of state-society relations in India, see Atul Kohli (ed.), *India's Democracy: An Analysis of Changing State-Society Relations* (Princeton: Princeton University Press, 1990). Also see Subrata Kumar Mitra, "Between Transaction and Transcendence: The State and the Institutionalization of Power in India," in Subrata Kumar Mitra (ed.), *The Post-Colonial State in Asia: Dialectics of Politics and Culture* (London: Harvester Wheatsheaf, 1990): 73–99.

5
The Third World, Bipolarity, and the Cold War

The Third World was born into bipolarity and the Cold War. Although most Latin American states had achieved formal independence a century before the end of World War II, the emergence of independent Asian and African states created the phenomenon of the weak, intruder majority in the system of states and, consequently, had the quantitative and qualitative impact on the international system discussed in Chapter 4. The latent consciousness among Latin American political and intellectual elites that their states belonged to a separate category from the states of Europe and North America gained saliency and became explicit as a result of Latin American interaction with Asian and African states in the 1950s and 1960s. This interaction augmented the feeling of many of the Latin American elites that South and Central American countries shared with those of Asia and Africa similar experiences of subjugation and exploitation by the European powers (and, in the case of Latin America, also by the United States), as well as the continued status of dependency vis-à-vis the industrialized countries. The tricontinental coalition evolved from common economic and political concerns of Asian, African, and Latin American states and helped to translate the concept of the Third World into an empirical reality.

The two organizations that came to symbolize the notion of the Third World—the Non-Aligned Movement (NAM) and the Group of 77 (G-77)—emerged in the 1960s. G-77, which was principally concerned with enhancing Third World interests in the areas of trade and development, had substantial Latin American membership from its inception. These two organizations reached the zenith of their popularity and effectiveness in the 1970s, both in the influence they asserted on the formulation of their members' foreign policies and in terms of their impact on the international system as a whole and on North-South relations in particular.[1]

If the Third World was born in the heyday of the Cold War, it came of age in the era of superpower détente. Détente, however, did not represent the end of the Cold War because it did not imply a radical reordering of superpower relations. All it signified was the ushering in of a more mature phase of the Cold War, one in which the superpowers refined their mode of managing their adversarial relationship[2] by acknowledging the cooperative as well as the competitive element in that relationship, although the latter continued to form the principal dimension of superpower interaction.[3]

There were several major effects of the bipolar character of the balance of global power after World War II on the security of Third World states and regions. First, Third World states—especially the larger and more important states such as India, Egypt, and Indonesia and those such as Iran and Pakistan that were geopolitically and geoeconomically strategically situated—obtained leverage in their individual dealings with the superpowers that might not have been possible had the distribution of power been more diffuse or the nature of the superpower relationship less competitive. This meant that Third World states involved in interstate or intrastate conflicts could often call upon one of the superpowers for political, military, or economic assistance—especially if they could portray their antagonists as clients or allies of the rival superpower.

Second, the fierce competition between the superpowers for political and military advantage in the Third World, coupled with the desire of Third World protagonists to draw their superpower patrons into regional disputes, dramatically increased the level of great power intrusion into the Third World and the impact of those powers on the course of regional conflicts among, and often within, postcolonial states.[4] Superpower involvement in Third World conflicts generally exacerbated these conflicts and escalated the level of destruction by providing regional contestants with increasingly sophisticated military hardware for which such conflicts provided ideal testing grounds. Several of these conflicts, such as those in Angola and Mozambique, turned into virtual proxy wars between the superpowers. In a few exceptional cases, such as Vietnam and Afghanistan, one superpower became directly involved in the fighting, and the other continued to operate through surrogates—an essential strategy to prevent the escalation of such conflicts into direct military confrontations between Washington and Moscow. In some cases, however, superpower involvement prevented Third World regional conflicts from crossing a threshold fixed by tacit agreement between the superpowers, especially if, as in the Middle East, Washington and Moscow shared the apprehension that uncontrolled escalation could easily lead to direct superpower confrontation.[5]

Third, despite the mutual interpenetration of superpower competition and regional conflicts in the Third World, a fundamental asymmetry, with very rare exceptions, continued to exist in the interaction between these two phenomena. Third World protagonists in regional conflicts could frequently borrow power from their superpower patrons to meet threats from, or to threaten, their domestic or regional adversaries. Sometimes, as in the case of India vis-à-vis the Soviet Union, they could also exercise much influence over the shaping of their superpower ally's regional policies. However, they rarely had the capacity to significantly affect the terms on which the global superpower rivalry was conducted or to determine the course of that rivalry. In other words, even the most important Third World states remained marginal to the central balance.

On the other hand, the superpowers had a major impact on the course of regional conflicts and the terms on which they were conducted. This impact was realized through a host of instruments. These included the exercise of their veto power in the UN Security Council against resolutions unacceptable to their Third World friends, the accelerated supply of weapons to allies engaged in conflicts in the Third World, and the imposition of arms embargoes on regional protagonists engaged in shooting wars.

Occasionally, concerns about superpower credibility circumscribed to some extent the autonomy of the superpower relationship from the dynamic of regional conflict in the Third World. This was the case when those concerns were interpreted in terms of the predictability of the superpowers to come to the assistance of regional clients in times of crisis and, in rare instances, in terms of the intrinsic economic and strategic value of certain regions of the Third World to one of the superpowers.

On the whole, however, superpower policies toward each other functioned largely independent of regional Third World concerns (certainly of the concerns of the overwhelming majority of Third World states) and, therefore, proved resistant to permeation even by the superpowers' closest Third World allies. These allies and friends, again with very rare exceptions, basically had an instrumental value to the superpowers inasmuch as they helped Washington and Moscow conduct their mutual adversarial relationship around the globe, but they were not in a position to crucially influence that relationship. Superpower interests in the Third World were derived mostly from the logic of the Cold War and functioned according to that logic. Conversely, Third World rivalries and conflicts had only a marginal effect on the central issues of the bilateral relationship that defined the nature of the global balance in the forty-five years following World War II.

Core and Peripheral States

The asymmetry and inequality in the interaction between the fundamental dynamic of the Cold War and that of Third World regional concerns and conflicts meant that strategically, the post–World War II world was divided into two distinct arenas that corresponded to the division between the primary and the secondary actors in the international system discussed in Chapter 4. This de facto division of the globe into core and peripheral states, in both strategic and economic terms, had major consequences for the security of Third World states in the context of nuclearized bipolarity. Moreover, the dichotomy between the core and the periphery had a direct impact on the level and destructive capacity of conflicts in the Third World.

The way the adversarial relationship between the superpowers affected Third World conflicts was a function of the clear distinction both superpowers made between regions of vital importance to them for both strategic and economic reasons (primarily the industrial and technological powerhouses of North America, Europe, and Japan) and the gray areas of the globe (the Third World). In the former, interstate conflict was ruled out in the epoch of nuclear weaponry. In the latter, violent conflict was permissible because it did not vitally affect the management of the dominant global relationship and was marginal to the maintenance of the central balance of power.[6]

Samuel Huntington pointed out that during the Cold War era, U.S. and Soviet involvement in the Third World increased not steadily and gradually but in alternating surges primarily in response to the activism of the rival superpower in the immediately preceding surge.[7] Such a pattern of superpower intervention clearly demonstrated the importance of the Third World as an arena of superpower competition while simultaneously providing evidence that the vital interests of the superpowers were not engaged in the periphery. This combination permitted surges and countersurges of superpower intervention in the Third World to take place without significantly destabilizing the central balance. That such a pattern of superpower interaction would have been permissible in Europe in the nuclear age was unthinkable.

We can argue indefinitely whether the strict discipline imposed by bipolarity on the behavior of major states or the fear of mass destruction that undergirded the nuclear balance of terror was primarily responsible for the "long peace" among the great powers during the Cold War era.[8] It is undeniable that the superpowers treated the possibility of conflict differently in the Third World than they did in Europe and Northeast Asia, where the two nuclear giants physically were vitally involved, their spheres of influence rigidly demarcated, and their major allies geographically located. Any external attempt to change the status quo, by force or subversion, in these vitally important areas was likely to immediately trigger the risk of global conflagration and nuclear devastation.

When such attempts were made from within the sphere of influence of one of the superpowers, as in Hungary in 1956 and in Czechoslovakia in 1968, the superpower that dominated that sphere was allowed a free hand to deal with anti–status-quo elements within its sphere. What the Soviet Union did in Hungary and Czechoslovakia was perceived globally (despite the declamatory rhetoric to the contrary) not as a violation of the rules of the game but as a reaffirmation of the rules by which the Cold War game was being played in Europe. In the case of Europe and Japan, the security of existing states (and regimes in East Europe) had become inextricably tied to the security of the superpowers and, therefore, to the security of the international system as a whole.

The situation in the Third World was a far cry from that in the industrialized world. Conflict in the Third World in the postwar period was widespread, as was the political and military involvement of the superpowers in supporting, and sometimes beyond supporting, roles in Third World conflicts. As Nicole Ball pointed out in 1988, "All interstate wars since the end of World War II have taken place in the Third World, although there have been industrialized country participants in some of these conflicts."[9] Evan Luard concluded that the Third World was the scene of 98 percent of all international conflicts between 1945 and 1984.[10] Kalevi Holsti calculated that nearly 97 percent of all major wars and armed interventions between 1945 and 1989 occurred in the Third World.[11] But conflict on such a large scale only marginally affected the stability of the central strategic balance that had effectively insulated itself from the gains achieved and the losses incurred by the superpowers in the Third World.

This insulation of the central strategic relationship from conflicts in the Third World, when superpower involvement was nearly universal, prompted some analysts to argue that conflict in the Third World during the postwar decades was actively encouraged by superpower policies largely aimed at testing each others' political will and power projection capabilities in areas of the globe peripheral to the superpowers' vital concerns. This point was made forcefully by Sisir Gupta almost a quarter of a century ago.

> The very stability of the global balance of power and the determination of the great powers to avoid a confrontation makes them prone to seek lower levels of conflict and less dangerous ways of conducting their rivalries, which in effect means a concerted attempt to confine their conflicts to problems that impinge on them less directly and to localize them in such areas as are far removed from the areas where their vital interests are involved. To fight out their battles in the Third World is one way of ensuring that their own worlds are not touched by their conflicts and that they retain a greater measure of option to escalate and de-escalate these conflicts according to the needs of their relationships. . . . To the extent that the central power balance has become immune from the contagious effects of Third World conflicts, to the extent that the stability of great power relations can be maintained in spite of local and regional disturbances, such conflicts and such disturbances have become permissible.[12]

Recent analyses have demonstrated that the Cold War possessed both a competitive and a cooperative dimension in superpower interaction. The cooperative characteristic of the Cold War applied especially to Third World conflicts. Both Washington and Moscow had to be extremely careful that despite their competition for power and influence in the Third World, crises in the periphery did not commit the superpowers irrevocably to policies that could draw them into direct confrontation with each other. This constraint on superpower policies during the Cold War was summed up well by Benjamin Miller.

> In noncrisis times during the cold war the superpowers might each have tried to reach a hegemonic position and to exclude the other power from having a voice in the international politics of various parts of the Third World. Nevertheless, in crisis situations both Washington and Moscow were more sensitive than previous great powers had been to the interests of the rival power. Moreover, even during the cold war the United States and the Soviet Union tended to collaborate tacitly in controlling wars in the Third World and in maintaining the status quo in world politics.[13]

As a result of the largely successful insulation of the central balance from the instabilities and insecurities prevalent in the periphery, leaders of many Third World states perceived themselves as having the worst of both worlds. They were unable to prevent the penetration of their polities and regions by superpower rivalries and conflicts; paradoxically, many of them collaborated with the superpowers to facilitate the penetration. They were equally incapable of affecting, except marginally and in selected cases, the global political and military equation between the superpowers and their respective alliance systems.

As a result of this dual impotence of Third World states, it was no surprise that, as Robert Litwak and Samuel Wells stated, "During the postwar era, the Third World has been a principal arena of East-West rivalry. From Southeast Asia to the Middle East to Southern Africa to Central America, the superpowers have found themselves on opposing sides of regional conflicts, locked in global competition for influence."[14] That the superpowers chose the Third World as the arena in which they could afford to be "locked in global competition for influence" in the thermonuclear age demonstrated the low priority they attached to gains and losses in the Third World and the vast distance that separated their Third World concerns from their vital interests, which were protected by the nuclear balance of terror. This state of affairs enhanced the insecurity of Third World states and regimes, because their security requirements seemed to have virtually no impact on the global security agenda fashioned by the Cold War concerns of the superpowers and their major allies.

The marginality of Third World conflicts to systemic security concerns was demonstrated convincingly during the eight-year-long war between Iran and Iraq, which was fought in the strategically important and oil-rich Gulf region with some of the most advanced conventional weaponry available to Third World countries and in which the scale of human and material destruction dwarfed all conflicts since World War II. To the uninitiated observer, the indifference of the great powers to the conflict appeared astounding. However, as long as the flow of oil from the noncombatant Gulf producers was assured, and as long as neither party—primarily Iran—

was in a position to win a decisive victory, the superpowers were content to allow Iran and Iraq to fight to the point of utter exhaustion.

The only sphere in which the major powers had a substantial impact on the fighting was that of arms supply. Here, the Soviets and the French (the latter with tacit U.S. approval) kept Iraq well supplied with some of the most sophisticated military hardware available while, at the same time, the superpowers "successfully pressured their allies and friends to restrict their deliveries [to Iran] to weapons that will not tilt the war in Iran's favor."[15] They did so in order to prevent a victory by Iran, which was perceived by both superpowers as the greater threat to their respective and overlapping conceptions of stability in the oil-rich Gulf and adjacent regions.

U.S. antagonism toward Iran originated primarily from its perception of the destabilizing impact Iran's radical version of political Islam, if it were victorious, could have on the pro-West conservative monarchies of the Gulf, especially Saudi Arabia. Soviet antipathy toward Tehran resulted largely from Iran's strident opposition to Soviet military intervention in neighboring Afghanistan, as well as from Moscow's apprehension regarding the impact of the Islamic Revolution on the Muslim republics of the Soviet Union. Therefore, "while the superpowers [were] in competition over the scope of their respective future influence in the Gulf and in Tehran, they [were] in substantial agreement on the fact that they [did] not wish to see Islamic Iran win the war."[16] Nevertheless, the indifference of the major powers to the massive destruction produced by the Iran-Iraq War was the most dramatic manifestation of the impotence of even some of the more important Third World states, in this case Iran and Iraq, in affecting the substance of the global security agenda.

It is tempting here to draw analogies between the stability of the central balance of power in the Cold War era, which was accompanied by high levels of conflict in the periphery, and the situation in the classical age of the balance of power in Europe in the nineteenth century when, in the words of Robert Tucker, "such moderation as the balance of power introduced in Europe depended upon the immoderation of its working in the world outside Europe."[17] In an even earlier age, as Martin Wight has pointed out, the same dichotomy between the core and the periphery had prevailed in the sixteenth century regarding the permissibility of conflict in the European-dominated state system, which was in the early stages of expanding outside its original European home. Wight traced this dichotomy to the Treaty of Cateau-Cambresis in 1559 between France and Spain, in which "in a verbal agreement, that formed no part of the treaty, the delegates decided on the meridian of the Azores and the Tropic of Cancer as a line, to the west and south of which acts of hostility would not violate the treaty nor constitute grounds for complaint, and whoever was strongest would pass for master. . . . 'No peace beyond the line' became almost the rule of international law, giving freedom to plunder, attack and settle without upsetting the peace of Europe." Wight concluded that "in the twentieth century states-system, divided still concentrically between the world city and the world rural district, the amity lines have reappeared. One of the unwritten understandings of the Cold War has been that the peace of Europe shall be warily preserved while the struggle is pursued for influence and position throughout the Third World."[18]

Third World Arms Transfers

In this highly stratified and divided world, a major instrument of influence the superpowers utilized in their relations with the Third World during the Cold War era was the supply of weapons and, on a more restricted scale, the transfer of weapons technology to Third World states that were either actively engaged in territorial disputes with their neighbors or were acutely apprehensive about the multiple sources of insecurity from which they suffered. Interstate wars and intrastate vulnerabilities being the hallmark of states in the early stage of state making, there was no dearth of Third World takers for arms from the developed countries, above all from the superpowers. Arms and weapons technology transfers to the Third World from the superpowers and the major European arms suppliers became so important in North-South relations during the decades of the Cold War that this form of the Third World's dependence on the industrialized countries came to be viewed as "the defining characteristic of post-colonial North-South military relations."[19]

The importance of weapons transfers in North-South relations during the Cold War era has been clearly demonstrated by Keith Krause's calculation that the developing countries' share in the global import of arms reached 80 percent in the 1980s. Whereas West Germany had headed the list of arms recipients in 1963 with 14.6 percent of the world total, Iraq achieved this distinction in 1982, with almost the same share of the global arms imports. In the 1980s the top ten arms recipients, who together accounted for about half of the world's total arms imports, did not include a single developed country.[20]

It is true that weapons are of instrumental value and are not in themselves the primary cause of war. But relatively sophisticated weapon systems, which provided a Third World state with temporary technological superiority—the so-called window of opportunity—over a regional rival, were often crucial in decisionmakers' calculations to escalate disputes to a point at which war became a distinct possibility. Pakistan's decision to go to war against India in 1965, with the objective of changing the status quo in Kashmir, was based substantially on the assessment that its edge in sophisticated weaponry—provided by the United States—over India was likely to be eroded during the next few years as India acquired comparable

Soviet weapon systems.[21] In this case, Pakistan decided to act before its window of opportunity was closed by the Indian decision to build up its armed forces following the disastrous performance of the Indian Army in the Sino-Indian border war of 1962.

The timing of Iraq's invasion of Iran in September 1980 was also crucially determined by Iraq's perception of its superiority over Iran in terms of its Soviet-supplied military hardware. Iran had lost much of its technical capability to operate the U.S. weapons in its arsenal after the 1979 Islamic Revolution. This loss had been a result of the disintegration of the Iranian military, the demoralization of its officer corps, and Washington's decision to cut off the supply of spare parts for U.S. weaponry following the overthrow of the pro-American shah and his replacement by an anti-Western, radical Islamic regime.[22]

Although major arms suppliers to the Third World have included European countries such as Britain, France, Germany, and Italy, as well as, more recently, China,[23] during the Cold War period the superpowers cornered the lion's share of the arms market in the Third World. According to Krause's data, between 1963 and 1988 the two superpowers were responsible for 70 percent of global arms deliveries, with the United States supplying 33 percent and the Soviet Union 37 percent of all arms transferred globally.[24] Michael Klare calculated that between 1975 and 1990 the United States and the Soviet Union together supplied $325 billion in military hardware to the Third World. Klare wrote, "The dominant position in the arms trade occupied by the United States and the Soviet Union during the Cold War era was a product of two key factors: first, their possession of a massive military-industrial complex capable of producing vast numbers of weapons of every type; and second, their willingness to use arms transfers as a mechanism for promoting diplomatic and military ties with emerging powers in the developing world."[25]

Richard Grimmett confirmed this trend in his annual study for the Congressional Research Service published in 1993, which covers the 1985–1992 period. According to Grimmett, "The United States has come to dominate the Third World arms market in the most recent period. From 1989–1992, the United States made $55.4 billion in arms transfer agreements with the Third World, or 43.7% of all such agreements. In the earlier period before the Cold War had ended (1985–1988), the former Soviet Union was the single leading supplier, making $88.9 billion [in] arms transfer agreements with the Third World, or 44.5% (in constant 1992 dollars)."[26] In both periods, as in earlier years, when one superpower ranked as the leading supplier, the other ranked second.

The analyses of Krause, Klare, and Grimmett corroborate Stephanie Neuman's thesis that in spite of the commercial value of arms sales to the major suppliers and the consequent competition among them in what was perceived by the 1980s to have become a buyer's market, the transfer of sophisticated weaponry during the Cold War period was essentially a political activity. Many political and strategic considerations were connected with superpower global rivalries and with the myriad political and strategic links between the superpowers and the leading nonsuperpower arms suppliers. These considerations had a major bearing on the pattern of arms trade and even more of an effect on the transfer of sophisticated weapons technology to Third World recipients.[27]

If during the Cold War years political and strategic considerations dominated arms transfer decisions on the suppliers' side, Third World regions that had the greatest potential for interstate conflict were clearly home to states that were the largest purchasers of military hardware. The Middle East (including the Gulf), with its unique combination of high conflict potential and vast amounts of petro dollars, headed the list of purchasers in the 1980s. It was followed by South Asia, a region whose political landscape continues to be dominated by the India-Pakistan cold war, occasionally punctuated by bouts of open warfare. As Klare pointed out, "Of the $341 billion worth of arms sold to developing countries between 1981 and 1988, some $235 billion worth, or 69 percent, were purchased by countries in the Middle East and South Asia. Among the biggest spenders in this group were India, Iran, Iraq, Israel, Libya, Pakistan and Syria—countries that went to war in this period and/or participated in regional arms races with contentious neighbors."[28] Grimmett has confirmed this trend for 1985 to 1992. His data on arms deliveries for this period show that Saudi Arabia and Iraq were the top two recipients of arms imports, followed by India, Afghanistan, Iran, Cuba, Vietnam, Syria, Angola, and Egypt.[29]

The figures regarding arms transfers from the superpowers to major Third World recipients demonstrate clearly the direct and far-reaching impact of weapons deliveries on conflicts in the Third World during the Cold War. Therefore, whereas weapons transfers even on such a large scale should not be seen as substituting for the root causes of conflicts inherent in Third World historical situations, the relatively easy availability of sophisticated weaponry certainly contributed to regional arms races and to the escalation and prolongation of conflicts in the Third World. The availability of superpower-supplied arms also frequently influenced and sometimes determined decisions about the timing of interstate wars by providing incentives to parties involved in Third World territorial disputes to escalate such disputes to shooting wars.

Nonalignment and the Search for Autonomy

Thus far I have analyzed the relationship of the Third World with the superpowers during the Cold War era principally as one in which Third World states were individually and collectively the objects of superpower machinations, to be used and discarded when it suited the dominant powers in the international system. Although this approach captures a major dimension of the international reality during the Cold War era, it does not represent the entire picture. Third World states, as mentioned at the beginning of this chapter, possessed a certain amount of leverage vis-à-vis the superpowers. This leverage was provided by the very logic of the intense competition for power and influence the Cold War symbolized.

Important Third World states used this leverage effectively in pushing their own domestic and regional security agendas. On occasion, as the examples of Egypt in the early and middle 1970s and of Ethiopia and Somalia in the late 1970s demonstrated, leaders of some Third World states concluded that their state or regime security interests could no longer be served by their alliance with the superpower with which they were aligned. Consequently, they switched sides dramatically and realigned themselves with the rival superpower.[30]

Many Third World states also responded at the collective level to nuclearized bipolarity in a highly stratified international system by banding together in the Non-Aligned Movement (NAM). This strategy was motivated by the states' desire to protect their autonomy of action from the dominant powers by creating and maintaining for themselves international political space that occupied a middle ground between the two major power blocs. It needs to be pointed out that nonalignment did not mean equidistance from the two superpowers; it merely denoted an attempt by the less powerful states to maintain their independence, as much as possible, from the superpowers in the formulation of their own foreign policies.

The nonaligned policy of each state turned out to be somewhat different from that of every other state, conditioned as the policy was bound to be by the geographic location, security needs, and economic dependence of the state in question. Therefore, membership in NAM only signified a particular foreign policy orientation; it did not prescribe any set of uniform policies that had to be followed by all members of the organization. Such concrete policies continued to be determined by the specific contexts in which individual states found themselves. From the early 1970s onward, NAM also became involved in pushing an economic agenda aimed at improving the Third World's position in the international economic system. This task was attempted in tandem with the G-77, whose membership overlapped that of NAM.

The concept of nonalignment in general, and membership in NAM in particular, also served to reconcile particular state interests of Third World countries with the general political and economic interests of the weak, intruder elements of the international system in a strategically polarized and economically stratified world. For the major Third World founders of NAM—India, Egypt, and Indonesia, which were also the preeminent powers in their respective regions—nonalignment was a means of minimizing, if not totally excluding, political and military intervention by the great powers in regional affairs. But even smaller and weaker powers, who needed great power patrons in part to resist the hegemonic tendencies of the regional influentials, subscribed to the philosophy of nonalignment and competed with each other to gain membership in NAM. To them, NAM's major attraction was that it symbolized and, to a certain degree, operationalized the "solidarity of the less powerful in global affairs."[31]

Whereas the NAM membership of states such as Cuba, Vietnam, Singapore, and Saudi Arabia may have appeared hypocritical to the outside observer, their membership did not flout the criteria laid down for membership. The third of the five criteria drawn up for the membership of NAM at the first nonaligned gathering, the Cairo Preparatory Meeting of Foreign Ministers in June 1961, which was authorized to issue invitations for the first NAM summit, clearly stated that those states that were not members of "a multilateral alliance concluded in the context of Great Power conflicts" were eligible for invitation to the NAM summit. The fourth and fifth criteria permitted the membership of those states that had bilateral military agreements with a great power and even of those that had leased military bases to a foreign power, as long as such military and basing agreements were not concluded "in the context of Great Power conflicts."[32]

The application of these criteria meant, in effect, that all states except members of NATO, the Warsaw Pact, the Australia–New Zealand–United States Pact (ANZUS), the Central Treaty Organization (CENTO), and the Southeast Asia Treaty Organization (SEATO) could become members of NAM. States such as Cuba that had bilateral security arrangements with a superpower were therefore eligible. Similarly, Malaysia and Singapore, which were members of the multilateral Five-Power Defense Arrangement (FPDA) with Britain, Australia, and New Zealand (the first a member of NATO and the other two members of ANZUS) and under this arrangement had British, Australian, and New Zealand troops stationed on their soil, were also eligible because the FPDA was ostensibly not concluded "in the context of Great Power conflicts." When SEATO and CENTO folded in the 1970s, many of the members of these multilateral alliances, which had been conceived in the context of the Cold War, also became eligible for membership in NAM; some such as Pakistan applied for membership almost immediately.

As a result of this broad interpretation of nonalignment, many members of NAM were able to retain the privileges of membership while maintaining security links with one of the superpowers. Although this undoubtedly gave rise to tensions within the movement (most clearly witnessed at the 1979 Havana summit when Cuba unsuccessfully tried to sell the thesis that the Soviet Union was NAM's "natural ally"[33]), the vast majority of the movement's membership obviously felt the benefits of continued membership outweighed the negative effects of tensions and bickerings within NAM.

These benefits lay not merely in collective economic bargaining with the developed countries. To be sure, economic issues became an increasingly important part of the NAM agenda in the 1970s and 1980s. Yet since the Third World's economic grievances and demands could be aired in other forums and through other agencies—for example, at meetings of the United Nations Conference on Trade and Development (UNCTAD) and the UN General Assembly and through the G-77—economic demands did not provide the fundamental rationale for the existence or even the popularity of NAM. The main reasons for NAM's existence and expansion were political and were closely related to the Third World's quest for autonomy from the dominant global powers during the Cold War era, even as many Third World states struggled to maintain their security links with one of the superpowers.

The contradictions perceived in the foreign policies of many NAM members between their commitment to nonalignment and their de facto alignment with one of the superpowers reflected the dual pulls of state and regime security and the inherent desire of most Third World state elites to retain as much flexibility and maneuverability internationally as possible so as not to compromise their newly acquired status as full members of the system of sovereign states. Membership in NAM helped even those countries most vulnerable to superpower pressure to reduce that pressure, if not to neutralize it totally. Fouad Ajami captured the essence of nonalignment when he wrote, "Behind the moral sermons of a Nehru [Indian prime minister from 1947 to 1964 and one of the founders of NAM] was a shrewd political instinct: if military might is not your strong suit, try to make the international system less of a jungle; raise the costs of superpower mischief; make the world more messy, for such a world will allow more room for maneuver to weak powers."[34]

Nuclear Nonproliferation and the Third World

Another instance of the struggle by some important Third World states to maintain their military and technological autonomy from the dominant global powers was the refusal of states such as India, Pakistan, Brazil, and Argentina (and, of course, Israel) to sign the Nuclear Non-Proliferation Treaty (NPT) and become parties to what they considered to be a highly unequal nuclear nonproliferation regime. Although their refusal was primarily determined by the nature of the threats emanating from their respective regional environments, it was, and continues to be, also related to their perception of their place within the international pecking order.[35]

Perceptions of the close connection between nuclear capability and international status were augmented by the Chinese experience. A country that for two decades had been considered an international pariah by one of the superpowers came to be accepted into the exclusive great power club because it attained nuclear weapons capability. This conclusion was strengthened because China's enhanced standing in the international system depended principally upon the superpowers' perceptions of Beijing's role in international affairs. China's standing was not affected adversely even by the turmoil during the Cultural Revolution, which closely followed its first nuclear explosion in 1964. In the light of the Chinese experience, no Third World state aspiring to graduate to the status of a primary actor in the international system could feel comfortable about giving up its nuclear option, since in the Cold War years the successful exercise of that option appeared to be the standard by which the status of international actors was judged.[36]

The controversy surrounding the NPT helped to highlight the resentment of leading Third World states toward what they considered to be a modern version of an unequal treaty because it was aimed at curbing horizontal proliferation among nonnuclear states while not effectively addressing the issue of vertical proliferation in the nuclear arsenals of the existing nuclear powers. Opposition to the NPT regime also suited the concrete state security interests of some major Third World actors such as India and Pakistan. This opposition demonstrated further that specific security interests could coincide with broader considerations of justice in the foreign policies of leading Third World states. The controversy surrounding the accession of several nuclear threshold powers such as Israel, India, Pakistan, and North Korea to the NPT did not end with the passing of the Cold War. The problem of nuclear proliferation in the Third World and its likely impact on international security remain major concerns of policymakers and strategic analysts in the post–Cold War era. I return to this subject in Chapter 7.

Shifts in Soviet and U.S. Policy

The winding down of the Cold War in the late 1980s, the formal end of political bipolarity in 1990, and the subsequent disintegration of the Soviet Union in 1991 have all had a great impact on the international politics of the Third World in general and on its conflicts in particular. This impact is discussed in greater detail in the next chapter. However, I cannot conclude here without a few remarks about the reasons that led to the end of the Cold War, especially those concerning the Third World.

The principal force driving the changes in superpower relations during the second half of the 1980s was Mikhail Gorbachev's and his associates' attempt to radically restructure the Soviet society, economy, and polity.[37] However, even they did not visualize how much the Soviet Union and its former satellites in Eastern Europe would change as a result of the momentum gained by the new forces they unleashed and by the constraints imposed on Soviet power by the very logic of Gorbachev's domestic and foreign policies. The internal political and economic dynamics of the Soviet Union, which were largely responsible for the remarkable thaw in superpower relations, the unraveling of the Soviet sphere of influence in East Europe, the emergence of a united Germany within NATO, and, finally, the disintegration of the Soviet state itself, had important effects on the international dimension of the security picture in the Third World.

Moscow's preoccupation with internal issues, above all the restructuring of its economy and the management of "international" relations within the Soviet Union, led to a retrenchment of Soviet involvement in the Third World—a trend dramatically symbolized by the Soviet military withdrawal from Afghanistan in early 1989.[38] Soviet retrenchment from the Third World had become inevitable even before the disintegration of the Soviet state, when Moscow decided to withdraw from East Europe. This decision completely undermined the strategic rationale for an active and interventionist Soviet policy in the Third World. If Gorbachev were to argue convincingly that Soviet security could be preserved without allies or client states in East Europe, he could not argue simultaneously that far-flung Third World states continued to be strategically significant for Soviet security. If East Germany and Poland were not indispensable to the maintenance of Soviet security, then Ethiopia, Angola, Cuba, and Vietnam could no longer be touted as essential to the maintenance of a global balance of power that would ensure the security of the Soviet heartland.

The inevitability of the retrenchment of Soviet involvement had been discernible in Soviet thinking regarding the Third World from the beginning of the 1980s and antedated Gorbachev's advent in power by several years.[39] However, it was only with the launching of the twin policies of perestroika and glasnost under Gorbachev and the subsequent impact of these policies on Moscow's foreign relations that a perceptible shift in Soviet Third World policy became evident. The Soviet decision to sign an agreement in April 1988 to withdraw Soviet troops from Afghanistan the following year was the most visible manifestation of this new policy. The policy was reflected simultaneously in many other areas of the Third World, especially where major regional conflicts were in progress. This new policy was summed up in 1988 by a close adviser to Gorbachev: "The main point . . . is that self-restraint by the external forces, the great powers above all, backed up by their joint or parallel action, is a necessary condition for eliminating regional conflicts on a just and lasting basis. The Soviet Union is prepared for such cooperation."[40] Stephen Larrabee's explanation of the new Soviet policy at the end of 1989 was similar:

"While Moscow has by no means given up on the Third World, it has become much more selective and cautious about its involvement. . . . The Soviets have begun to take a new and more constructive approach toward regional conflicts. . . . Rather than exploiting these conflicts militarily, they now seem more intent on finding political solutions to them."[41]

This Soviet policy was reflected diversely in the late 1980s and was seen in different Soviet stances toward almost all major regional conflicts in the Third World, including those in Central America (Nicaragua), Southern Africa (Angola, Namibia), the Horn of Africa (Ethiopia), the Middle East (Arab-Israel), the Gulf (Iran-Iraq), and Southeast Asia (Cambodia). At that time, Moscow clearly signaled to its clients that it could no longer commit itself to supporting them indefinitely. In several instances, such as in Angola, Moscow actively collaborated with Washington in trying to find ways to reconcile the conflicting demands of the local protagonists and help warring parties reach negotiated settlements. Overt superpower cooperation was aimed at settling Third World conflicts on terms acceptable to all parties and not at merely preventing the superpowers from being sucked directly into these conflicts, as had been the case earlier. This policy helped move many of these regional conflicts toward temporary deescalation, although not necessarily toward permanent resolution.[42]

The new Soviet policy was, however, most dramatically visible in the Soviet approach to the crisis in the Gulf stemming from Iraq's invasion of Kuwait in August 1990 and to the U.S.-led war against Iraq that ensued. In this instance, the Soviet Union actively collaborated with the United States to force Iraq to disgorge Kuwait, which Baghdad had annexed shortly after the invasion. Ironically, in 1972 the Soviet Union had signed a Treaty of Peace, Friendship, and Cooperation with Iraq. It had also acted as the major arms supplier to Iraq for two decades and had supported Iraq's claim on Kuwait in 1961 when Kuwait became independent. According to a scholar from the former Soviet Union, "The changes in Soviet policy [witnessed during the Gulf crisis] were driven by the political transformation of the Soviet Union. By 1990, cooperation with the West was a major aim of the Soviet leadership, which was concerned with ending the arms race, obtaining Western understanding for Soviet policies toward republics seeking independence, and seeking economic and technical assistance for the crucial goal of the economic restructuring of the Soviet Union."[43]

The changing nature of Soviet policy also brought about shifts in U.S. strategies in the late 1980s, with Washington responding favorably to Soviet offers of cooperation in the management and attempted resolution of several Third World conflicts. However, U.S. policy toward the Third World continued to be subject to contrary ideological and strategic pulls and pressures, despite clear indications of Soviet retrenchment. Therefore, even while reacting to shifts in Soviet policy under Gorbachev, U.S. policy was not as clear in its sense of direction and its ultimate goals as the policy of its Soviet counterpart appeared to be during the Gorbachev years.[44]

One set of pressures on U.S. policymaking in the Third World emanated directly from the perceived retrenchment of Soviet power and the consequent dramatic change in the superpower equation. Proponents of this view argued that the Third World was important—if it was important at all—to U.S. strategy primarily, if not exclusively, in the context of superpower competition. They argued further that the Soviet threat to the West had been dramatically reduced and that Washington should not be overly concerned with events in the Third World, including its conflicts, which had autonomous origins and dynamics that were only minimally influenced by the United States.

On the other side were those who argued that the Third World, or at least certain regions of it, such as the Gulf and Central America, were important to U.S. security regardless of the superpower equation. Therefore, they felt the United States should maintain and increase its interventionist capability in these selected regions. Some even argued that in the changed strategic context the Third World should replace the Soviet Union as the leading U.S. security concern. This argument received added strength in 1990 from the Iraqi invasion of Kuwait, its consequent perceived threat to Saudi and other Gulf oil reserves, and the impact of the episode on oil production and prices.

This argument was made forcefully by Steven David, who wrote just before the unraveling of the Soviet sphere in Eastern Europe that "the Third World matters [to the United States] because of the strategic-military threat from the Soviet Union and, *more importantly, because of the threat from the Third World states themselves*."[45] David concluded, with foresight corroborated by the events of 1990, "American allies in Japan and Western Europe are threatened far more by developments in the Persian Gulf than by any direct threat against these allies themselves. . . . It is . . . far more likely that any call upon the United States to defend its interests in Western Europe and Japan will be in response to threats in the Persian Gulf, rather than to a Soviet invasion of its allies."[46]

Michael Desch provided the rationale for selective, yet major, U.S. strategic concerns with an expanded number of regions in the Third World by arguing, "There are areas outside the homeland that have little intrinsic value, but are nonetheless strategically vital because they contribute to the defense of the homeland or of other intrinsically valuable areas. A great power must protect its interests in such areas, i.e., control them, have access to them, or be able to deny them to an adversary. . . . These areas have what I term *extrinsic* value."[47] Desch concluded:

> To defend intrinsically valuable areas such as Western Europe, the Persian Gulf, and Northeast Asia, the United States must also integrate other areas into

> its grand strategy. The Caribbean, the Indian Ocean littoral, and a base in the Western Pacific have extrinsic value because of their proximity to important lines of communication, because of the nature of current anti-shipping and transportation technology, and because forward defense is currently the best strategy for U.S. defense of intrinsically valuable areas of the world.[48]

The 1990–1991 Gulf crisis led to the deployment overseas of the largest number of U.S. military personnel since the Vietnam War. The crisis also augmented the arguments and conclusions that parts of the Third World are very important to the United States, despite the disappearance of the Soviet threat, and that U.S. interventionist capabilities in these regions should not be reduced in response to the improvement in relations between Washington and Moscow.[49] These arguments have had a strong impact on U.S. strategic thinking in the post–Cold War era, as witnessed by discussions of U.S. strategic needs at the highest levels of the administration during the past few years.[50] This debate in the U.S. strategic community, sometimes expressed as a commitment to the spread of human rights and democracy,[51] is not only very relevant to the future of Third World security but also may be the crucial external factor concerning the security of the Third World in the post–Cold War era. This subject is analyzed in greater depth in Chapter 6.

Notes

1. For details, see Robert A. Mortimer, *The Third World Coalition in International Politics,* 2d ed. (Boulder: Westview Press, 1984).

2. For détente as "a mode of management of adversarial power," see Coral Bell, *The Diplomacy of Détente* (New York: St. Martin's Press, 1977). The quote is from page 1.

3. For details of this argument, see Roger Kanet and Edward Kolodziej (eds.), *The Cold War as Cooperation* (Baltimore: Johns Hopkins University Press, 1991). Also see Benjamin Miller, "Explaining Great Power Cooperation in Conflict Management," *World Politics* 45, no. 1 (October 1992): 1–46.

4. For case studies of the interaction between superpower competition and regional conflicts in the Third World, see Robert S. Litwak and Samuel F. Wells, Jr. (eds.), *Superpower Competition and Security in the Third World* (Cambridge: Ballinger, 1988).

5. For an analysis of superpower cooperation in the Middle East, see Galia Golan, "Superpower Cooperation in the Middle East," in Kanet and Kolodziej, *Cold War as Cooperation,* 121–146.

6. That the Soviet leadership thought along these lines is borne out by the evidence and analysis presented by a leading Russian analyst of international relations, Victor Kremenyuk. According to him, the "system of beliefs" that informed Soviet foreign policymakers during the Cold War included the following: "(a) Third World regions were progressively regarded as 'safer' places for rivalry than Europe was. . . . (b) At the same time these areas were regarded as integral parts of the global superpower rivalry. . . . (c) Rivalry in Third World areas had a dual meaning:

geopolitical and ideological. . . . (d) The combination of geopolitical/ideological as well as 'spheres of influence' thinking in the general context of rivalry in the Third World produced a kind of symmetrical vision of the entire strategic and regional relationship between the US and USSR on the Soviet side, a view vehemently rejected by the American side. . . . For the United States the idea of 'balance' was generally unacceptable, since it contradicted the original idea of 'containment' which in practice meant the achievement of American superiority." Victor A. Kremenyuk, "The Cold War as Cooperation: A Soviet Perspective," in Kanet and Kolodziej, *Cold War as Cooperation,* 39–40.

7. Samuel P. Huntington, "Patterns of Intervention: America and the Soviets in the Third World," *National Interest* (Spring 1987): 39–47.

8. For an analysis of the essential underpinnings of the "long peace" in the Cold War era, see John Lewis Gaddis, "The Long Peace: Elements of Stability in the Postwar International System." For opposing points of view on the relevance of nuclear weapons to stability in the central balance and the "long peace," see John Mueller, "The Essential Irrelevance of Nuclear Weapons: Stability in the Postwar World," and Robert Jervis, "The Political Effects of Nuclear Weapons: A Comment," all in Sean M. Lynn-Jones and Steven E. Miller (eds.), *The Cold War and After: Prospects for Peace,* expanded ed. (Cambridge: MIT Press, 1993): 1–80.

9. Nicole Ball, *Security and Economy in the Third World* (Princeton: Princeton University Press, 1988): 33.

10. Evan Luard, *War in International Society* (London: I. B. Tauris, 1986): Appendix 5, 442–446.

11. Kalevi J. Holsti, *Peace and War: Armed Conflicts and International Order, 1648–1989* (Cambridge: Cambridge University Press, 1991): Table 11.1, 274–278.

12. Sisir Gupta, "Great Power Relations and the Third World," in Carsten Holbraad (ed.), *Super Powers and World Order* (Canberra: Australian National University Press, 1971): 125–126.

13. Benjamin Miller, "Explaining Great Power Cooperation in Conflict Management," *World Politics* 45, no. 1 (October 1992): 43.

14. Robert S. Litwak and Samuel F. Wells, Jr., "Introduction," in Robert S. Litwak and Samuel F. Wells, Jr. (eds.), *Superpower Competition and Security in the Third World* (Cambridge: Ballinger, 1988): ix.

15. Stephanie G. Neuman, "Arms, Aid and the Superpowers," *Foreign Affairs* 66, no. 5 (Summer 1988): 1055.

16. Shahram Chubin and Charles Tripp, *Iran and Iraq at War* (Boulder: Westview Press, 1988): 240.

17. Robert W. Tucker, *The Inequality of Nations* (London: Martin Robertson, 1977): 7.

18. Martin Wight, *Systems of States* (Leicester: Leicester University Press, 1977): 124–125.

19. Andrew L. Ross, "Arms Acquisition and National Security: The Irony of Military Strength," in Edward E. Azar and Chung-in Moon (eds.), *National Security in the Third World: The Management of Internal and External Threats* (College Park: Center for International Development and Conflict Management, University of Maryland, 1988): 156.

20. Keith Krause, *Arms and the State: Patterns of Military Production and Trade* (Cambridge: Cambridge University Press, 1992): Tables 27 and 28, 184–185.

21. Gowher Rizvi, "The Rivalry Between India and Pakistan," in Barry Buzan et. al., *South Asian Insecurity and the Great Powers* (London: Macmillan, 1986): 107–108.

22. Chubin and Tripp, *Iran and Iraq at War,* 28.

23. For an analysis of trends in Chinese arms sales to the Third World, see Richard A. Bitzinger, "Arms to Go: Chinese Arms Sales to the Third World," *International Security* 17, no. 2 (Fall 1992): 84–111.

24. Krause, *Arms and the State,* Table 8, 87.

25. Michael T. Klare, "Adding Fuel to the Fires: The Conventional Arms Trade in the 1990s," in Michael T. Klare and Daniel C. Thomas (eds.), *World Security: Challenges for a New Century,* 2d ed. (New York: St. Martin's Press, 1994): 139.

26. Richard F. Grimmett, *Conventional Arms Transfers to the Third World, 1985–1992* (Washington, D.C.: Congressional Research Service, Library of Congress, July 19, 1993), 6.

27. For details of this argument, see Neuman, "Arms, Aid, and the Superpowers," 1044–1066.

28. Michael T. Klare, "Deadly Convergence: The Arms Trade, Nuclear/Chemical/Missile Proliferation, and Regional Conflict in the 1990s," in Klare and Thomas (eds.), *World Security,* 1st ed, 1991; 172.

29. Grimmett, *Conventional Arms Transfers,* Table 2I, 69.

30. For details of alignment and realignment in the cases of Egypt and the states of the Horn of Africa, see Steven R. David, *Choosing Sides: Alignment and Realignment in the Third World* (Baltimore: Johns Hopkins University Press, 1991): Chapters 3 and 4, 55–142.

31. Ali Mazrui, "Foreword," in Peter Willetts, *The Non-Aligned Movement: The Origins of a Third World Alliance* (London: Francis Pinter, 1978): xiii.

32. Willetts, *Non-Aligned Movement,* 18–19.

33. For an insightful analysis of this episode, see William M. LeoGrande, "Evolution of the Nonaligned Movement," *Problems of Communism* 29, no. 1 (January–February 1980): 35–52.

34. Fouad Ajami, "The Fate of Nonalignment," *Foreign Affairs* 59, no. 2 (Winter 1980–1981): 382.

35. For a more detailed analysis of Third World reactions to the NPT regime, see Caroline Thomas, *In Search of Security: The Third World in International Relations* (Boulder: Lynne Rienner Publishers, 1987): 121–145.

36. A leading Indian strategic thinker gave expression to this feeling in these words: "In 1954, the US Assistant Secretary of State, Walter Robertson, declared that it was the policy of the US government to adopt such a posture in Asia to break up the communist regime in China. Richard Nixon was the Vice President of that administration. The United States threatened China with nuclear weapons in 1953 and 1958, and Quemoy and Matsu were declared vital to US interests. But in 1972 Taiwan was quietly abandoned and President Nixon became solicitous about China's 'legitimate interests' in South Asia. Herbert Klein, the presidential aide, pointed out that 800 million Chinese armed with nuclear weapons could not be ignored. That is quite correct; *800 million Chinese could be ignored, as they were all these years, but not after 15 nuclear blasts at Lopnor and two earth satellites.*" K. Subrahmanyam, "Indian Attitudes Towards the NPT," in SIPRI (ed.), *Nuclear Proliferation Problems* (Stockholm: Almsqvist and Wiksell, 1974): 263.

37. For a forthright account of the origins of change within the Soviet Union by a senior Soviet academic, see Oleg T. Bogomolov, "The Origins of Change in the Soviet Union," in *The Strategic Implications of Change in the Soviet Union, Part I,* Adelphi Paper no. 247 (London: International Institute for Strategic Studies, Winter 1989–1990): 16–28. For an explicit account by a senior Soviet academic (and close confidant of and policy adviser to Gorbachev) of the impact of the new

thinking on Soviet policy toward the Third World, see Yevgeni Primakov, "USSR Policy on Regional Conflicts," *International Affairs* (Moscow) (June 1988): 3–9.

38. For a good account of the Soviet intervention in and withdrawal from Afghanistan, see Olivier Roy, *The Lessons of the Soviet/Afghan War,* Adelphi Paper no. 259 (London: International Institute for Strategic Studies, Summer 1991).

39. For details, see Elizabeth Kridl Valkenier, "New Soviet Thinking About the Third World," *World Policy Journal* 4 no. 4 (1987): 651–674. Also, David E. Albright, "The USSR and the Third World in the 1980's," *Problems of Communism* 38, nos. 2–3 (1989): 50–70.

40. Primakov, "USSR Policy on Regional Conflicts," 9.

41. Stephen F. Larrabee, "Regional Conflict: Cooperation and Competition: Paper II," in *The Strategic Implications of Change in the Soviet Union, Part II,* Adelphi Paper no. 248 (London: International Institute for Strategic Studies, Winter 1989–1990): 63.

42. For an analysis of the impact of the new Soviet policy and the consequent superpower collaboration on Third World conflicts, see S. Neil Macfarlane, "The Impact of Superpower Collaboration on the Third World," in Thomas G. Weiss and Meryl A. Kessler (eds.), *Third World Security in the Post–Cold War Era* (Boulder: Lynne Rienner Publishers, 1991): 125–145; and James G. Blight and Thomas G. Weiss, "Must the Grass Still Suffer? Some Thoughts on Third World Conflicts After the Cold War," *Third World Quarterly* 13, no. 2 (1992): 229–253.

43. Yelena S. Melkumyan, "Soviet Policy and the Gulf Crisis," in Ibrahim Ibrahim (ed.), *The Gulf Crisis: Background and Consequences* (Washington, D.C.: Center for Contemporary Arab Studies, Georgetown University, 1992): 76.

44. The contending philosophies that attempted to shape U.S. Third World policy during the 1980s were lucidly presented in two articles with self-explanatory titles that are essential reading for all analysts interested in this subject: Robert H. Johnson, "Exaggerating America's Stakes in Third World Conflicts," *International Security* 10, no. 3 (Winter 1985–1986): 32–68; and Steven R. David, "Why the Third World Matters," *International Security* 14, no. 1 (Summer 1989): 50–85. For additional analyses from different perspectives of the same subject, see Charles William Maynes, "America's Third World Hang-ups," *Foreign Policy,* no. 71 (1988): 117–140; Michael C. Desch, "The Keys That Lock Up the World: Identifying American Interests in the Periphery," *International Security* 14, no. 1 (Summer 1989): 86–121; and Stephen Van Evera, "Why Europe Matters, Why the Third World Doesn't: American Grand Strategy After the Cold War," *Journal of Strategic Studies* 13, no. 2 (June 1990): 1–51.

45. David, "Why the Third World Matters," 61. Emphasis added.

46. Ibid., 77, 78.

47. Desch, "The Keys That Lock Up the World," 98, 99. Emphasis in the original.

48. Ibid., 121.

49. For an eloquent statement of the argument that despite the end of the Cold War the Third World continues to be important to U.S. global strategy, see Steven R. David, "Why the Third World Still Matters," in Sean M. Lynn-Jones and Steven E. Miller (eds.), *America's Strategy in a Changing World* (Cambridge: MIT Press, 1992): 328–360.

50. For a major example of high-level thinking on U.S. strategic needs in the post–Cold War era, see Colin L. Powell, "U.S. Forces: Challenges Ahead," *Foreign Affairs* 72, no. 5 (Winter 1992–1993): 32–45. General Colin Powell, who was chair of the U.S. Joint Chiefs of Staff during the war against Iraq and the disintegration of the Soviet Union, described the new U.S. national strategy in these words: "The

central idea in the strategy is the change from a focus on global war-fighting to a focus on regional contingencies. No communist hordes threaten western Europe today and, by extension, the rest of the free world. So our new strategy emphasizes being able to deal with individual crises without their escalating to global or thermonuclear war. . . . Prudent planning requires that we be able to deal simultaneously with two major crises of this type" (35). He went on to describe the future U.S. military structure as both "capabilities oriented" and "threat oriented." According to General Powell, "We must concentrate on the capabilities of our armed forces to meet a host of threats and not on a single threat. . . . Conceptually we refer to our new capabilities-oriented armed forces as 'the Base Force.' This concept provides for military forces focused on the Atlantic region, the Pacific region, contingencies in other regions and on continued nuclear deterrence" (41). Also, see details of the Pentagon's "Defense Planning Guidance for the Fiscal Years 1994–1999" published under the heading "US Strategy Plan Calls for Insuring No Rivals Develop: A One Superpower World," *New York Times* (March 8, 1992): 1, 4.

51. For an example of the genre of analysis in which concerns about human rights and democracy and those relating to U.S. strategic interests converge, see Brad Roberts, "Democracy and World Order," in Brad Roberts (ed.), *U.S. Foreign Policy After the Cold War* (Cambridge: MIT Press, 1992): 293–307.

■ 6 ■
The Third World and the Post–Cold War Global Balance

The end of superpower rivalry and the reduced competition for influence on the global periphery has given analysts the opportunity to view the dynamic of Third World conflict more clearly. This situation has been made possible by the removal of the Cold War overlay, which obscured the fundamental causes of conflict in the Third World by presenting such conflicts as part of a Manichaean global tussle between good and evil. At the same time, the end of bipolarity has left many specialists bewildered by the numerous ostensibly unique factors that seem to determine the course of individual conflicts in the Third World. Dazzled by the revelation of underlying forces that contribute to Third World conflict, some analysts have hastily concluded that the fundamental dynamics of those conflicts have been changed by the end of the Cold War. Some analysts have leaped to the assumption that with the removal of the restraints imposed by nuclear bipolarity, the Third World is bound to descend into even worse anarchy than that which prevailed during the preceding four decades.

Such a conclusion is flawed for two major reasons. First, as I argued in Chapter 2, instabilities and insecurities in the Third World are largely a function of the historical juncture at which most Third World states find themselves. The disorder within and among Third World states is primarily the product of the early stage of state making; as the European experience has shown, violence and conflict are inevitable at this stage. Furthermore, as was demonstrated in Chapter 4, the Third World states' insecure condition is related to their late entry into the international system, which made them vulnerable to systemic forces that transcend momentary manifestations of the global balance of power. The intensity of conflicts in the Third World can be increased or reduced by the policies of the great powers, but the fundamental causes that lead to conflict are largely disconnected from transitory configurations of the global balance of power. Therefore, these causes of conflict are affected only marginally by transformations in that balance, such as the end of the Cold War.

Second, the conclusion that Third World conflict was fundamentally changed by the end of the Cold War is also flawed because it assumes that the bipolar distribution of power during the Cold War era almost always mitigated conflicts in the Third World. On the contrary, in many instances superpower rivalry exacerbated tensions in the Third World by providing external sources of political, military, and economic support to regional disputants; this support prompted local protagonists to adopt more rigid postures and provided them with the wherewithal to prolong conflicts. Frequently, conflict-prone areas of the Third World were also used by the superpowers to fight proxy wars, to test each others' political will, and to assess the efficacy of new weapons systems. This point was discussed at considerable length in Chapter 5, especially in the context of arms transfers to the Third World, and needs no further elaboration.

Nonetheless, by marking a fundamental transformation in the global balance of power, the end of the Cold War has had a major impact on conflicts in the Third World and on the way great powers attempt to manage conflicts. To tackle the issue of the impact of the post–Cold War configuration of global power on the Third World, we must first attempt to decipher the emerging contours of the new global balance.

The Post–Cold War Global Balance

There is no firm consensus among scholars, analysts, and statesmen on what the post–Cold War world will ultimately look like in terms of the distribution of the various dimensions of power—political, military, and economic—among the major claimants to the status of great power, which is defined as "a country possessing the will and the capability to alter events throughout the international system."[1] Neither is there a consensus on the interaction among these various dimensions of power and their fungibility nor on the nature of future relations among the established and aspiring great powers.[2] Predictions have ranged from unipolarity[3] through concert[4] to a return to the old days of a genuine multipolar balance[5] and everything in between.

The only conclusion scholars in the field agree upon is that with the end of the U.S.-Soviet Cold War, the world is no longer bipolar in the comprehensive sense of the past four decades. However, Cold War perceptions of global bipolarity were in any case exaggerated. Whereas the Soviet Union had achieved essential equivalence with the United States in the nuclear weapons arena by about 1960, the Soviet-led bloc never achieved global political equilibrium with the United States and its allies, and Moscow was never a major player in the international economic arena. The rather simplistic perception of the global balance to which many analysts subscribed during the Cold War era arose from the obsession with the nuclear dimension of the global balance coupled with inflated U.S. perceptions—partly from naïveté and partly by calculation—of the Soviet Union's global political reach.

With the end of the Cold War, a number of analysts seem to be falling into the same trap of converting one dimension of the multidimensional global balance of power into the criterion for defining that global balance. The economic rather than the strategic dimension is now used to describe the dominant pattern of global relationships. We are in danger, therefore, of substituting economic determinism for strategic determinism.[6] The Russian republic, the largest successor state to the Soviet Union, possesses essential nuclear equivalence with the United States today, and it will retain that equivalence even after reductions from the most recent strategic arms limitation treaties are implemented. We should not, therefore, confuse Russian political retrenchment, whether from East Europe or from the Third World, with the total dissipation of Moscow's strategic capabilities. As Kenneth Waltz has convincingly argued, despite Russia's dire economic condition and its inability to keep up with the United States in the field of nuclear technology, strategic bipolarity endures because "with nuclear weapons . . . short of a breakthrough that would give the United States either a first-strike capability or an effective defense, Russia need not keep pace militarily with American technology. So long as a country can retaliate after being struck, or appears to be able to do so, its nuclear forces cannot be made obsolete by an adversary's technological advances."[7]

In fact, Moscow's reliance upon its nuclear armory has increased in the post-Soviet phase. This fact is borne out by Russia's new military doctrine, adopted by President Boris Yeltsin's Security Council on November 2, 1993. The new doctrine "drops Moscow's long-standing pledge not to strike first with nuclear weapons; instead Russia reserves its right to use nuclear weapons first against nuclear states and against nonnuclear states that are in alliance with nations that have nuclear weapons. . . . The change reflects the Russian view that nuclear weapons are needed to compensate for new weaknesses in conventional forces."[8] Moreover, given the continuing turmoil in Russia, we cannot confidently project the future course that country is likely to adopt in the strategic and foreign policy spheres.[9] The strong showing of the xenophobic Liberal Democrats in the Russian parliamentary elections of December 1993 has further confounded pundits trying to predict the future evolution of the nuclear-armed Russian republic.

If the future of Russian foreign policy cannot be predicted with any certainty, the same is the case when we set out to predict the likely role of other major powers in the post–Cold War world. Although it is an economic superpower, for the moment Japan is a strategic midget and a political dilettante. Japan's economy, the strongest weapon in its diplomatic armory, is in the throes of a major recession that is further crippling its capacity to undertake political initiatives. Furthermore, as Peter Katzenstein and

Nobuo Okawara have argued, "Most Japanese are convinced that nuclear weapons and a strong military would generate neither wealth nor strength but, at great economic cost, immense political and military risks instead." They conclude that "recent changes in world politics will not translate into sharp breaks in Japan's security policy."[10]

On the other hand, Kenneth Waltz has argued that the structural imperatives of the international system determine the emergence of great powers, as well as their policies. Waltz concluded, "Japanese and German nuclear inhibitions arising from World War II will not last indefinitely; one might expect them to expire as generational memories fade. The probability of both countries becoming nuclear powers in due course is all the higher because they can so easily do so. . . . For Germany and Japan the problems of becoming a nuclear power are not economic or technological; they are political."[11] The fall from power of the long-ruling Liberal Democratic Party, the ensuing confusion in the Japanese domestic political arena, and threatened changes in Japan's regional security environment as a result of suspected North Korean nuclear ambitions have further clouded the prognosis about Japan's role in the post–Cold War world.[12]

United Germany, suffering from the economic and political problems of unification and acutely aware of the latent suspicions of its neighbors, is not fully able to take advantage of the clout it has mustered as the most populous state in Europe (excluding Russia) with the strongest economy and currency within the European Union.[13] Germany's early political muscle flexing in European affairs, especially over the disintegration of Yugoslavia, and the way it led Western policy during the crucial early stages of the unraveling of the Soviet Union seem to have given way to introversion bordering on inertia in international affairs.[14] So far, the country has failed to live up to the prediction that "economically, politically and intellectually, Germany is uniquely a country whose time has come in a continent whose time has come again."[15] However, the structural imperatives of the international system and unanticipated changes in its regional security environment could prompt Germany to assert a great power role by the turn of the century.

China, as Nicholas Kristof has pointed out, "is the fastest growing economy in the world, with what may be the fastest growing military budget. It has nuclear weapons, border disputes with most of its neighbors, and a rapidly improving army that may—within a decade or so—be able to resolve old quarrels in its own favor."[16] Its booming economy and nuclear weapons notwithstanding, China is mired in too many political and economic contradictions and continues to have too much of a Third World socioeconomic profile for us to confidently predict it will be able to play a global great power role on par with Japan and Germany in the immediate future. However, when combined with its major regional role in Asia and its possession of nuclear weapons, China's veto power in the Security

Council will place it in a position of considerable advantage in the post–Cold War world compared with other major Third World countries. Furthermore, given its ability to manufacture and export sophisticated weaponry, China has the capacity to act as the major spoiler in U.S.-led efforts to impose effective controls on the export of missiles, missile technology, and sensitive nuclear technology to Third World countries such as Pakistan and Iran.[17] All of these factors mean that China will have to be taken seriously by the major global powers, even as its role as a major global strategic and political player remains in some doubt.

The United States, the principal beneficiary of the disintegration of the Soviet Union and the main victor in the Gulf War, is the only country with conventional military capabilities—including high mobility—that give it a truly global reach. The United States is also the only major power that defines its political as well as its economic interests in global terms. In this sense, it qualifies as the lone superpower in the post–Cold War era, especially if we accept the contention that "being a superpower involves more than owning nuclear weapons: it requires a state of mind that has the will to project power."[18] The current diplomatic and military hobbling of Japan and Germany and the disarray in Russia have thrown into sharper relief the twin U.S. advantages—its military capabilities and its political will—and have bolstered the worldwide perception that the United States falls into a separate and superior category from the other major powers.

The United States is, however, mired in its own problems of budgetary and balance-of-payment deficits, which will make it very difficult, if not impossible, for any U.S. administration to undertake global policing that cannot be justified as a vital national interest to an increasingly skeptical domestic constituency.[19] This difficulty has been borne out by both the vacillation of U.S. policy on Bosnia and the lack of U.S. resolve in Somalia. The U.S. decision to withdraw from Somalia by March 31, 1994, when confronted militarily by a warlord's relatively meager forces, was a clear indication of the heightened domestic pressures on Washington to retrench from its global commitments.[20]

However, as I pointed out toward the end of Chapter 5, contrary pressures on foreign policymakers are pushing the United States into an activist policy abroad, in the Third World as well as in Europe and Northeast Asia. Such activist compulsions have been summed up succinctly by Joseph Nye: "In realist terms the United States will remain the world's largest power well into the next century. Economists have long noted that if the largest consumer of a collective good, such as order, does not take the lead in organizing its production, there is little likelihood that the good will be produced by others." Nye argued further that "the United States will have to combine both traditional power and liberal institutional approaches if it is to pursue effectively its national interest."[21]

Nye's argument represents the most sophisticated post facto defense of

U.S. policy in the Gulf following its use of the UN Security Council during the Gulf War to achieve ends that were primarily determined in Washington. His argument also represents an essentially quasi-hegemonic approach—even if clothed in the vocabulary of transnational interdependence—to world order in the post–Cold War era on the assumption that the United States, as the only true great power, is "bound to lead" in the quest for a new world order.[22] The contradictory economic and political pressures on Washington have, however, created a considerable degree of confusion in U.S. foreign policy and have led the Clinton administration to settle "on an approach that might be described as maintaining the global pretense politically while adopting a more regional posture economically."[23]

Complexities of Multipolarity

As the debate about the U.S. role and the uncertainties surrounding the roles of other major powers demonstrate, the post–Cold War world, although still dominated by great powers, will be far more complex than the era of strategic bipolarity that preceded it. With a return to the simple bipolarity of the Cold War era not likely, the new world order is likely to consist of four or five great powers (with the United States leading the pack) that possess different attributes in the various dimensions by which power is measured in the international system.

Just as there is much room for debate about the great powers' capabilities in the post–Cold War international system, there is much scope for argument about the relationships of the great powers with each other. In the immediate aftermath of the Cold War, the 1991 Gulf War left the impression that a new world order would be dominated by the sole surviving superpower, the United States, and that a tripolar international economic system would serve the goals of U.S. political unipolarity by underwriting the costs incurred by the global policeman. The Gulf War following on the heels of the Cold War left the further impression that major international organizations—the UN Security Council (political) and the International Monetary Fund (IMF) and the World Bank (economic)—would become vehicles for the promotion of U.S. political and economic objectives, which would also be shared by the other industrialized countries.

This preliminary vision of a new world order had grave implications for the Third World. It implied the creation, if not the existence, of an international directorate composed of the major industrialized powers, dominated by the United States, and positioned to determine the political and security contours of the post–Cold War world. Barry Buzan called this scenario one of unipolarized multipolarity; "multipolar in the sense that several independent great powers are in play, but unipolarized in the sense that there is a single dominant coalition governing international relations."[24] In official U.S. perceptions, such a vision of unipolarized multipolarity is little different from that of continued U.S. preponderance. This situation seeks to "preserve unipolarity by persuading Japan and Germany that they are better off remaining within the orbit of an American-led security and economic system than they would be if they became great powers. The strategy of preponderance assumes that rather than balancing against the United States, other states will bandwagon with it."[25] If a concert of powers dominated by the United States becomes a long-term reality and effectively controls the political, security, and economic agendas in the post–Cold War world, the limited degree of political and economic autonomy the developing countries enjoyed during the era of bipolarity will be further eroded.[26] I return to this topic later.

Lessons of the Gulf War

A concert of powers dominated by the United States and consisting of the major industrialized democracies, but also including the Soviet Union at the margins, operated quite effectively during the war against Iraq over its annexation of Kuwait. This episode, therefore, deserves greater exploration to understand the most significant trends likely to unfold over issues of conflict and security in the international system in general and in the Third World in particular.

In addition to being the principal example of the operation of the concert of powers in the security arena, the war against Iraq must be analyzed for two further reasons. First, the entire episode, beginning with the Iraqi invasion of Kuwait in August 1990, could provide a preview of what might happen in the Third World if the interests of an aspiring regional hegemon clash with those of the global political hegemon. Second, the U.S.-led war against Iraq was the first major post–Cold War crisis. The military action against Iraq, blessed by an apparently reinvigorated UN Security Council, was portrayed as a successful application of the collective security doctrine for the first time since the Korean War. Since collective security has been touted as the preferred way of dealing with aggression in the post–Cold War world, the Gulf War needs to be analyzed for the pointers it might provide for future collective action undertaken in the name of the international community, especially in the Third World.

Despite the fact that the most visible facet of the Gulf crisis was its international dimension, its causes and beginnings can be found in the intrastate, interstate, and regionwide dynamics of conflict in the Gulf and in its parent region, the Middle East. It is true that the most dramatic manifestation of the crisis was the U.S. decision to confront Iraqi ambitions by landing troops in Saudi Arabia and expelling Iraq from Kuwait by the use of force. Further, the immediate provocation for the Iraqi attack on Kuwait was related to oil, particularly Kuwait's initial defiance of the OPEC pricing policy and its reluctance to share its tremendous oil wealth with its more populous and war-devastated neighbor. However, Iraqi ambitions regarding Kuwait date back to the founding of the Iraqi state in the aftermath of World War I as one of the Arab successor states to the Ottoman Empire. Iraqi attempts in 1961 and 1973 to annex or subordinate Kuwait were based on the claim that until World War I the Ottomans had exercised formal authority over Kuwait and had aspired at various times to bring it under their control by making its ruler subordinate to the Ottoman authorities in the *vilayet* (province) of Basra, which now forms the southernmost part of Iraq.[27]

Furthermore, the Iraqi invasion of Kuwait in 1990 was linked to Iraqi ambitions of leadership in both the Gulf and the wider Arab world. The complex interplay of boundaries inherited from colonial days, Iraqi irredentism, inter-Arab rivalry, Baghdad's quest for predominance in the Gulf, Baghdad's search for resources in the wake of the devastating war with Iran, and the issue of oil pricing and production constituted the Iraqi decisionmaking process that led Iraq to invade and annex the emirate.

The end of the Cold War also influenced the Iraqi decision. This decision seemed to have been based at least in part on the Iraqi leadership's perception that given the relaxed nature of superpower relations, an Iraqi move into a small, neighboring country would not be viewed by Washington as a major shift in the bipolar equation in the Middle East in favor of the Soviet Union. Therefore, the Iraqi leadership apparently concluded that the invasion of Kuwait would not invite severe reprisals by the United States and its allies.

It was unfortunate for Saddam Hussein that Iraq and Kuwait happened to be located within a region defined by U.S. strategists as having intrinsic importance for U.S. security regardless of the state of great power relations at a particular point in time. Had such an invasion taken place in another, less strategically important region of the Third World, and had it involved countries that lacked the massive oil reserves controlled by Kuwait, Iraq, and Saudi Arabia, the U.S. outcry would have been much diminished, and the outcome would almost certainly have been very different. Iraq and Kuwait together possess 20 percent of the proven world oil reserves, which would have come under the direct control of Baghdad had it been able to annex Kuwait. In addition, by dominating the Arab littoral of the Gulf, Iraq would have been able to determine the production, pricing, and direction of flow of the oil produced by the other Gulf Arab oil producers, who together possess 37 percent of the proven world oil reserves, with Saudi Arabia alone accounting for over 26 percent. Thus, 57 percent of the world's proven oil reserves could conceivably have come under some form of Iraqi control.[28]

The most important U.S. objective in the Gulf crisis was to prevent a single Arab state—especially one such as Iraq that could become a pole for attracting radical Arab nationalists—from controlling, directly or indirectly, the vast exportable oil resources of the Gulf and thereby dominating the process that determined oil prices, production levels, and direction of oil exports. Second, the renewed U.S. perception that Iraq threatened Israeli security, especially after Saddam Hussein's warning in April 1990 that "we will make the fire eat up half of Israel if it tries to do anything against Iraq," resulted in a major reassessment of U.S. attitudes toward Iraq, which had been benign to the extent of being actively supportive during most of the time when Saddam Hussein's Iraq was fighting the Ayatollah's Iran.[29]

Intelligence reports that Iraq was moving toward the acquisition of nuclear weapons capability combined with its possession of Soviet missiles that could deliver chemical warheads against Israel fueled apprehension in Washington that Iraq might be tempted to use its newly acquired capabilities to extract concessions from Israel on the Palestinian issue, thus bringing about a direct Iraqi-Israeli confrontation. From Washington's point of view, the prospect of Iraq controlling the vast Gulf oil reserves, becoming engaged in an eyeball-to-eyeball confrontation with Israel, and, in the process, threatening to cut off the industrialized world's access to Gulf oil made the Arab oil embargo of 1973 pale by comparison. Iraq had to be stopped before it was too late.[30]

This reading of U.S. objectives has been corroborated by the U.S. insistence after the war that Iraq's war-making capabilities be decimated so totally that Baghdad would be prevented from attempting to dominate the Arab littoral of the oil-rich Gulf for at least the next half century, if not longer. This objective is being achieved in the guise of implementing UN resolutions that demand the destruction of all facilities remotely connected with Iraq's future capability to launch a major war.[31] These resolutions and the attempt to implement them to the last punctuation mark have resulted in the violation of state sovereignty on a scale unprecedented since the occupation of Germany and Japan at the end of World War II.

The Iraqi annexation of Kuwait gave a considerable degree of legitimacy to U.S. actions, especially since it reminded most Third World states of their own vulnerabilities in the face of internal and external challenges to their juridical sovereignty. More important, however, was the universal perception that after the contraction of Soviet commitments and in the context of the Soviet Union's impending demise, the United States was the only superpower remaining in the international system. The perception was that it would be unwise to defy Washington on a matter the United States considered to be of vital concern at a time when it was at the zenith of its power after having finally "won" the Cold War. This perception was shared equally by members of the Western alliance system—some of whom had initially had reservations about the Gulf venture—by the traditionally non-aligned states of the Third World, and even by China, which wanted to rebuild the bridges with the United States that had been damaged by the Tiananmen Square massacre in June 1989. The fortuitous convergence of these perceptions both within and outside the United Nations allowed the U.S.-led war against Iraq to be portrayed as a shining example of the success of a revitalized United Nations that was once again in a position to fulfill its original collective security mission.

However, discerning observers quickly realized that the war against Iraq was conducted in the name of the United Nations but not by the UN. Command and control of operations rested securely in the hands of the United States and its allies. Washington and its allies also continued to set the military and, therefore, the political objectives of the war. If "the UN was used both to get into the war and to get out of it,"[32] its role was reduced to that of an endorsement agency; it merely legitimized the military venture against Iraq without allowing the international community any major input into a war that was extolled as an outstanding example of collective security at work.

This realization led two U.S. observers to characterize the conduct of the war against Iraq as "a procedure in which action is taken on behalf of the [Security] council but without any council control over the nature, timing or extent of the action." They further asserted that "none of the 12 Security Council resolutions called for eliminating Iraq's war-making capability or deposing Saddam Hussein. But the former clearly became a goal of some coalition members, and the latter was widely suspected." Finally, they raised the crucial question: "In any operation, if the Security Council has asserted no control over the military action authorized, will it be possible for it to assert control over the terms of peace?"[33] If the answer to this question is negative, as was the case in the Gulf War, we can legitimately ask whether the notion of collective security had not been hijacked by a concert of powers led by the United States to serve its own ends.

Collective Versus Selective Security

In light of the fact that the U.S.-led war against Iraq was touted as a successful exercise in collective security, the next important question is, Will actions such as this become routine in the lone superpower's dealings with the Third World, with or without the participation of the other major powers, or was the Gulf War the result of a unique conjunction of circumstances that cannot be easily replicated?

With time it has become clear that the United States will not easily be able to repeat its success in the Gulf elsewhere because of a unique combination of two crucial elements in the prelude to the Gulf War that cannot be reproduced unless the same exceptional circumstances occur again. The first factor was the clear perception in Washington that vital U.S. interests were at stake in the Gulf; this made U.S. military action to reverse Iraq's annexation of Kuwait imperative. Despite its current lone superpower status, the financial and political constraints on U.S. resources seem to rule out future open-ended commitments by Washington to the indiscriminate deployment of U.S. forces in the Third World to reverse aggression by a powerful regional state against a weaker neighbor.

What is more, even if Washington believes major U.S. strategic and economic interests are imperiled in a hypothetical future crisis, it is unlikely that the president would receive as free a hand as was allowed in 1990 to deploy large numbers of U.S. troops to a Third World region. Financial costs were not well understood at the beginning of the Kuwait crisis and were serendipitously made up by generous handouts from Japan, Germany, Kuwait, and Saudi Arabia. Financial considerations are, however, expected to play a strong part in any future U.S. decision. Such a decision would be made on the basis of a much more rigorous cost-benefit analysis and with the clear understanding that Germany and Japan may be unwilling or unable to help pay for future U.S.-led ventures.

The second unique factor, touched upon earlier, was the coincidental timing of the Gulf crisis and the U.S. ascension to unipolar status. The suddenness of the Soviet collapse had left the international community astounded by what was perceived as the U.S. victory in the Cold War. The collapse of the second pole of power in a bipolar global balance was a crucial variable that determined the response of important members of the international community to the Gulf crisis. Many were numbed into inaction; several others decided there was no alternative but to comply with U.S. wishes. Several votes in the UN Security Council during the crisis, especially those cast by Third World members, can be explained in light of this factor. Once countries around the world have adjusted to the changes in the global balance of power and have taken stock of U.S. strengths and weaknesses, it will be extremely difficult for the United States to construct the sort of international consensus it achieved during the Gulf crisis to help give international legitimacy to U.S. objectives.

Much will also depend on the future configuration of global power and on the perception by the great powers of the new distribution of power. This perception will provide the key to how much leeway the United States will have to exercise unilateral initiatives in future Third World crises. It has become common among analysts of the post–Cold War international system to assume that the disappearance of the Soviet threat to the Western allies, combined with the growing economic muscle of Western Europe and Japan, will soon fundamentally reshape the great power relationships, if it has not already done so. It is further assumed that the end of the Cold War will inevitably lead to the rewriting of the global agenda by radically shifting the emphasis to economic rather than military concerns in the areas of cooperation and conflict.[34] On the basis of such assumptions, analysts project that the U.S. importance to the maintenance of the global political and economic order will diminish and that its major problems in the remainder of the 1990s will emanate from its competition with Europe and Japan for a fair share of the global economic cake.[35]

In the context of the growing perception that economic factors will determine the post–Cold War international pecking order, crises in the Third World serve a useful U.S. purpose. These crises help refocus attention on the variable of military power and its continuing usefulness in assuring the industrialized countries access at reasonable prices to scarce commodities such as oil. Third World crises also help demonstrate that the United States is the only major power with the will and the military capabilities to perform the role of policeman for the developed world and that without its global military reach and its decisive political leadership Europe and Japan would be at the mercy of Third World "extortionists" such as Saddam Hussein.

Coming on the heels of the end of the Cold War, the Kuwait crisis helped to remind Europe and Japan of their continuing need for the U.S. military shield, if not against the Soviet threat then against future Third World "predators." The crisis performed a valuable function for Washington—namely, that of decelerating the shifts of power within the Western alliance. This situation has allowed the United States to remain in control, at least for the moment, of Western strategic and security concerns in general and Western security policies in relation to the Third World in particular. However, the continuing legitimacy of U.S. primacy, if not hegemony, rests on convincing the other major powers that "a world without U.S. primacy will be a world with more violence and disorder and less democracy and economic growth than a world where the United States continues to have more influence than any other country in shaping global affairs."[36]

What, therefore, are the lasting lessons of the Gulf War? First it should be clear that U.S.-led actions such as the one against Iraq are exercises in selective, not collective, security. This was true of the Gulf War and will be true in other cases as long as the decision to intervene militarily against a recalcitrant state is made because one or more major powers have determined that their vital strategic and economic interests are involved. It was this involvement of great power interests that formed the crucial difference in the case of aggression committed against Kuwait compared with that against Bosnia; it dictated the international community's decision to intervene forcefully against the aggressor in Kuwait and not in Bosnia.

If such selectivity in the enforcement of collective security persists, it is likely to reduce the moral stature of the very international institutions (above all, the UN Security Council) that are used to give international legitimacy to these actions. Third World states, the weak and vulnerable members of the international system, depend upon these institutions more than the developed, industrialized states do to protect their sovereign status membership in such institutions gives them. Therefore, any threat to the legitimacy of international institutions, especially those in the UN system, that arises from their selective and partisan manipulation by the great powers is likely to translate into Third World perceptions of greater insecurity and vulnerability. Collective security must pass the test of consistency in its application; otherwise, it may greatly weaken the foundations of international society in which "state interaction is influenced by a set of shared norms about permissible and impermissible behavior."[37] An ineffective Security Council, as in the Cold War era,[38] poses less threat to international society than does a Security Council that may routinely become an instrument of one great power or a concert of great powers to be used for their own ends.[39]

John Goldgeier and Michael McFaul have predicted, if not advocated, the emergence of a "great power society" in the post–Cold War world, because "rather than balancing, core states are seeking to bandwagon, not around a power pole but around a shared set of liberal beliefs, institutions, and practices."[40] The emergence of such a "great power society," a euphemism for a concert of the major industrialized powers, as a substitute for the much broader concept of international society—thus excluding the majority of members of the international system—is likely to be less legitimate and more unstable than most proponents of the idea seem to realize.

A further factor militates against the applicability of the collective security doctrine to conflicts in the Third World, which may now be defined as including the Balkans and the Soviet successor states in the Caucasus and in Central Asia. This reason, as valid in the post–Cold War period as it was during the Cold War, arises because conflicts in the Third World, which account for the overwhelming number of conflicts since 1945, are "a ubiquitous corollary of the birth, formation, and fracturing of Third World states."[41] As envisaged in the UN Charter and by the proponents of a strengthened collective security system, collective security has and will continue to have little relevance for this category of war—a category that will continue to comprise the bulk of armed conflicts well into the twenty-first century. The validity of this assertion is demonstrated by the ongoing conflicts in the Balkans, the Caucasus, and Central Asia, in addition to conflicts raging from Sudan to Sri Lanka in regions traditionally considered to be part of the Third World.

Finally, the realities of conflict in the post–Cold War world, combined with the paucity of financial resources at the UN's command and U.S. reluctance to get involved in places where its vital interests are not at stake, have applied a brake to the expansion of UN peace enforcement operations and to UN enthusiasm for undertaking such missions in a large number of cases around the globe. In fact, the U.S. attitude toward multilateral interventions was very ambiguous from the beginning of the post–Cold War era. Washington found the United Nations useful in legitimizing international interventions that suited its interests but was extremely reluctant to place its forces under UN command even in these cases, as was clear in the instance of Somalia. When it did not suit its interests to intervene, the United States insisted on maintaining its right to remain aloof while dumping such cases into the UN's lap.[42]

This conjunction of forces and factors in the post–Cold War era has led Adam Roberts to conclude that "the possibility that has been opened up in the past few years is not of a completely new system of collective security, nor of an entirely new agenda, nor indeed of peace other than in the limited form of a possible reduction of major interstate conflicts. Rather, it is of a coexistence of unilateral, alliance-based and UN-based uses of force in almost the entire gamut of circumstances in which force has traditionally been deployed."[43] The new world order, in this case, looks little different from the old one.

Humanitarian Intervention and the Third World

Third World concerns about the increasing frequency of international intervention in conflicts, many of them intrastate rather than interstate in character, go beyond the apprehension that such intervention may be used to serve the political objectives of one or more of the great powers.[44] The concerns are rooted in "the tension between the new-found activism of the UN with regard to internal conflicts (and especially humanitarian intervention) and the cardinal principle of the international society of states—the sovereign equality of states—and its corollary, the duty of nonintervention by states in the internal affairs of each other."[45] Such concerns were eloquently expressed by India in an April 1993 submission to the UN Special Committee on Peacekeeping. India argued that it had become "a new responsibility for the UN and its member states to ensure that . . . new departures in peacekeeping operations are in conformity with the principles and provisions of the UN Charter. . . . Most important among these principles and guidelines are respect for the sovereignty of the State, non-interference in matters under the domestic jurisdiction of a State and the requirement of consent of all concerned parties for such operations."[46]

Humanitarian intervention undertaken within the UN framework, as in Iraq, Yugoslavia, and Somalia, has been justified by an extremely elastic definition of the phrase "threats to international peace and security," thereby permitting the Security Council to act under Chapter VII of the Charter. This form of intervention has created the greatest amount of unease in Third World capitals. This was especially true following the U.S.-led intervention in the Kurdish areas of Iraq, which resulted in a substantial portion of Iraqi territory being declared out of bounds to forces of the Iraqi state. James Jonah, the former UN Undersecretary-General for Political Affairs, has stated clearly that following the Western intervention to provide safe havens for Iraqi Kurds, "Most small and medium-sized states, particularly in the Third World, have expressed concern at the way the concept of humanitarian intervention has been applied in Iraq. They fear that this precedent could be used in [the] future as a pretext for old-fashioned political and military intervention in weak states."[47] This fear goes beyond the insecurity felt by repressive and unrepresentative Third World regimes, as is borne out by the widely held perception that "the practice of intervention has diverged from international law with respect to 'less civilized,' 'non-Western,' 'developing' states, leaving intervention linked with imperialism and colonialism in historical memory."[48]

The next major confrontation between the North and the South may well take place over the issue of humanitarian intervention if the major industrialized powers insist on exercising the right to such intervention on behalf of the international community. The fundamental reason for Third World apprehension on this score is that the logic of humanitarian intervention runs directly counter to the imperatives of state making, which is defined as "primitive central state power accumulation."[49] This is the primary political enterprise in which most Third World countries are currently engaged. As the Indian example demonstrates clearly, state building, even when undertaken by primarily persuasive means, inevitably entails a certain amount of coercion against segments of the population that remain irreconcilably opposed to the consolidation of the power of the central state. Equally inevitably, such coercion on the part of the state leads to the violation of human rights of the target population, to a greater or lesser degree. To most Third World states, therefore, the U.S.-UN intervention in Somalia is likely to appear as the thin end of the wedge that could allow for the future expansion of such interventionist activities, justified by humanitarian considerations, beyond the confines of the category of failed states. In the perception of most Third World state elites, this condition could present a potential threat to every Third World state's efforts at state consolidation.

A second important reason for Third World resentment of humanitarian intervention on the part of great powers was encapsulated in a remark made by Martin Wight a quarter century ago that "all such historical examples of intervention show the powerful correcting the weak. The moral interdependence of peoples has never been so strong, nor the circumstances so favorable, that there has been collective intervention to suppress the iniquities of a Great Power."[50] Wight's assertion is corroborated by Thomas Weiss's conclusion about post–Cold War activism on the part of the UN Security Council: "The Security Council takes decisions to intervene not according to objective criteria but rather to what the international political traffic will bear."[51] The very fact that even in the case of humanitarian intervention "what international political traffic can bear" is determined by great power interests leads one to ponder with Noam Chomsky "whether the category exists," or whether "in this world [it merely] means intervention authorized or directed by the United States."[52]

The selective nature of humanitarian interventions, even among the many cases in the Third World that could qualify for them, has also raised doubts about the real reasons for such interventions. As Adam Roberts has pointed out, "The fact that mass slaughter in Cambodia, shootings in Beijing, ruthless dictatorship in Myanmar (Burma) or catastrophe in Sudan did not lead to humanitarian interventions suggests that some other factors are involved in decision-making."[53] We can add the civil war in Burundi and the near-total anarchy in Zaire to Roberts's examples.

However, with the reversals suffered by the U.S. and UN forces in Somalia and the clearly demonstrated unwillingness of the United Nations, the United States, and the major European powers to intervene in Bosnia, the major powers seem to be losing their initial post–Cold War enthusiasm for humanitarian intervention. This is the case primarily because of the change of attitude on the part of the United States. U.S. humanitarian intervention in Somalia was undertaken in part to neutralize the criticism that U.S. intervention in northern Iraq to create a safe haven for the Kurds was an act of political retribution against Iraq rather than a genuinely humanitarian venture. Washington wanted to demonstrate that the lone superpower had the will and the capability to promote a new world order by intervening for purely altruistic purposes in a remote place that was of little strategic or economic significance to the United States.

But U.S. domestic reactions, including those in Congress, to the loss of a handful of American lives in combat in Somalia made it very clear that the U.S. public and politicians had no stomach for such politically disinterested intervention if it resulted in even very few casualties. Meanwhile, U.S. failure to concretely follow up its repeated threats of military intervention against Serbia and the Bosnian Serbs further eroded the credibility of the U.S. commitment to humanitarian intervention for its own sake and dampened any remaining enthusiasm in the UN corridors for such intervention on a large scale.[54]

Finding a Multipolar Balance

Does this mean great power intervention in the affairs of Third World states will dwindle, if not cease, after having reached a new high immediately following the Cold War? Or does it mean great powers will intervene strongly but more selectively when they perceive that their interests are threatened by forces within a Third World region or state? The answers to these questions will lie in the nature of the multipolar balance that is likely to evolve over the rest of this decade and into the next.

It is too early, however, to predict whether great power relations at the turn of the century will be primarily competitive or cooperative or whether they will constitute a true balance, a concert, or a hybrid containing elements of both. However, two things can be predicted at this stage. First, the next ten years will constitute a bridging or transitional decade, during which the contours of the future balance will gradually take shape. Second, the new balance will be more explicitly multidimensional than the previous balance, which was perceived and defined in largely unidimensional—that is, nuclear-strategic—terms.

In a world in which economic capabilities are being radically realigned, the economic dimension of the balance will play an important, but not exclusive, role in defining the configuration of power in the post–Cold War epoch. However, even if we accept the importance of the economic dimension in the evolving global balance, this dimension alone does not automatically define the nature of great power relationships in that balance. A group of researchers belonging to the Berkeley Roundtable on the International Economy (BRIE) has argued that the economic dimension "creates the possibility of fundamentally new relationships among great powers, and the regions that they dominate." These new relationships could range from "true multilateral cooperation [in which] the United States would continue to be *primus inter pares*" to the peaceful coexistence of self-contained regional trading blocs to mercantilist regional rivalry based on the fundamental premise of strategic trade theory, which "proposes that governments can by unilateral action permanently alter the competitive balance of trade in critical industries . . . [a] dynamic . . . reminiscent of the 'cult of the offensive' among European military organizations prior to World War I." This last tendency, according to the BRIE analysts, could well "be reinforced by a new dynamic developing between military and commercial technology . . . [in which the Cold War] dynamic is frequently reversed—that is, advanced commercial technologies 'spin on' into military applications."[55]

The range of economic relationships presented here also applies to the political arena of great power relationships, which can range from concert to acute competition. Great power political relations will likely operate in tandem with the character of their economic relationships and vice versa. What do these different scenarios of great power interaction portend for the Third World, especially for the security of Third World regions?

If the global balance of power in the post–Cold War era turns out to be genuinely multipolar—that is, if the four or five great powers are competitive in the economic as well as the political arena—the balance of power may be able to restore a substantial degree of equilibrium to the international system. At the same time, it may curb the interventionist tendencies of the major powers, thus providing weaker states with more political and military autonomy within a setting of managed great power rivalry. Great power rivalry in the nuclear age will continue to be managed in order to avoid direct military confrontation, even if not all of the great powers possess the nuclear capability that had underwritten nuclear deterrence in the Cold War era. The latent nuclear capabilities of two potential great powers, Japan and Germany, combined with the explicit nuclear capabilities of the United States, Russia, and China will prevent any of these states from escalating conflicts to the stage of open warfare. As Waltz has pointed out, "In the presence of nuclear weapons, any challenge to a leading state, and any attempt to reverse a state's decline, has to rely on political and economic means."[56]

The possibility of a genuine multipolar balance emerging by the beginning of the twenty-first century cannot be ruled out, because, as Christopher Layne has observed, "the historical evidence strongly supports the hypothesis derived from neorealist theory: unipolar moments cause geopolitical backlashes that lead to multipolarity."[57] Moreover, if the economic competition among the major industrial powers is accentuated and new security threats in Europe and Northeast Asia—ranging from the assertion of xenophobic Russian nationalism to the acquisition of a credible nuclear capability by North Korea—emerge, they are likely to alter the political and security calculations of Japan and Germany and accelerate their move toward strategic independence, the first step toward genuine multipolarity.

If, however, genuine multipolarity does not evolve from this transitional era, and a concert of the major industrialized powers—dominated by the United States—continues to operate as it did in the Gulf War and is intensified in the economic arena by multilateral cooperation among the great economic powers, this situation is bound to circumscribe the political, military, and economic autonomy of the weaker members of the system. It would do so by greatly limiting the political and economic maneuverability of even the largest Third World states by concentrating both political and economic power in a coalition of industrialized states that cannot be played off against one another. Furthermore, Third World states that fall foul of this dominant coalition would be vulnerable to hostile intervention carried out with nearly total impunity by the concert of great powers. For whereas the grass suffers when elephants fight, it suffers immeasurably more when they make love.

The two major powers facing exclusion in this scenario of a world dominated by a concert of industrialized democracies would be Russia and China. On the one hand, they will face the strong temptation of being coopted into the concert, albeit as less than full members, thereby deriving economic and technological benefits from their collaboration with the Group of Seven (G-7) powers. On the other hand, if they become acutely conscious of their subsidiary position in the concert and conclude that their political and security interests cannot be protected when they play second fiddle to the industrialized democracies, Moscow and Beijing may find it in their interest both to cooperate with each other economically and militarily and to build their own constituencies in the Third World to oppose the concert's "hegemonic" designs.[58] They could also paralyze the Security Council by exercising their veto power, thereby forcing the concert of industrialized powers to act in the security arena outside the UN framework. Both Russia and China would, however, be hamstrung in their attempt to counter the G-7's control of the international security agenda because of their continuing dependence upon the industrialized countries for investments, technology, and markets.

However, the Third World's security problems in the post–Cold War era would arise only partially from the emerging balance of power among the great powers. These problems would arise even more from the weaknesses and vulnerabilities within Third World states and from the conflicts among them. As stated at the beginning of this chapter, these weaknesses and conflicts have surfaced with greater force in the post–Cold War era. Whereas some of these problems have acquired or will acquire salience because of the transformations in the global security environment wrought by the end of the Cold War, others are thrown into sharper relief because of the changes in international norms that are just beginning to become perceptible. I turn to these issues and problems in the next two chapters.

Notes

1. John M. Goldgeier and Michael McFaul, "A Tale of Two Worlds: Core and Periphery in the Post–Cold War Era," *International Organization* 46, no. 2 (Spring 1992): footnote 1, 467.

2. For a sampling of some of the most sophisticated scholarly attempts to predict the configuration of global power in the post–Cold War era and the lack of consensus among them, see Robert Jervis, "The Future of World Politics: Will It Resemble the Past?" *International Security* 16, no. 3 (Winter 1991–1992): 39–73; Joseph S. Nye, Jr., "What New World Order?" *Foreign Affairs* 71, no. 2 (Spring 1992): 83–96; Christopher Layne, "The Unipolar Illusion: Why New Great Powers Will Rise," *International Security* 17, no. 4 (Spring 1993): 5–51; and Kenneth N. Waltz, "The Emerging Structure of International Politics," *International Security* 18, no. 2 (Fall 1993): 44–79.

3. Charles Krauthammer, "The Unipolar Moment," *Foreign Affairs* 70, no. 1 (Winter 1991): 23–33.

4. Richard Rosecrance, "A New Concert of Powers," *Foreign Affairs* 71, no. 2 (Spring 1992): 64–82.

5. John J. Mearsheimer, "Back to the Future: Instability in Europe After the Cold War," *International Security* 15, no. 1 (Summer 1990): 5–56.

6. The thesis that the economic dimension will be the determining dimension of the global balance of power in the post–Cold War era has found advocates rang-

ing from economists to geostrategists. For example, see Lester C. Thurow, *Head to Head: The Coming Battle Among Japan, Europe and America* (New York: William Morrow, 1992); and Edward N. Luttwak, *The Endangered American Dream: How to Stop the United States from Becoming a Third World Country and How to Win the Geo-Economic Struggle for Industrial Supremacy* (New York: Simon and Schuster, 1993).

7. Waltz, "The Emerging Structure," 51.

8. Michael R. Gordon, "The Guns May Be a Bit Rusty but the Nuclear Arms Are Still Polished," *New York Times* (November 29, 1993): A10.

9. For different scenarios of the future course of Russian policy, see Alexei G. Arbatov, "Russia's Foreign Policy Alternatives," *International Security* 18, no. 2 (Fall 1993): 5–43. Also see Alexei K. Pushkov, "Letter from Eurasia: Russia and America: The Honeymoon's Over," *Foreign Policy* 93 (Winter 1993–1994): 76–90. According to Pushkov, the school of thought represented by the group he terms *statist democrats* will determine the future direction of Russian foreign policy: "Statist democrats considering themselves students of realpolitik insist that partnership with the West should not sacrifice Russia's national interests and security" (79).

10. Peter J. Katzenstein and Nobuo Okawara, "Japan's National Security: Structures, Norms, and Policies," *International Security* 17, no. 4 (Spring 1993): 116, 118.

11. Waltz, "The Emerging Structure," 66–67.

12. For an analysis of the contradictory pressures on, and contrary trends in, Japan's post–Cold War foreign policy even before the fall of the Liberal Democratic Party (LDP) government, see Takashi Inoguchi, "Japan's Role in International Affairs," *Survival* 34, no. 2 (Summer 1992): 71–87. Although Inoguchi concluded that "the pressures on Japan to play a greater role in world affairs are beginning to overwhelm the countervailing obstacles," he qualified this conclusion by insisting on two conditions that must be met when charting out Japan's future role in international affairs: "First, Japan's policies must be in harmony with those of the international community as a whole. In practice, this means that Japan's actions should be linked to multilateral undertakings wherever possible. Second, Tokyo's initiatives need to be grounded by a solid domestic consensus about the broad course and content of Japan's foreign policy" (71). Inoguchi's conclusions epitomize the ambivalence among the Japanese elite regarding Japan's future international role.

13. For problems facing the united Germany, see Fritz Stern, "Freedom and Its Discontents," *Foreign Affairs* 72, no. 4 (September–October 1993): 108–125.

14. For a well-rounded analysis of Germany's future role, see Wolfram F. Hanrieder, "Germany, the New Europe, and the Transatlantic Connection," *International Journal* 46, no. 3 (Summer 1991): 394–419.

15. Elizabeth Pond, "Germany in the New Europe," *Foreign Affairs* 71, no. 2 (Spring 1992): 115.

16. Nicholas D. Kristof, "The Rise of China," *Foreign Affairs* 72, no. 5 (November–December 1993): 59.

17. For a discussion of the controversy surrounding China's supplying sophisticated weaponry to Third World countries, see Nayan Chanda, "Red Rockets' Glare," *Far Eastern Economic Review* (September 9, 1993): 10–11.

18. *The Economist* (March 9–15, 1991): 15.

19. For a scathing attack on the new U.S. "imperial role" in the wake of the Gulf War of 1991, see Robert W. Tucker and David C. Hendrickson, *The Imperial Temptation: The New World Order and America's Purpose* (New York: Council on Foreign Relations Press, 1992).

20. For an incisive commentary on the U.S. mission in Somalia and on humanitarian intervention in general, see Thomas L. Friedman, "U.S. Pays Dearly for an Education in Somalia," *New York Times* (October 10, 1993): section 4, 1, 3.

21. Nye, "What New World Order?" 95, 96.

22. Joseph S. Nye, Jr., *Bound to Lead: The Changing Nature of American Power* (New York: Basic Books, 1990).

23. Charles William Maynes, "A Workable Clinton Doctrine," *Foreign Policy,* no. 93 (Winter 1993–1994): 6.

24. Barry Buzan, "New Patterns of Global Security in the Twenty-First Century," *International Affairs* 67, no. 3 (July 1991): 437.

25. Layne, "The Unipolar Illusion," 7.

26. The Group of Seven Summit, as John Kirton has argued, could form an effective vehicle for the institutionalization of this new concert of the leading industrial powers because it has already begun to perform "an increasingly central role in the efficacious management of the international security order." John Kirton, "The Seven-Power Summit as a New Security Institution," in David Dewitt, David Haglund, and John Kirton (eds.), *Building a New Global Order: Emerging Trends in International Security* (Toronto: Oxford University Press, 1993): 342.

27. For a concise and penetrating analysis of the historical background, see Theodore Draper, "The Gulf War Reconsidered," *New York Review* 39, nos. 1 and 2 (January 16, 1992): 46–53.

28. Figures for oil reserves, confirmed as of 1990, are drawn from Bahgat Korany, Paul Noble, and Rex Brynen (eds.), *The Many Faces of National Security in the Arab World* (New York: St. Martin's Press, 1993): Appendix, Table A.5, 308.

29. For one account of U.S. and other Western powers' policies that augmented Iraq's military capabilities during the Iran-Iraq War, see Alan Friedman, *Spider's Web: The Secret History of How the White House Illegally Armed Iraq* (New York: Bantam Books, 1993).

30. For an analysis of U.S. reasons for intervening in the Iraq-Kuwait crisis, see Michael C. Hudson, "Washington's Intervention in the Gulf: Toward a New Middle East Order?" in Ibrahim Ibrahim (ed.), *The Gulf Crisis: Background and Consequences* (Washington, D.C.: Center for Contemporary Arab Studies, Georgetown University, 1992): 61–62.

31. As Freedman and Karsh have pointed out, "By the time war came, the Bush administration had concluded that an important advantage would be the opportunity to cut Iraq's military power down to size. It was less successful in the military campaign in this objective than was assumed at the time. However, the deficit, at least with regard to mass destruction capabilities, was made up in the enforcement of the cease-fire demands for the destruction of these capabilities." Lawrence Freedman and Efraim Karsh, *The Gulf Conflict, 1990–1991: Diplomacy and War in the New World Order* (Princeton: Princeton University Press, 1993): 439.

32. Theodore Draper, "The True History of the Gulf War," *New York Review* 39, no. 3 (January 30, 1992): 45.

33. Bruce Russett and James S. Sutterlin, "The U.N. in a New World Order," *Foreign Affairs* 70, no. 2 (Spring 1991): 76–77.

34. For one example, see Theodore C. Sorensen, "Rethinking National Security," *Foreign Affairs* 69, no. 3 (Summer 1990): 1–18.

35. For example, see Jeffrey T. Bergner, *The New Superpowers: Germany, Japan, the U.S. and the New World Order* (New York: St. Martin's Press, 1991).

36. Samuel P. Huntington, "Why International Primacy Matters," *International Security* 17, no. 4 (Spring 1993): 83.

37. Goldgeier and McFaul, "A Tale of Two Worlds," footnote 5, 468. For a discussion of the notion of international society, see Hedley Bull, *The Anarchical Society: A Study of Order in World Politics* (New York: Columbia University Press, 1977): 12–14.

38. It should be noted that whereas the Soviet Union was primarily responsible for the Security Council's ineffectiveness in the 1950s and the early 1960s, the United States cast the largest number of vetoes in the Security Council in the second half of the 1960s and especially in the 1970s, thus rendering the Security Council ineffective in the areas of peace and security.

39. For an elaborate statement of these arguments regarding collective security in the post–Cold War world, see Mohammed Ayoob, "Squaring the Circle: Collective Security in a System of States," in Thomas G. Weiss (ed.), *Collective Security in a Changing World* (Boulder: Lynne Rienner Publishers, 1993): 45–62.

40. Goldgeier and McFaul, "A Tale of Two Worlds," 480.

41. K. J. Holsti, "International Theory and War in the Third World," in Brian L. Job (ed.), *The Insecurity Dilemma: National Security of Third World States* (Boulder: Lynne Rienner Publishers, 1992): 38.

42. The U.S. reluctance to participate in UN peacekeeping and peace enforcement operations except when it suits U.S. interests and Washington's unwillingness to put U.S. troops under UN command have been formally adopted as U.S. policy by the Clinton administration in "Presidential Decision Directive 25" announced on May 5, 1994. For details, see Elaine Sciolino, "New U.S. Peacekeeping Policy De-Emphasizes Role of the U.N.," *New York Times* (May 6, 1994): A1, A7.

43. Adam Roberts, "The United Nations and International Security," *Survival* 35, no. 2 (Summer 1993): 27–28.

44. International intervention has been defined by Thomas Weiss as "those coercive actions (economic and military sanctions) taken by the community of states to alter the domestic affairs, behavior, or policies of a targeted government or insurgency that flouts international norms and resists the expressed will of the international community." Thomas G. Weiss, "Intervention: Whither the United Nations?" *Washington Quarterly* 17, no. 1 (Winter 1994): 110. Other forms of international interference—ranging from the imposition of economic conditionality by the IMF to human rights monitoring—although irksome to Third World states, do not fall into the category of international intervention, narrowly defined.

45. Mats R. Berdal, *Whither UN Peacekeeping?* Adelphi Paper no. 281 (London: International Institute of Strategic Studies, October 1993): 74.

46. Quoted in Ibid., 75.

47. James O.C. Jonah, "Humanitarian Intervention," in Thomas G. Weiss and Larry Minear (eds.), *Humanitarianism Across Borders: Sustaining Civilians in Times of War* (Boulder: Lynne Rienner Publishers, 1993): 69.

48. Kimberley Stanton, "Pitfalls of Intervention: Sovereignty as a Foundation for Human Rights," *Harvard International Review* 16, no. 1 (Fall 1993): 16.

49. Youssef Cohen, Brian R. Brown, and A. F. K. Organski, "The Paradoxical Nature of State Making: The Violent Creation of Order," *American Political Science Review* 75, no. 4 (December 1981): 902.

50. Martin Wight, "Western Values in International Relations," in Herbert Butterfield and Martin Wight (eds.), *Diplomatic Investigations: Essays in the Theory of International Politics* (Cambridge: Harvard University Press, 1968): 120.

51. Weiss, "Intervention: Whither the United Nations?" 114.

52. Noam Chomsky, "Humanitarian Intervention," *Boston Review* 18, no. 6 (December–January 1993–1994): 3, 4.

53. Adam Roberts, "The Road to Hell . . . : A Critique of Humanitarian Intervention," *Harvard International Review* 16, no. 1 (Fall 1993): 12.

54. This mood was best summed up in two statements made by the U.S. president and the UN Secretary-General in 1993. In his address to the UN General Assembly in September 1993, President Clinton declared, "The United Nations simply cannot become engaged in every one of the world's conflicts. If the American people are to say yes to peacekeeping, the United Nations must know when to say no." UN Secretary-General Boutros Boutros-Ghali lamented, however, that "politically and economically the international community is now in retreat." Both statements are quoted in Paul Lewis, "Reluctant Peacekeepers: Many U.N. Members Reconsider Role in Conflicts," *New York Times* (December 12, 1993): 22. Also see Elaine Sciolino, "The U.N.'s Glow Is Gone: After Months of Frustrations and Setbacks, U.S. Turns Away from Joint Peacekeeping," *New York Times* (October 9, 1993): 1, 7.

55. Michael Borrus, Steve Weber, and John Zysman, with Joseph Willihngnaz, "Mercantilism and Global Security," *National Interest* (Fall 1992): 23–27. For a detailed version of the BRIE analysis, see Wayne Sandholtz et. al., *The Highest Stakes: The Economic Foundations of the Next Security System* (New York: Oxford University Press, 1992).

56. Waltz, "The Emerging Structure," 76.

57. Layne, "The Unipolar Illusion," 32.

58. For an analysis of Chinese unease at the end of bipolarity and the projected future direction of Chinese foreign and security policies, see David Shambaugh, "China's Security Policy in the Post–Cold War Era," *Survival* 34, no. 2 (Summer 1992): 86–106. According to Shambaugh, "China would prefer to find itself in a multipolar world in which U.S. global power declines absolutely and regional powers, such as China, are able to resist external interference in their respective regions" (92).

■ 7 ■

The Third World's Post–Cold War Security Predicament: The External Dimension

The end of the Cold War, the current transitional phase in the global balance of power that is likely to last at least for another decade, and the gradual emergence of a new global equilibrium in the first decade of the next century should have a major effect on the security situation in the Third World, even if they do not transform the fundamental dynamic of conflict within and among the developing countries. Some dynamics, especially those pertaining to the autonomy of Third World states in two possible scenarios of the evolving global balance of power—genuine multipolarity and a concert of major powers—were touched upon in Chapter 6. However, the impact of recent changes in the international arena on the course of interstate and intrastate conflicts in the Third World may be more immediately visible than the erosion or augmentation of the Third World's autonomy in the post–Cold War era. The latter is a complex process that will take years to play out, and it will be several more years until analysts can determine with any certainty whether the role of the Third World in the international system has been weakened or strengthened under a new global political dispensation.

By removing the element of superpower rivalry from Third World conflicts, the end of the Cold War can affect the intensity and frequency of these conflicts in contradictory ways. On the one hand, it has the potential to dampen such conflicts and to reduce their intensity by removing the major sources of external political and military support to the participants. The most dramatic example of superpower retrenchment from contested situations in the Third World was the Soviet military withdrawal from Afghanistan, which was completed in February 1989. This withdrawal removed the major bone of contention between the warring domestic parties and eventually led to the fall of the pro-Soviet Najibullah regime in April 1992. That superpower reconciliation could have positive effects even on Third World conflicts in which a superpower was not militarily engaged was demonstrated, to different degrees, in such cases as Namibia,

Angola, Mozambique, and Cambodia. It should be pointed out, however, that the solutions imposed in all these cases have been partial, fragile, and, in most instances, temporary.

Afghanistan, despite the removal of the Soviet-Russian factor, is as far away from national reconciliation as it was during the 1980s. In fact, the central government in Kabul has become even weaker since the Soviet withdrawal, and the country has been carved into several fiefdoms, based largely on ethnic and sectarian lines. This has occurred primarily because even during the war against the Soviet-backed regime,

> the Afghan resistance was at no point a homogeneous social movement: it embraced a diverse range of political parties, commanders, combat units and sympathizers, fragmented on the basis of ethnic identity, segmentary lineage or locality. As long as a common enemy provided a focus for popular mobilization, this problem of fragmentation was to an extent kept under control. . . . The circumstances surrounding the establishment of Islamic rule in Kabul have brought this issue to the forefront of concern.

Continued and persistent interference by neighboring countries, principally Pakistan but also Iran and Saudi Arabia, which "are now actively seeking to secure returns on their investments" in the Afghan resistance, has further complicated the already messy situation inside Afghanistan.[1]

The conflict in Angola, after an initial period of apparent national reconciliation, has also taken a turn for the worse. The refusal of the National Union for the Total Independence of Angola (UNITA) to accept the results of the internationally supervised elections, which it lost, and its subsequent unleashing of the latest phase of civil conflict have led to human and material destruction that has surpassed that of the fifteen years of civil war between the Popular Movement for the Liberation of Angola (MPLA) and UNITA.

The conflict in Cambodia, whose resolution has been overseen by the United Nations, has wound down enough to allow the establishment of a government of national reconciliation following UN-supervised elections. However, with the Khmer Rouge unwilling to abide by the UN-mediated solution and the Cambodian government itself riddled with divisions between the Sihanoukists and the former pro-Vietnam communists, the situation is marked by a fragile and limited peace that may be violated massively at any time. This could especially be the case if the Thai military continues to supply the Khmer Rouge with weaponry, gasoline, and cash in exchange for logs, gems, and priceless ancient Khmer statues.[2]

There is reason to be more optimistic about the outcome in Mozambique, although the situation in that country is also unstable because of the reluctance of the rival government and Mozambique National Resistance (RENAMO) forces to disarm and demobilize. Namibia has been a success story thus far, and the transfer of power from South African to South West African People's Organization (SWAPO) hands has gone relatively smoothly. However, any deterioration in the political and security situation in South Africa following the introduction of multiracial democracy in April 1994 is likely to destabilize Namibia.[3]

Despite the frequent backsliding into anarchy and violence, the initial impact of the end of the Cold War on Third World conflicts has been positive on the whole and has led initially to the temporary alleviation of some major conflicts in Asia, Africa, and Central America. However, by removing the restraints that had been imposed upon local protagonists by the parallel conflict management policies followed by the superpowers, the end of superpower rivalry may have simultaneously signaled the beginning of an era of less restrained and more bloody conflicts in the Third World. In this sense, the current conflicts in the Balkans, the Caucasus, and Central Asia may be the precursors of a pattern that might prevail more widely throughout the Third World.

Superpower involvement in Third World conflicts during the Cold War exacerbated many of these conflicts, but it also prevented many from becoming truly zero-sum games. This was the case because the two dominant powers did not push each other's allies to the wall, thereby forcing the rival superpower to intervene directly to maintain its credibility. Superpower policies blocked conclusive outcomes of many Third World conflicts by preventing the stronger party from winning.

The primary example of such joint superpower restraint on regional combatants was the way the 1973 October War between Israel and Egypt was brought to an end without the total decimation of the Egyptian Third Army and the fact that it was concluded on the basis of a formula that allowed Egypt to maintain its foothold on the eastern bank of the Suez Canal and, eventually, to proceed step by step toward reclaiming the Sinai Peninsula.[4] Although their arguments are based on less conclusive evidence, some policymakers and analysts have claimed that joint superpower pressure on India during the closing stages of the India-Pakistan War in December 1971 was responsible for New Delhi's not attempting to score a clear military victory against West Pakistan after it had defeated the Pakistan Army in what was then East Pakistan (now Bangladesh).[5] As these two cases demonstrate, the stronger and victorious party in such conflicts was the preeminent military power in the region. Superpower cooperation in restraining victorious parties in regional conflicts usually prevented the clear assertion of regional hegemony by the most powerful states in the Third World.

The end of the Cold War may lead to a clearer assertion of hegemony by the preeminent powers in their respective regions by removing the most important external brakes on the aspirations of potential regional hegemons.[6] This conclusion may be true in theory, but the experience of the past few years has established that it deserves to be heavily qualified in two major ways.

First, it has become clear that attempts to assume regional hegemonic roles must not conflict with the global interests of the lone superpower as long as the United States continues to enjoy that status. This fact was demonstrated more than adequately by the abysmal failure of Iraq to assert its hegemony in the Arab littoral of the Gulf in 1990–1991. Although it may not be possible to easily replicate the massive U.S. intervention in the Gulf in a similar future crisis,[7] the Gulf War forcefully made the point that Washington will not tolerate the emergence of regional hegemons in the Third World that have the potential to threaten the vital economic and strategic interests of the United States and its allies in the industrialized world. If the U.S. unipolar moment is succeeded by a concert of major industrialized powers that is in a position to act as the international security directorate over a long period, then the same restriction will apply to the role of potential regional hegemons toward the interests of the concert. Global managers, if they have the will, can usually bring superior capabilities to bear in a conflict of wills with aspiring regional hegemons.

Second, potential regional hegemons must possess not only the military but also the economic means and the domestic political capacity to sustain a dominant regional role over a relatively long period of time. Even when respectable military force has been present, the Achilles' heel of regionally preeminent powers in the Third World aspiring to managerial roles has been a combination of sluggish economic performance and weak domestic political capacity. Israel is a very special case because its demographic, territorial, and economic resources are totally out of sync with its military prowess and with its political influence with the United States. But even states such as India and Nigeria—in theory, potential regional hegemons par excellence in the Third World—suffer differently from a combination of economic and political weaknesses. For example, Nigeria, with its floundering economy and a highly unstable political situation, is a very weak candidate for the role of regional manager, despite its lead in deploying Economic Community of West African States (ECOWAS) forces into Liberia in August 1990 following the outbreak of civil war in that West African country.[8]

India has been often perceived as the strongest contender for regional predominance in the Third World in the post–Cold War era. However, its one major attempt at conflict resolution in the region by applying military force in Sri Lanka ended in failure and detracted from its credibility as regional security manager. India has also consistently recorded only a modest economic growth rate and during the past few years has witnessed a dramatic deterioration in its domestic political arena. This situation resulted from a proliferation of ethnic insurgencies and the erosion of the fundamental consensus that was the basis of the Indian secular and democratic polity for four decades. The Indian case illustrates that internal political decay, even if it is not terminal, greatly erodes the managerial capacity of aspiring regional hegemons because of the perennial eruption of domestic crises.[9]

This analysis shows that preeminent regional powers in the Third World, even if they are militarily capable, are largely incapable of managing the security problems of their respective regions. In addition, their weaknesses leave them open to political and military challenges from other regional states. The removal of the superpower rivalry, especially the cooperative dimension that affected the management of regional conflicts, may have left a void in the Third World that may encourage greater interstate conflict linked to regional balance of power.

Russia's Role as Regional Conflict Manager

Russia could be the major exception to the general rule of the preeminent regional powers' relative ineffectiveness in managing their regional security environments in the Third World. However, Russian activism on its periphery does not necessarily rule out interstate conflict in the sphere of influence between Russia and one or more regional states or among the regional states themselves. As noted in Chapter 3, Russia, which is not a Third World country but which has a periphery of prototypical Third World states, will continue its attempt to impose a regional order on the Caucasus and Central Asia that will conform to Moscow's political and military interests.

The Russian strategy results in part from what one analyst has called "Russia's greatest post-Soviet nightmare . . . the possibility that former republics will eventually seek alliances or special relations with outside powers."[10] In part the strategy is also the result of Russian historical memories, particularly of the Muslim republics of the former Soviet Union. As Ronald Dannreuther has pointed out, "Ever since Muscovy's subjection to two centuries of Tatar rule under the vassalage of the Golden Horde [incidentally, before the Tatars converted to Islam], Russia has tended to view the southern Muslim world as a threat to the security and integrity of the Russian state. . . . This sensitivity to the security threats from the south continued throughout the Soviet period and reached its final apotheosis in the folly of the Soviet invasion of Afghanistan in December 1979."[11]

The proclamation by the Chechen and Tatarstan Republics, components of the Russian Federation with predominantly Muslim populations, of state sovereignty in November 1991 and March 1992, respectively, threatened to reverse the last of the gains imperial Russia had made during four hundred years of subjugating Muslim populations. With around 20 million Muslims continuing to live within Russia's current borders, such assertions of Muslim independence, especially in the context of the unraveling of Russian rule in Central Asia, have further increased Moscow's nervousness about its southern periphery.

So far, Russian attempts to manage regional conflicts and problems between and within the Soviet successor states in Central Asia and the Caucasus have had the blessings of the United States and the major European powers. Policymakers in these states fear opposing the Kremlin's policies on this score may lead to an intensification of Russian xenophobia and may thus derail the Russian move toward economic liberalization, democratization, and accommodation with the West. Russia's "legitimate" right to a sphere of influence that includes most of the Soviet successor states—especially those in Central Asia and the Caucasus—and that is comparable to the U.S. sphere in Central America has been strongly advocated by several Washington pundits. One pundit, while endorsing Boris Yeltsin's proposal that "Russia might serve as the arbiter of disputes in the former Soviet Union, provided that it acted with the formal blessing of the United Nations," argued, "If force had to be used [to 'solve' regional ethnic conflicts], a . . . common path would be for the international community to search for and legitimate some individual state to serve as the enforcer for the international community. In most cases, that would turn out to be a neighbor state with a direct interest in the outcome."[12]

One suspects that the U.S. endorsement of Russian regional hegemony serves a dual function. First, it helps impose a political order acceptable to the Western powers on the predominantly Muslim republics of the former Soviet Union, which in Western perceptions are in danger of falling prey to "Islamic fundamentalism."[13] Second, it helps relieve Russian feelings about the loss of superpower status by acknowledging Moscow's legitimate role as a regional great power and accepting its right to control its own fief in most of the territories of the former Soviet Union, which some pundits believe may ease Russia's transition into a subordinate role in a future world order dominated by the major industrialized powers. Incidentally, Moscow's preoccupation with the Caucasus and Central Asia could also help divert Russian attention from its former possessions and satellites in Eastern Europe, thus reducing the possibility that Russia's renewed ambitions may clash directly with the interests of the leading Western powers in Central and Eastern Europe.

It is too early to predict whether Russia will succeed in imposing order on Moscow's former colonies or whether it will cause a backlash of major proportions and introduce greater disorder into the Caucasus and Central Asia. If the latter scenario unfolds, it could strengthen militant Islamic forces in Central Asia, because they are increasingly perceived by the local populations as the only viable alternative to continued Russian domination. This may in fact be true, especially since most of the current rulers in Central Asian states are former communists who are to varying degrees dependent on Moscow for their political survival.[14] Such a scenario could also set off interethnic strife between Russian settlers—10 million of whom still live in Central Asia—and the indigenous inhabitants, especially in states such as Kazakhstan and Uzbekistan, which have very sizable Russian minorities.[15]

Interethnic strife involving Russian settlers in Central Asia could, in turn, prompt a Russian government, under pressure from hardline nationalists, to intervene directly and transform intrastate conflicts into interstate ones. In this case, such a transformation will be more threatening to international order because it would involve a nuclear-armed, but psychologically insecure, great power. The threat could increase if the Western powers intervened to dissuade Russia from asserting its domination by force, thus setting off a crisis of systemic proportions.[16] If this happens, regional order issues in at least one part of the Third World may become enmeshed with those of global political and military order, importing the instabilities of the periphery into the core of the international system.

Arms Transfers and Interstate Conflict

The one variable that can presumably help neutralize the tendency toward greater interstate conflict in the Third World in the post–Cold War era is the reduction in the supply of sophisticated weapons to Third World states, especially to those in conflict-prone regions. The importance of this variable is emphasized by the fact that "regional actors' perceptions of security threats are in part determined by the military capabilities of other actors in the same security complex."[17] Analysts generally perceive that the end of the Cold War should positively affect Third World security by removing the principal political motivation for such arms transfers on the part of the major suppliers. This perception needs to be addressed and its validity confirmed or denied before we can further predict the level and intensity of conflict in the post–Cold War Third World.

Two major shifts in the pattern of arms transfers to the Third World have become visible since the end of the Cold War. These shifts are depicted in the arms delivery figures for 1992 and even more in arms transfer agreements signed in that year. First, states such as Cuba, Vietnam, Angola, and Syria, which were major recipients of Soviet arms at concessional prices, have dropped off the list of major arms importers, and even India's position on that list is no longer secure. Iraq also dropped out following the Gulf War and the international restrictions imposed upon it as a result of its defeat in that war. Second, these states have been replaced by the newly industrialized countries (NICs) of East and Southeast Asia, with Taiwan jumping ahead of even Saudi Arabia in the value of arms transfer agreements signed in 1992. Other major new recipients include Indonesia,

Malaysia, Singapore, and Thailand, all of which are either NICs or near NICs (NNICs) with booming economies and increased spending power.[18]

The latter trend demonstrates the increased purchasing power of the East and Southeast Asian NICs and NNICs. It also reflects renewed feelings of insecurity among the ASEAN states and Taiwan, particularly since these countries seem concerned that the end of the Cold War may lead to U.S. disengagement from the region. Such disengagement would leave the regional states vulnerable to pressure from the two major Asian powers in their vicinity, China and Japan. Moreover, the presence of unresolved disputes in the region—especially those between China and Taiwan over the relationship between the two countries and the competing claims of China, Malaysia, the Philippines, Taiwan, Vietnam, and Brunei to the islands of the Paracel and Spratly archipelagoes in the South China Sea—makes this region potentially volatile. As one analyst claimed, "The most likely site for a war [involving China] is probably the South China Sea, which China claims as its own 1,000-mile-long pond. This huge sea, encompassing the Paracel and Spratly Island groups, covers major international shipping routes, including those that carry oil from the gulf to Japan."[19]

The recent Chinese acquisition of Su-27 fighters from Russia and the U.S. decision to sell F-16 fighters to Taiwan are major indications of a renewed arms race between the two neighbors, whose regimes do not accept each other's legitimacy. According to a seasoned observer of arms trade, "The China-Taiwan nexus probably constitutes the most vibrant arms market in the world today, with leaders of both countries signing multibillion dollar contracts for the acquisition of modern weapons."[20]

Richard Grimmett pointed out that the value of all 1992 arms transfer agreements with the Third World, at $23.9 billion, was the lowest for the 1985 to 1992 period. This development resulted from a drastic reduction in the value of Russia's arms transfer agreements, which at $1.3 billion fell to just over one-fifth the 1991 figure achieved by the former Soviet Union.[21] In 1992 the value of all arms delivered to the Third World—$12.7 billion—also showed a significant decline, the fifth consecutive decline since 1987.[22]

The decline in arms imports was also related in part to the saturation of many Third World markets in the 1980s and in part to the fall in the price of oil during that decade. However, these facts should give little comfort to analysts who might feel such a trend portends a more peaceful Third World. First, much of the decline is tied to the almost total halt in Russian arms supply to Third World clients, which in the former Soviet days was paid for either at concessional prices or through barter. As Russia settles down in the post-Soviet phase and begins to play the arms market using capitalist logic, its share is expected to rise once again but this time bringing badly needed hard currency to Moscow. The latest deals Russia has struck with China for the supply of sophisticated weapons and weapons technology amount to $2 billion and are an indication of things to come. According to one observer, "The Chinese . . . have been taking advantage of hard times in Russia by acquiring a wide range of sophisticated Soviet weapons at rock-bottom prices; among the items mentioned in recent reports of Chinese bargain hunting are MiG-31 interceptors, Tu-22 bombers, T-72M main battle tanks, A-50 airborne warning and control planes, and S-300 ground-based antiballistic missiles."[23]

Second, the Iraqi invasion of Kuwait in 1990 and the subsequent Gulf War have heightened Saudi concerns, as well as those of the other oil-producing Gulf monarchies, about their continuing vulnerability to regional predators such as Saddam Hussein. This concern has led to a renewed demand for sophisticated weaponry by the Gulf states, especially Saudi Arabia, and to the signing of major arms deals between these countries and the Western powers, especially the United States. This demand is reflected in the data on arms transfer agreements signed in 1992, which show Saudi Arabia, Kuwait, and the United Arab Emirates as three of the top ten recipients. In 1992, among the Gulf countries, Saudi Arabia signed arms transfer agreements worth $4.5 billion; Kuwait followed with $1.1 billion and the UAE with $500 million.[24]

Third, the fall in the value of weapons imports into the Third World from 1987 onward masks a different and growing form of weapons transfer from developed to developing countries: the transfer of sophisticated arms production technology, which is now an integral part of the arms trade.[25] Since the 1980s, transfer of weapons technology, at first politically driven by the requirements of the Cold War, has acquired a primarily economic rationale as competition among suppliers has become more intense, giving recipients greater leverage with the arms-exporting countries. Package deals—including the transfer of finished weapons, weapons assembled in the recipient countries, and licensed production that entails the transfer of weapons technologies—have often been worked out between suppliers and recipients, especially those recipients with a sufficiently developed technological and industrial base to absorb or adapt to the technology transferred.[26] As a result, certain Third World states such as Argentina, Brazil, India, and South Korea have increased their capacity to produce—and, in some cases—even export indigenous arms.[27]

This problem predates the end of the Cold War. The transfer of weapons technology, however, could have important consequences for the post–Cold War world order if, with the end of the bipolar competition in the Third World, weapons and weapons technology transfers are determined by commercial considerations that tend to give the recipient country considerable leverage over the supplier. Such a situation is likely to increase the autonomy of decisionmaking in regard to war and peace, at least in the more developed Third World countries, because transfers of weapons technology strengthen the fighting capacity of the technologically more advanced Third World states. In addition, such technology frees these countries from having to obtain spare parts and ammunition from the original suppliers and increases the sophistication of the technology their war machines can command indigenously.

As a result, wars in the Third World, especially among major regional actors, could now be started without the protagonists being overly concerned about supplier reactions; further, such wars could be sustained for longer periods of time and could be far more costly in human and material terms than wars in the past. Paradoxically, the increased autonomy of important Third World actors in this instance may lead to an increase in the duration and intensity of interstate conflicts, thanks to the weapons and technology transferred by the major powers during the Cold War and thereafter.

Prospects for the creation of successful regional arms control regimes in the Third World appear to be slim, because they are dependent upon the willingness of all major suppliers to, and recipients in, a particular security complex to cooperate in the setting up of such regimes.[28] Furthermore, the success of arms control regimes also requires detection instruments and the mandatory punishment of defectors, whether suppliers or recipients. But these are conditions impossible to impose in an international system organized around the concepts of state sovereignty and national interest.[29]

Additionally, many major Third World recipients of sophisticated arms do not define their security dilemma in a single dyad. For example, Indian acquisitions of military hardware and weapons technology are justified by New Delhi with reference to threats from both Pakistan and China. Similarly, during the 1980s Pakistan's military needs were defined by Islamabad in relation to the threats from India and from the Soviet military presence in Afghanistan. Before the Gulf War, Iraq's acquisition of military hardware was determined, according to Baghdad, by both the Iranian and Israeli threats. The oil-rich countries of the Gulf and the NICs of East and Southeast Asia, two leading categories of arms purchasers in the post–Cold War world, tend to define their defense needs not by a particular threat (although Taiwan can point to China) but more generally as emanating from their unstable security environments. In such cases, even the basic requirement for the construction of arms transfer regimes—the identification of a security complex—is conspicuously absent.

The absence of well-defined threats, or the presumed existence of more than one threat, also suits the purposes of the major arms suppliers, who can always deny that they were fueling a particular arms race by pointing to the multiplicity or the undefinable character of the source of threats to their clients in the Third World. The end of the Cold War is unlikely to change this situation, which both the suppliers and the recipients of military hardware and weapons technology believe to be mutually advantageous.

Nuclear Proliferation in the Post–Cold War Era

A major subset of the problems connected with the transfer of sophisticated weapons technology, one that has reached the top of the international security agenda in the post–Cold War era, is the threat of nuclear weapons proliferation and the related phenomenon of the proliferation of ballistic missiles. Nuclear proliferation is possibly the only Third World security issue that directly ties Third World security concerns to those of global security, because the possession of nuclear weapons can give selected Third World states the capability to gravely endanger the human environment if they decide to use such weapons in combat. More important to the major powers, even short of the actual use of these weapons, nuclear-capable countries in the Third World can in theory target the forces and even the population centers of the major industrialized states, especially if they also possess the capability to produce and operate ballistic missiles. This situation, in the perception of major powers, could alter the power balance between them and some Third World states.

It is no wonder that concern about nuclear and missiles proliferation in the Third World cut across the East-West division even during the height of the Cold War and led to superpower collaboration in an attempt to institutionalize international controls on Third World behavior in the nuclear realm through the instrument of the NPT. Aimed at delegitimizing and thereby preventing horizontal proliferation beyond the five established members of the nuclear club, the NPT was opened for signature in 1968 and came into force in 1970. In combination with the safeguards administered since the 1950s by the International Atomic Energy Agency (IAEA), the NPT was seen as the most effective method of keeping in check the nuclear ambitions of important Third World states that were on the verge of attaining the technical capability to manufacture nuclear weapons.

However, anxious to maintain their autonomy of decisionmaking on nuclear matters, the states with nuclear weapons potential refused to adhere to the NPT. Leading members of this group—Israel, India, Pakistan, and South Africa until it signed the NPT in 1991—attempted with considerable success to circumvent the controls on the transfer of nuclear weapons, related materials, and technology imposed by the nuclear club. Such controls have been imposed primarily through the medium of the London Suppliers' Group, which is made up of the principal industrialized countries that possess nuclear technology and materials. This group was formed in 1974 following India's detonation of a nuclear device in May of that year.

The policies of the near-nuclear powers on the acquisition of nuclear weapons capability have been shrouded in cloaks of deliberate ambiguity (although some of these cloaks are more transparent than others) in order to keep in suspense both regional adversaries and the international nuclear establishment and to prevent technological and economic retribution by that establishment.[30] However, there is little doubt among informed observers that Israel currently possesses dozens of nuclear weapons, that India and Pakistan are, for all practical purposes, nuclear-capable powers, and that North Korea is close to acquiring such capacity. South Africa's voluntary abdication of nuclear ambitions, the decimation of Iraq's embryonic nuclear capacity, and the commitment by Brazil and Argentina to avoid a nuclear arms race by putting all their nuclear facilities under IAEA safeguards have removed the other former aspirants from the list of likely immediate proliferators.

The breakup of the Soviet Union has left large quantities of strategic nuclear weapons within the territories of Belarus, Ukraine, and Kazakhstan, although the overwhelming majority of these weapons remain under the control of Russian Strategic Rocket Forces. Soviet tactical nuclear weapons were distributed more widely across nine or ten of the former Soviet republics. By May 1992, all Soviet tactical nuclear weapons were withdrawn to Russia. Although John Mearsheimer argued that "Ukraine is likely to keep its nuclear weapons, regardless of what other states say and do,"[31] there are clear indications that Ukraine's major objective in dragging its feet on the dismantling or transfer of strategic nuclear weapons to Russia is to use the weapons as bargaining chips in negotiations with Moscow and as a form of leverage to acquire Western security guarantees and gain additional economic assistance from the Western powers.[32]

Whereas the post-Soviet proliferation of nuclear powers may have introduced temporary instability into the nuclear arena, the all-but-acknowledged possession of nuclear weapons by Israel, India, Pakistan, and, more recently, North Korea is perceived as far more destabilizing and dangerous by the international nuclear establishment. These unacknowledged but nonetheless credible instances of nuclear proliferation pose more than merely abstract problems of managing a world that includes a dozen or so nuclear powers. They pose the more acute problem of the probability that some of the most sensitive and conflict-prone regional environments in the Third World will become nuclearized because the four de facto nuclear powers—Israel, India, Pakistan, and North Korea—have all been engaged in protracted disputes with their neighbors that were punctuated by intense bouts of armed conflict.[33] The superpowers' experience shows that nuclear powers tend to act responsibly and that mutual nuclear deterrence prevents the outbreak of shooting wars. However, skeptics believe such restraint may not equally apply to Third World contexts for several reasons.[34]

First, a situation of nuclear deterrence and relative symmetry does not exist in the most volatile region of the Third World—the Middle East—where Israel is widely believed to possess up to one hundred nuclear warheads[35] and monopolizes nuclear weapons capability. Israel is on record—

not merely in words but also in practice, with its 1981 attack on the Osirak nuclear reactor in Iraq—as saying it will not allow any Arab country to attain nuclear weapons capability. Such nuclear monopoly is extremely dangerous because in a time of acute crisis, when vital interests appear to be threatened, it is likely to provide the major incentive as well as the prime justification for unleashing nuclear weaponry on a nonnuclear adversary that may temporarily appear to have an advantage in conventional power.[36] It is also dangerous in the sense that nonnuclear adversaries of a nuclear monopolist are tempted to take grave risks to acquire nuclear capability themselves. The evidence from Iraq after the Gulf War regarding its attempt to circumvent IAEA restrictions to acquire nuclear weapons that would match those of Israel demonstrates the validity of this assertion.

But even an ostensibly balanced case of nuclear proliferation, such as that projected in South Asia between India and Pakistan, carries risks of miscalculation and adventurism that may end in catastrophe.[37] In this case, the India-Pakistan nuclear and conventional balances are fundamentally unstable and asymmetrical. There are also serious doubts about the countries' second-strike capabilities, even after they overtly acquire first-strike capacity. The highly emotionally charged atmosphere that surrounds the two countries' bilateral disputes, principally over Kashmir, adds to the danger of proliferation in South Asia.[38]

In the post–Cold War period the United States has stepped up its pressure on both India and Pakistan to sign the NPT and give up their nuclear ambitions. Yet it is increasingly apparent to Washington that it is too late to turn back the clock and eliminate the undeclared nuclear capabilities of the two South Asian states. For the first time, this has led the United States under President Clinton to change its emphasis from eliminating to capping Indian and Pakistani nuclear capabilities, thus giving some legitimacy to these undeclared but widely presumed capabilities.[39]

The latest presumed proliferator is North Korea. Recent evidence has been mounting that North Korea, isolated in the post–Cold War world and with an increasingly paranoid leadership, has embarked seriously on the road to nuclear weapons capability. This conclusion has been augmented by Pyongyang's refusal to abide by the terms of IAEA inspection mandated by the NPT, which it has signed. The evidence coming out of North Korea is too confusing to categorically conclude whether North Korea is trying to use the threat of acquiring nuclear weapons capability to gain political, economic, and military concessions from the United States and South Korea or whether it is engaged in a serious attempt to become a nuclear-armed state.[40]

The International Institute for Strategic Studies concluded from North Korean actions that "the simplest, but not necessarily the correct, reason is that the government has something to hide and is, perhaps, despite U.S. warnings, far closer to producing a nuclear weapon than had been supposed."[41] The Central Intelligence Agency's (CIA) classified assessment, which is supported by other U.S. intelligence agencies but with which the U.S. State Department continues to disagree, has gone even further and has surmised that North Korea has already developed one or two nuclear bombs.[42] If this is true, it would be the first time a nonnuclear signatory to the NPT, albeit one that has unilaterally suspended its treaty membership, has taken the fateful step of developing nuclear weapons and directly contravening the terms of the treaty.

The problem is further complicated by the fact that "North Korea is developing an intermediate-range ballistic missile, the No-Dong 1, a system too expensive . . . to equip with a conventional warhead; Japan, in particular, fears that a nuclear warhead is planned for the system."[43] The tense relationship between North and South Korea, the presence of over 30,000 U.S. troops in South Korea, and Japanese apprehensions about the nuclear arming of the Korean peninsula create a very unstable situation in Northeast Asia. Moreover, the situation may have a major impact on the global balance if it leads to Japan's reassessing its defense policies in conventional and nuclear matters.

Ballistic Missile Proliferation

The North Korean case illustrates the fact that in the last decade, prospects of nuclear weapons proliferation (even if covert or ambiguous), especially in the most volatile and conflict-prone regions of the Third World, have caused much greater concern than they had previously because there has been a simultaneous proliferation of ballistic missile technology that is concentrated in the same regions and among many of the same countries that aspire to possess nuclear weapons.[44] Foremost among these regions is the Middle East, where, as one analyst noted,

> within a setting . . . inherently unstable . . . ballistic missiles . . . accentuate insecurities by undermining long-standing deterrent postures, and by emphasizing the benefits of preemptive counter-force action. The virtual certainty that enemy ballistic missiles will penetrate defensive systems may lead to conclusions that first-strike attacks aimed at destroying opposing missile forces are preferable to absorptive and second-strike strategies. Regional crisis stability may be further jeopardized, and the preference for pre-emptive assault transformed into a strategic imperative, should fears arise that enemy missiles may be used to deliver nuclear or chemical warheads. In the Middle East, this concern is real as the spread of surface-to-surface systems has in some countries been accompanied, and in others predated, by an interest in nuclear, chemical and bacteriological weapons.[45]

The intensity of the Middle East problem is underscored by the fact that, according to a study conducted in 1988 by the U.S. Congressional

Research Service, nine of the seventeen Third World countries then considered to be in possession of, or in the process of developing or procuring, ballistic missiles were located in the Middle East.[46] Israel's impressive nuclear arsenal and the known (but now decimated) Iraqi chemical weapons capability—which Egypt, Israel, Libya, Syria, and Iran are also suspected of having—make the possession of missile technology an extremely destabilizing factor in political and military equations in the Middle East.

The South Asian region is not far behind. India, which had already test fired short-range missiles, dramatically demonstrated its capacity to develop sophisticated delivery systems in May 1989 by test firing its first domestically produced Intermediate Range Ballistic Missile (IRBM), which could deliver a payload of a thousand pounds up to a distance of fifteen hundred miles.[47] This has been followed by further successful test firings of the Indian IRBM, the *Agni.* Whereas the Indian ballistic missiles program is primarily a delayed response to the development of IRBMs by China, Pakistan has undertaken its own missile development program in response to the buildup of Indian capabilities in this field. It has done so with the help of China, which has emerged as one of the leading missile exporters with its sale of missiles to Iran and Saudi Arabia. More recently, China has been accused by the United States of supplying Pakistan with the technology and components of the M-11 short-range tactical missile.[48]

The attempt to check the transfer of missile technology, undertaken through the Missile Technology Control Regime (MTCR) announced in April 1987 after four years of negotiations and based on a voluntary agreement among the leading Western industrial powers, has thus far been limited in its success because of the nonparticipation, until recently, of the Soviet Union (Russia) and of China and Third World missile producers such as Brazil and Argentina. However, the post–Cold War changes in Russian attitudes toward MTCR, as toward many other issues relating to global and regional conflict management, have paved the way for U.S.-Russian cooperation on this issue. This might still be a case of too little too late, given the spread of missile technology across many parts of the globe and the reluctance of above all China to fully conform to the restrictions imposed by the MTCR.[49]

The proliferation of chemical weapons and the evidence of the political will to use them in defiance of international conventions (for example, by the Iraqis in their war with Iran and against the Kurdish insurgents in Iraq) have provided a terrifying weapons alternative for many Third World countries, which are not in a position, either technologically or financially, to launch a serious nuclear weapons program. Steve Fetter has estimated that fourteen Third World countries already possess chemical weapons, and four may also possess biological weapons.[50] Given the high cost and cumbersome nature of the protective gear that is essential in defending against a chemical weapons attack, a preemptive, first-strike counterforce strategy in conflicts involving two countries known to possess such weapons might appear attractive to policymakers on one or both sides. Combined with short-range and medium-range missile capability, which most countries engaged in producing chemical weapons already possess, these weapons may not only wreak havoc on civilian populations but may also destabilize local balances of power and make Third World crises more difficult to manage. Again, it would be extremely difficult to enforce a ban on such weapons, because the relatively simple technology required to manufacture them is readily available.[51]

Following the Iraqi use of Scud missiles against U.S.-led forces in Saudi Arabia and against Israel during the Gulf War, the United States has become very concerned about the threat to its forces and installations from Third World countries that possess ballistic missiles, some of which are also near-nuclear powers.[52] However, it needs to be reiterated that the major threat from the spread of weapons of mass destruction and of sophisticated delivery systems will not be to the United States or other industrialized powers but to Third World states engaged in bilateral disputes with their neighbors. The threat is especially acute if one or both countries possess nuclear weapons. Even when both parties to a dispute are nuclear capable, this may be insufficient to mutually deter them from using such weapons. The lack of second-strike capability, the absence of well-developed strategic doctrines, the unrepresentative and personalized nature of regimes in likely proliferators, and the visceral and apparently zero-sum nature of several Third World conflicts make the proliferation of weapons of mass destruction in the Third World an extremely dangerous and potentially devastating proposition.

This statement is not an indictment of Third World leaders as irrational or otherwise lacking. It is merely an honest cataloging of factors that are fundamentally the products of the historical juncture at which Third World states and their leaders find themselves. These factors are related, on the one hand, to the early stage of state making and, therefore, to the primitive nature of decisionmaking institutions and procedures in the Third World. On the other hand, they are related to the relative technological backwardness of even the most advanced Third World states, including those that are capable of producing untested nuclear devices.

Weak institutions permit the personal idiosyncrasies of decisionmakers to intrude significantly in the formulation of vital decisions. When these decisions are made in the midst of high-stake territorial conflicts that are direct products of the state-making process and in the context of the possession of nuclear weapons, they can be highly dangerous. Similarly, primitive forms of nuclear weapons technology and the absence of strategic doctrine encourage the first use of nuclear weapons and make nuclear preemption appear attractive to decisionmakers.

In the context mapped out in the previous paragraph, the availability of weapons of mass destruction in highly conflict-prone regional environments can be catastrophic. This assertion also has relevance for post-Soviet Russia. Its relevance is demonstrated by both the increasingly volatile and conflictual nature of Russia's regional environment, particularly the complex relationship between Russia and a still nuclear-armed Ukraine, and the instability of the Russian regime, which was dramatically foreshadowed by the abortive August 1991 coup against Soviet President Mikhail Gorbachev. During that critical episode, the rest of the world was greatly concerned, and rightly so, about who was in control of the Soviet nuclear arsenal. To this day, there has been no clear answer to that crucial question.[53] Therefore, if Soviet and Russian nuclear decisionmaking, after decades of meticulous planning and streamlining, could become an object of serious speculation during a critical period such as this, it is legitimate to worry about the untried structures and the unknown calculus of nuclear decisionmaking in nuclear-capable Third World states.

Managing Interstate Conflict

Most Third World states, even those in the most conflict-prone regions, will not have nuclear weapons capability in the foreseeable future. However, there are enough states with actual or putative nuclear and chemical weapons capability that also possess relatively advanced delivery systems, ranging from aircraft to ballistic missiles, to raise serious apprehensions about the destructive potential of future interstate conflicts in the Third World. Moreover, as the 1980–1988 Iran-Iraq War demonstrated, the destructive capacity of conventional weaponry available to Third World disputants has increased in geometric progressions in the past two decades. Consequently, the growing concern about the destructive capabilities of interstate conflict in the Third World has increased the amount of discussion in recent years regarding the role of regional organizations in the management of such conflicts.

This discussion has gained momentum in the context of both the end of superpower rivalry and the newfound activism of the United Nations in the field of peace and security, which has been made possible by greater agreement among the permanent members of the Security Council. Together, these events have spurred the notion of common security and its presumed increased relevance in the post–Cold War world at the global and regional levels. At the global level, common security is virtually indistinguishable from the concept of collective security. I have analyzed the pros and cons of the collective security idea earlier in this book. At the regional level, the notion of common security in its operational form has evolved to mean the augmentation of regional organizations so they are able to provide institutional and political frameworks within which regional conflicts can be resolved or at least managed.[54]

However, to be effective conflict managers, regional organizations need to fulfill two essential conditions. First, they must coincide with regional security complexes so the parties that are central to regional conflicts are encompassed in their membership. Second, they also need the political, military, and financial capacity to undertake such conflict management, which may entail the deployment of troops for peacekeeping purposes for relatively long periods of time. If a regional organization does not coincide with a regional security complex, as was the case with the GCC in relation to the Iraq-Kuwait crisis, it cannot even begin to cope with the task of conflict management and is likely either to be rendered marginal to the conflict or to become a protagonist in the conflict. The latter outcome was demonstrated clearly by the role played by ASEAN in the Cambodian conflict during the 1980s.

As I pointed out earlier, subregional organizations such as the GCC or ASEAN, since they are unlikely to coincide with regional security complexes, are ineffective instruments to provide common security to conflict-prone regions. At best, they work as alliances that help member states, especially their regimes, to maintain their security in the face of internal and external challenges. At worst, they contribute to regional polarization by institutionalizing and solidifying political and military cleavages within regional security complexes.

On the other hand, if a regional organization such as SAARC coincides with a regional security complex, it is usually rendered impotent because of the unwillingness of the protagonists to use it for conflict resolution or conflict management purposes and because of the apprehension that any attempt to use the organization for such purposes could lead to its disintegration. Continental-size regional organizations have fared no better in conflict management. The OAU is ineffective because of its diverse and unwieldy membership and the conflicting interests of its major members. The OAS seemed to have had a better track record until its expulsion of Cuba following the Castro revolution and its endorsement of U.S. intervention in the Dominican Republic in 1965. The dominating presence of the United States has been the major stumbling block for the OAS in managing regional conflict, especially those conflicts to which the United States has been a direct or an indirect party. The fact that an informal group of Central American presidents was instrumental, despite strong signs of U.S. displeasure, in finding solutions to the conflicts in Nicaragua and El Salvador in the 1980s is an indication of both the efficacy of traditional methods of informal multilateral diplomacy and the ineffectiveness of institutionalized regional arrangements in resolving or managing regional conflicts. The end of the Cold War is unlikely to substantially change this position.

This assertion is corroborated by S. Neil MacFarlane and Thomas

Weiss who, after analyzing several cases of regional organization involvement in Third World conflicts—including ASEAN in Cambodia, the OAU in the Horn of Africa and Southern Africa, ECOWAS in Liberia, the OAS in Central America, and the role of the European Community in the Serb-Croat conflict—concluded that "regionalism is not a promising approach to conflict regulation." They arrived at this pessimistic conclusion based on data that demonstrated that "the so-called comparative superiority of organizations in the actual region in conflict—familiarity with the issues, insulation from outside powers, need to deal with acute crises—[is] more than offset by such practical disadvantages as partisanship, local rivalries, and lack of resources." They stated further that "the end of the Cold War does little to change this conclusion."[55]

MacFarlane and Weiss were accurate in pointing out the two main reasons inclusive regional organizations, whether subcontinental such as SAARC or continental such as the OAU and the OAS, have been generally unsuccessful in conflict regulation. The first reason is the fact that "regional organizations replicate within themselves power imbalances." Second, "In numerous instances the reluctance to become involved in civil conflict [which often lies at the root of interstate conflicts in the Third World] reflects the sensitivity of regional powers to the creation of precedents that might subsequently justify intervention in their own countries."[56]

With regional organizations largely impotent, there has been a tendency in the post–Cold War period to look to the United Nations as the major instrument for the management and resolution of conflicts in the Third World. However, as I argued in Chapter 6, after the first flush of optimism following the end of the Cold War, the United Nations has increasingly found itself unable to manage regional conflicts for a variety of political and financial reasons. When international intervention has been successful militarily, as in the Iraq-Kuwait crisis, the United Nations has played the role of an endorsing agency for actions already decided upon by a great power or a concert of powers rather than the role of an active enforcer of the will of the international community. As such, it has run the grave risk of being seen merely as an instrument for the imposition of a regional order favored by a concert of great powers, with little regard for regional interests and concerns. Any credibility the United Nations might have had in the aftermath of the Gulf crisis has been seriously eroded by its incapacity to act firmly in the Balkans, especially to prevent the forcible disintegration of the Bosnian state. Even when the United Nations has been relatively successful politically, such as in Cambodia, its inability to disarm the Khmer Rouge has left a potentially very dangerous situation that can explode at any time. As a result, the prospects for conflict management (let alone conflict resolution) in the Third World, whether through regional organizations or the United Nations, do not seem to be appreciably greater than they were during the Cold War era.

This is admittedly a pessimistic conclusion. Some of this pessimism stems from the difficulty that is bound to be experienced by any multilateral organization in resolving issues intimately and vitally connected with regional balance-of-power concerns. Much of the pessimism, however, is the result of the fact that, as I have stated repeatedly throughout the book, interstate conflicts in the Third World are often rooted in intrastate conflicts. The latter are mostly a function of the early stage of state making at which many Third World states currently find themselves. To expect these conflicts to be resolved by regional or global external agents, even if they act in the spirit of pure altruism—which they seldom do—flies in the face not only of hard evidence but also of sound political logic.

To make matters worse, some recent changes in the international normative environment that are partially related to the end of the Cold War have increased the possibility that the frequency and intensity of internal conflicts within Third World states may rise dramatically. These changes, and how they affect the Third World's security predicament, form a major theme of the next chapter.

Notes

1. William Maley, "The Future of Islamic Afghanistan," *Security Dialogue* 24, no. 4 (December 1993): 386, 394. For a detailed discussion of the rivalries among the various Afghan factions opposed to the pro-Soviet regime in Kabul, see Olivier Roy, *Islam and Resistance in Afghanistan* (Cambridge: Cambridge University Press, 1990). For an analysis of regional powers' involvement in Afghanistan after the Soviet withdrawal, see Rasul Bakhsh Rais, "Afghanistan and the Regional Powers," *Asian Survey* 33, no. 9 (September 1993): 905–922.

2. For details, see Philip Shenon, "In Big Threat to Cambodia, Thais Still Aid Khmer Rouge," *New York Times* (December 19, 1993): 1, 16.

3. For the effects of the end of the Cold War on the conflicts in Angola, Mozambique, and Namibia, see the relevant chapters in Thomas G. Weiss and James G. Blight (eds.), *The Suffering Grass: Superpowers and Regional Conflict in Southern Africa and the Caribbean* (Boulder: Lynne Rienner Publishers, 1992). For the Cambodian case, see Steven R. Ratner, "The United Nations in Cambodia: A Model for Resolution of International Conflicts?" in Lori Fisler Damrosch (ed.), *Enforcing Restraint: Collective Intervention in International Conflicts* (New York: Council on Foreign Relations Press, 1993): 241–273.

4. For details of U.S.-Soviet cooperation in the management of the Arab-Israeli conflict, see Harold H. Saunders, "Regulating Soviet-US Competition and Cooperation in the Arab-Israel Arena, 1967–86," in Alexander L. George, Philip J. Farley, and Alexander Dallin (eds.), *US-Soviet Security Cooperation: Achievements, Failures, Lessons* (New York: Oxford University Press, 1988): 540–580.

5. Henry Kissinger, then national security adviser to President Nixon, has argued that India's war aims included West Pakistan's disintegration. Henry Kissinger, *White House Years* (Boston: Little, Brown, 1979): 842–918, deals with the Bangladesh crisis. This assertion has been denied by Indian decisionmakers and

has been disputed by both U.S. and other analysts. It is plausible, however, that Indian policymakers were interested in decimating the war-making capacity of the Pakistan Army in the western wing but were deterred from doing so by their perception that such an action would be unacceptable to both the United States and the Soviet Union. Such a conclusion can be derived from the argument put forward by Richard Sisson and Leo Rose that "the most important issue for both Washington and Moscow in the 1971 conflict was not East Pakistan, but rather the fate of West Pakistan. On this subject there was a broad congruence of Soviet and American perceptions and interests. These interests were seen, for different reasons, as being best served by maintaining the integrity of West Pakistan, including the Pakistani-held areas of Kashmir, and by encouraging New Delhi to limit its military actions on the western front." Richard Sisson and Leo E. Rose, *War and Secession: Pakistan, India, and the Creation of Bangladesh* (Berkeley: University of California Press, 1990): 246.

6. According to Amitav Acharya, a regional power can be defined with reference to the following attributes: "(1) a relative lead in most indicators of political, military and economic power among all actors within the region; (2) a supportive as well as coercive power projection capability within the region; (3) a capacity, whether exercised or not, to deny outside powers direct or indirect control over regional security arrangements." Amitav Acharya, "Third World Conflicts and International Order After the Cold War," Working Paper no. 134 (Canberra: Peace Research Centre, Australian National University, August 1993): footnote 69, 21.

7. As Lawrence Freedman and Ephraim Karsh have stated, "The West may not find many conflicts with principles so clear-cut, enemies so ready to take on Western military power on its own terms and circumstances so favourable to its application." Lawrence Freedman and Ephraim Karsh, *The Gulf Conflict: Diplomacy and War in the New World Order* (Princeton: Princeton University Press, 1993): 442.

8. For details, see Julius O. Ihonvbere, "Nigeria as Africa's Great Power: Constraints and Prospects for the 1990s," *International Journal* 46, no. 3 (Summer 1991): 510–535.

9. For details, see Mohammed Ayoob, "India as Regional Hegemon: External Opportunities and Internal Constraints," *International Journal* 46, no. 3 (Summer 1991): 420–448.

10. Bruce D. Porter, "A Country Instead of a Cause: Russian Foreign Policy in the Post-Soviet Era," *Washington Quarterly* 15, no. 3 (Summer 1992): 45.

11. Ronald Dannreuther, "Russia, Central Asia and the Persian Gulf," *Survival* 35, no. 4 (Winter 1993–1994): 92.

12. Charles William Maynes, "A Workable Clinton Doctrine," *Foreign Policy,* no. 93 (Winter 1993–1994): 15.

13. The fallacious nature of the premise on which such perceptions are based—that "Islamic fundamentalism" is a monolithic phenomenon and that all Islamic political movements are viscerally anti-Western—has now been accepted even by Bernard Lewis, a leading historian of the Middle East, who has not been averse on occasion to demonizing political Islam as a monolithic force threatening Judaeo-Christian values. According to Lewis, "Islamic fundamentalism is a loose and inaccurate term that designates a number of different, and sometimes contrasting, forms of Islamic religious militancy. . . . The more oppressive the regime, the greater help it gives to the fundamentalists by eliminating competing oppositions." Bernard Lewis, "Rethinking the Middle East," *Foreign Affairs* 71, no. 4 (Fall 1992): 115–116. For Lewis's earlier views, which tended to convey the impression that Islamic political activism was monolithic and, by definition, anti-Western, see

Bernard Lewis, "The Return of Islam," *Commentary* 61, no. 1 (January 1976): 39–49; and Bernard Lewis, "The Roots of Muslim Rage," *Atlantic Monthly* (September 1990): 47–60.

14. For an incisive analysis of political conditions in the Muslim republics of the former Soviet Union, see Shireen T. Hunter, "The Muslim Republics of the Former Soviet Union: Policy Challenges for the United States," *Washington Quarterly* 15, no. 3 (Summer 1992): 57–71.

15. It is instructive to note in this context that at a summit meeting of the Commonwealth of Independent States (CIS) in December 1993, held in Turkmenistan, the former Soviet republics rebuffed a Russian attempt to persuade them to grant special status to Russians living within their borders, including the right to hold dual citizenship. See Steven Erlanger, "Ex-Soviet Lands Rebuff Yeltsin on Protecting Russians Abroad: Tension on Nationalism at Commonwealth Talks," *New York Times* (December 25, 1993): 1, 4.

16. The contradiction inherent in Western policy toward Russia's Muslim periphery is well brought out by Ronald Dannreuther: "It is right for the West to continue to see Central Asia as a region where Russian interests are engaged and where Russia has a right to be the dominant external power. However, such assertions must be counterbalanced by a commitment to the independence of the Central Asian states. These states must be treated as fully independent entities and not as some imperial appendages. A corollary of this is that the West should make clear that it expects Russia to act in accordance with the norms and principles of international law, both in its development of bilateral relations and in specific operations such as CIS peacekeeping." Dannreuther, "Russia, Central Asia and the Persian Gulf," 110–111.

17. Keith Krause, "Constructing Regional Security Regimes and the Control of Arms Transfers," *International Journal* 45, no. 2 (Spring 1990): 388.

18. Richard F. Grimmett, *Conventional Arms Transfers to the Third World, 1985–1992* (Washington, D.C.: Congressional Research Service, Library of Congress, July 19, 1993): Tables 1J and 2J, 59, 70.

19. Nicholas D. Kristof, "The Rise of China," *Foreign Affairs* 72, no. 5 (November–December 1993): 67.

20. Michael T. Klare, "The Next Great Arms Race," *Foreign Affairs* 72, no. 3 (Summer 1993): 141.

21. Grimmett, *Conventional Arms Transfers,* 5, 7.

22. Ibid., 5.

23. Klare, "The Next Great Arms Race," 141. For further details of Sino-Russian arms deals, see Tai Ming Cheung, "China's Buying Spree," *Far Eastern Economic Review* (July 8, 1993): 24–25.

24. Grimmett, *Conventional Arms Transfers,* Table 1J, 59.

25. For a detailed discussion of this issue, see Michael T. Klare, "The Unnoticed Arms Trade: Exports of Conventional Arms-Making Technology," *International Security* 8, no. 2 (Fall 1983): 68–90.

26. For conceptual analyses and case studies that address the issues of weapons technology transfer, absorption capability, and the interplay between supplier and recipient interests, see Kwang-Il Baeck, Ronald D. McLaurin, and Chung-in Moon (eds.), *The Dilemma of Third World Defense Industries* (Boulder: Westview Press, 1989).

27. For a discussion of recent trends in arms supplies to, and weapons production in, the Third World, see Amit Gupta, "Third World Militaries: New Suppliers, Deadlier Weapons," *Orbis* 37, no. 1 (Winter 1993): 57–68.

28. "A security complex is defined as a group of states whose primary security

concerns link together sufficiently closely that their national securities cannot realistically be considered apart from one another." Barry Buzan, *People, States and Fear: An Agenda for International Security Studies in the Post–Cold War Era,* 2d ed. (Boulder: Lynne Rienner Publishers, 1991): 190.

29. For details of the problems and prospects of regional arms control regimes in the Third World, see Krause, "Constructing Regional Security Regimes," 386–423.

30. For a comprehensive overview and assessment of the leading threshold powers' nuclear capabilities, see Leonard S. Spector and Jacqueline R. Smith, *Nuclear Ambitions: The Spread of Nuclear Weapons, 1989–1990* (Boulder: Westview Press, 1990). For an update on nuclear proliferation trends, see Leonard S. Spector, *A Historical and Technical Introduction to the Proliferation of Nuclear Weapons* (Washington, D.C.: Carnegie Endowment for International Peace, June 1992). Also see Robert D. Blackwill and Albert Carnesale (eds.), *New Nuclear Nations: Consequences for U.S. Policy* (New York: Council on Foreign Relations Press, 1993).

31. John J. Mearsheimer, "The Case for a Ukrainian Nuclear Deterrent," *Foreign Affairs* 72, no. 3 (Summer 1993): 58.

32. For a discussion of post-Soviet nuclear dilemmas, see Steven E. Miller, "Western Diplomacy and the Soviet Nuclear Legacy," *Survival* 34, no. 3 (Autumn 1992): 3–27.

33. For a balanced analysis of the pattern of nuclear proliferation in South Asia, see Brahma Chellaney, "South Asia's Passage to Nuclear Power," *International Security* 16, no. 1 (Summer 1991): 43–72; for a rather alarmist analysis, see Seymour Hersh, "On the Nuclear Edge," *New Yorker* (March 29, 1993): 56–73. For the Middle East, where a situation of de facto nuclear monopoly prevails, see Helena Cobban, "Israel's Nuclear Game: The U.S. Stake," *World Policy Journal* 5 (1988): 415–433; and Avner Cohen and Marvin Miller, "How to Think About—and Implement—Nuclear Arms Control in the Middle East," *Washington Quarterly* 16, no. 2 (Spring 1993): 101–113. For a discussion of North Korea's nuclear status and its impact on regional and global politics, see Ronald F. Lehman, "A North Korean Nuclear-Weapons Program: International Implications," *Security Dialogue* 24, no. 3 (September 1993): 257–272.

34. For an analysis of different factors affecting various nuclear equations in the post–Cold War world, see Lewis A. Dunn, "Rethinking the Nuclear Equation: The United States and the New Nuclear Powers," *Washington Quarterly* 17, no. 1 (Winter 1994): 5–25.

35. *The Military Balance 1993–94* (London: International Institute for Strategic Studies, 1993): 118.

36. There has been considerable speculation, some of it well-informed, that Israel was contemplating the use of nuclear weapons during the initial stages of the 1973 October War. This is argued by, among others, Seymour M. Hersh in *The Samson Option* (New York: Random House, 1991): 225–240.

37. For three different likely scenarios in a nuclear exchange between India and Pakistan, see S. Rashid Naim, "Aadhi Raat Ke Baad (After Midnight)," in Stephen Philip Cohen (ed.), *Nuclear Proliferation in South Asia: The Prospects for Arms Control* (Boulder: Westview Press, 1991): 23–61.

38. The case for continuing asymmetry and instability in the India-Pakistan nuclear relationship, even after both have demonstrated nuclear weapons capability, has been put forth best by a perceptive Pakistani scholar who has argued that "the development of operational nuclear weapon systems in South Asia might not produce a stable strategic environment as advocated by the proponents of the bomb

option in both India and Pakistan. The outdated NATO doctrine of massive retaliation and nuclear option to augment meager conventional defense sources is hardly relevant in Pakistan's case because of the vast and unbridgeable disparities in the conventional and assumed nuclear capabilities of the adversaries." Rasul B. Rais, "Pakistan's Nuclear Program: Prospects for Proliferation," *Asian Survey* 25, no. 4 (April 1985): 472.

39. Susumu Awanohara, "Clinton's New Line: US Changes Terms of Indo-Pakistan Debate," *Far Eastern Economic Review* (December 23, 1993): 22.

40. David E. Sanger, "North Korea's Game Looks a Lot Like Nuclear Blackmail," *New York Times* (December 12, 1993): sec. 4, 6.

41. *The Military Balance 1993–94,* 233.

42. Stephen Engelberg with Michael R. Gordon, "Intelligence Study Says North Korea Has Nuclear Bomb," *New York Times* (December 26, 1993): 1, 8.

43. Leonard S. Spector, "Repentant Nuclear Proliferants," *Foreign Policy,* no. 88 (Fall 1992): 29.

44. For details, see Janne E. Nolan, *Trappings of Power: Ballistic Missiles in the Third World* (Washington, D.C.: Brookings Institution, 1991). Also see Martin Navias, *Ballistic Missile Proliferation in the Third World,* Adelphi Paper no. 252 (London: International Institute for Strategic Studies, Summer 1990).

45. Martin S. Navias, "Ballistic Missile Proliferation in the Middle East," *Survival* 31, no. 3 (1989): 225.

46. *Missile Proliferation: Survey of Emerging Missile Forces,* Congressional Research Service Report 88-642-F, October 3, 1988; quoted in ibid., 226.

47. For details of India's missile development program, see Nolan, *Trappings of Power,* 38–48.

48. Nayan Chanda, "Red Rockets' Glare," *Far Eastern Economic Review* (September 9, 1993): 10–11.

49. For a somewhat more optimistic assessment of the MTCR, see Albert Legault, "The Missile Technology Control Regime," in David Dewitt, David Haglund, and John Kirton (eds.), *Building a New Global Order: Emerging Trends in International Security* (Toronto: Oxford University Press, 1993): 358–377.

50. Steve Fetter, "Ballistic Missiles and Weapons of Mass Destruction: What Is the Threat? What Should Be Done?" *International Security* 16, no. 1 (Summer 1991): Table 2, 14.

51. For details, see Kathleen C. Bailey, *Doomsday Weapons in the Hands of the Many: The Arms Control Challenge of the '90s* (Urbana: University of Illinois Press, 1991): Chapters 4–6. Also see Brad Roberts, *Chemical Disarmament and International Security,* Adelphi Paper no. 267 (London: International Institute for Strategic Studies, Spring 1992).

52. According to Lewis Dunn, a "possibility, of particular concern to the United States and its friends abroad, is that some new nuclear powers will seek to use the implicit or explicit threat to use nuclear weapons to undermine U.S. readiness to deploy forces to protect critical interests or allies. . . . At the least, U.S. freedom of action could be severely constrained, for example, in a future confrontation with a nuclear-armed Iran or Iraq. At worst, a country might successfully use nuclear threats to hold the ring against U.S. involvement. Other countries might also be the target of nuclear blackmail, including U.S. allies in Europe and Japan, whose support would be critical for intervention in the Middle East, the Gulf, and Asia." Dunn, "Rethinking the Nuclear Equation," 9–10.

53. Steven Miller has conveyed the confusion surrounding the issue of the control of Soviet nuclear weapons during the abortive coup of August 1991: "Various published reports suggested that the leaders of the coup held control of the

arsenal for several days, that Gorbachev had possessed critical launch codes even during his brief exile, that senior military leaders loyal to Gorbachev were in a position to prevent the leaders of the coup from using nuclear weapons, and that top military commanders had full control of the arsenal during certain periods of the coup." Miller, "Western Diplomacy and the Soviet Nuclear Legacy," 3–4.

54. For a discussion of regional organizations as instruments of conflict management, see Thomas Perry Thornton, "Regional Organizations in Conflict Management," *Annals of the American Academy of Political and Social Science* 518 (November 1991): 132–142.

55. S. Neil MacFarlane and Thomas G. Weiss, "Regional Organizations and Regional Security," *Security Studies* 2, no. 1 (Autumn 1992): 7, 11.

56. Ibid., 31.

■ 8 ■

The Third World's Post–Cold War Security Predicament: The Internal Dimension

Even more important to the crucial internal dimension and, therefore, to the future of Third World security than issues of regional hegemony, arms transfers, nuclear weapons, and ballistic missiles are two other factors that have achieved great prominence since the end of the Cold War: the increasing legitimacy accorded to ethnonationalism by the international community, and the increasing incidence of failed states. These two phenomena, which are frequently interrelated, have emerged as the major post–Cold War challenges to the security and integrity of Third World states.

The renewed acceptance in Europe of ethnonational self-determination, symbolized by the prompt recognition of Slovenia and Croatia by the European Community and the separation of Slovakia from the Czech Republic, is likely to give a fillip to demands for ethnic separatism in the Third World. The acceptance in principle by the major European powers and UN representatives of the division of Bosnia into three ethnonational states is bound to strengthen the legitimacy accorded to the right of ethnic groups to self-determination. The breakup of the Soviet Union and the ethnic strife that has accompanied its demise have provided greater evidence of the increasing popularity and destructiveness of the ethnonationalist ideal.

The excesses of ethnonationalism in the Balkans, especially the atrocities perpetrated by the Serbs against the Bosnian Muslims, are also likely to affect parties engaged in ethnic conflict in the Third World.[1] This situation could be aggravated by the failure of the great powers to stop the carnage in Bosnia. Such a failure is likely to leave a strong impression in parts of the Third World where ethnic conflict is acute that if ethnonationalists can get away with such excesses in Europe, then similar behavior on other continents will bring even less opposition from the major powers.

As I pointed out in Chapter 2, tensions among ethnicity, ethnonationalism, and state-defined nationalism have plagued most postcolonial states, nearly all of which encompass several ethnic groups, from their inception.

However, the difference between ethnicity and ethnonationalism needs to be emphasized at this point. Ashutosh Varshney has explained this difference with great clarity in the context of India.

> An ethnic group may function without a state of its own; a nation [ethnonation in my terms] implies bringing ethnicity and statehood together. In principle, this congruence may be satisfied in a federal arrangement, in which case the concerned nationalism becomes a subnationalism or an ethnicity. The larger federal entity, then, has the highest claims on that group's loyalty. Alternatively, one may opt for nothing short of sovereignty. That is what Sikh nationalists aimed at and Kashmiri nationalists are still fighting for. A Bengali can be both a Bengali and an Indian, so can a Gujarati. Bengalis and Gujaratis are ethnic groups: for separatists, Sikhs and Kashmiris are nations. However, for Indian nationalists . . . the Sikhs and the Kashmiris are ethnic groups, not nations.[2]

Given the latent tensions between ethnicity and state-defined nationalism, even in functioning federal polities such as India, and the clear contradiction between ethnonationalism and state-defined nationalism in much of the Third World, any development anywhere in the world that encourages ethnic separatist demands in the context of fragilities prevalent in the Third World is bound to add to the strains that already exist there. This is the reason the revival and renewed legitimation of ethnonationalism in the Balkans and in the former Soviet republics could damage the fragile ethnic balances in many Third World states.

Amitai Etzioni has pointed out correctly that even though "historians tend to treat as distinct the emergence of nation-states from the Ottoman and Hapsburg empires and the liberation of former colonies in Asia and Africa following World War II, there are actually great sociological similarities between the two movements."[3] Above all, these similarities are symbolized by the multiethnic nature of both sets of states and the inadequate integration of the different ethnic groups with each other. Even though the successor states to the Ottoman and Hapsburg Empires were ostensibly created on the basis of national self-determination, almost all of those states were multiethnic in character with low levels of interethnic integration, much like the empires from which they emerged.

The one major factor that distinguished the new "nation-states" from the old empires was that each of the new states had a dominant ethnonational group that arrogated to itself the right to define the national identity of the new state and to impose that identity over the ethnic minorities. As one observer of the Balkans has pointed out, "The old empires were by no means perfect, but the national states that followed them were almost invariably worse. . . . In the more confined space of some of the new nation-states established after both empires [Ottoman and Hapsburg] broke up, minorities became exposed to a variety of dangers—from discrimination and assimilation to expulsion or even physical annihilation."[4]

The current Serb attempt to dominate with brute force the large Albanian majority in the province of Kosovo and the Bulgarian attempt in the late 1980s to "nationalize" its sizable Turkish minority demonstrate the continuity of a policy followed by Balkan state elites since the inception of their states. This is little different from what has been happening, for example, in Sudan or Myanmar.

The sociological similarity mentioned by Etzioni also extends to the ideology used to legitimate the dominant nationalisms of the post–World War I Balkan states and the postcolonial states of the Third World. The idea of national self-determination was accepted at the peace settlement following World War I and was applied, with certain qualifications, to the subject European peoples of the defeated Hapsburg and Ottoman Empires. In the interwar period and during the first quarter century following World War II, the doctrine of national self-determination also played an important role in legitimizing the anticolonial struggles of peoples in Asia and Africa who were subjected to European colonial rule.

In an interesting twist, the colonial territories' self-determination following World War II became linked to the territorial rather than the ethnic imperative, since by common consent it had to be exercised so that the colonially demarcated boundaries of postcolonial states were not disturbed. As one scholar has pointed out, "UN and state practice . . . provides evidence that the international community recognizes only a very limited right to 1) external self-determination, defined as the right to freedom from a former colonial power, and 2) internal self-determination, defined as independence of the whole state's population from foreign intervention or influence."[5]

As I pointed out in Chapter 4, in addition to helping to justify the end of European colonialism, the doctrine of national self-determination provided much of the ideological underpinning for state making and nation building in the Third World. For the past four decades, when leaders of Third World states talked about nation building, they usually did not mean the augmentation of ethnonational identities; they meant the consolidation of the loyalties of Third World populations to the postcolonial states within their colonially crafted boundaries. In the Third World, as in the earliest national states in Western Europe during the seventeenth and eighteenth centuries, the state was the given; the future nation was expected to fit the geopolitical realities of the existing state.

However, since 1990 there has been a renewed attempt to interpret the notion of national self-determination in order to legitimize ethnonational self-determination, much as Woodrow Wilson had originally envisaged for the Balkans and Eastern Europe.[6] This attempt, however, runs directly counter to the imperatives of state making in multiethnic polities. Since the boundaries of almost all Third World states encompass more than one ethnic group (some contain dozens of such groups), the legitimation of ethnonational self-determination in any part of the globe could be catastrophic for several Third World states, because "under the banner of self-determination, there are active movements in more than sixty countries—one third of the total roster of nations—to achieve full sovereignty or some lesser degree of 'minority' rights. A number of these movements have developed into ongoing civil wars."[7]

Ethnicity, Ethnic Self-Determination, and the Third World State

In this context, the international community's endorsement of the doctrine of ethnonational self-determination, even if limited to exceptional cases, is bound to challenge the principle that postcolonial states in their present form are territorially inviolable. This would be the case especially if ethnonational self-determination were able to successfully assert itself in even a few significant cases in the Third World. The Eritrean case is unique in the sense that Eritrea's independence in 1993 has really meant a reversion to its original postcolonial boundaries. However, this fine point is likely to be missed or deliberately ignored by ethnonational separatists looking for precedents to justify their struggle for secession from postcolonial states. The effects of the spread of such contagion were summed up in a Council on Foreign Relations study, which concluded that "while the creation of some new states may be necessary or inevitable, the fragmentation of international society into hundreds of independent territorial entities is a recipe for an even more dangerous and anarchic world."[8]

Recent events, especially in the Balkans and the Caucasus, have also demonstrated two major problems that stand out when we attempt to put into practice the concept of ethnonational self-determination. These problems apply with equal or greater force to much of the traditional Third World and make this ideology extremely dangerous for the stability of Third World states.

First, given the ethnic mixtures of populations in most Third World countries, few pure ethnic homelands still exist. This fact contradicts the ethnonationalists' assumption that "the earth's entire population, or most of it, divides into a finite number of distinct, homogeneous peoples. It follows that the world's ideal condition consists of that finite number of nation-states."[9] Attempts at ethnonational self-determination are, therefore, bound to run into resistance from ethnic minorities in presumed ethnic homelands. As William Pfaff has succinctly put it, "The ethnic state is a product of the political imagination; it does not exist in reality. . . . The idea of the ethnic nation thus is a permanent provocation to war."[10] This is the reason, as Rupert Emerson pointed out more than three decades ago, "it is no accident that self-determination . . . should be associated in its practical manifestations with wars and the aftermath of wars. . . . The great run of cases are linked to violence or to such fundamental changes in power relationships as occur most notably as a result of wars."[11]

New states carved out in the name of ethnic nations that in reality encompass sizable ethnic minorities can address the contradiction between their claims to ethnonationalism and the existence of ethnic minorities in one of three ways: They can continue balancing ethnic demands and interests, they can assimilate ethnic minorities into the dominant ethnonation, or they can try to wipe out the ethnic minorities. The first method has been attempted by several Third World states, most successfully by those such as India and Malaysia that have maintained functioning, if imperfect, federal and democratic polities. The second strategy has been practiced by states with dominant ethnic groups such as Turkey and Thailand, which refuse to accept the multiethnic nature of their societies and relegate ethnic minorities to secondary status or define them as inferior variants of the dominant ethnonational group. The third option has been most efficiently implemented by the Serbs in Bosnia.

If the first route—balancing ethnic groups' demands—has to be taken, it does not make sense to divide established states into ministates or microstates, to escalate ethnic tensions, and then to go back to the same old strategy with even less chance of success than exists in Third World states that openly call themselves multiethnic. Additionally, the creation of many new ministates and microstates can add to the vulnerability of Third World states, increase conflict among them, and contribute to greater anarchy in the world as a whole. The conclusion one observer of the mess in Yugoslavia reached in connection with that ill-fated federation is then likely to apply with equal force to the Third World: "Since everybody wishes to exercise sovereignty, and since virtually every claim to sovereignty is disputed, no overall solution can contain the magic formula of fulfilling national aspirations within the territories claimed. This alone, if nothing else, was the reason why the breakup of Yugoslavia was always a monstrous idea."[12] If the Yugoslav experience is repeated elsewhere, it would create pure mayhem, and the already weak distinction between intrastate and interstate conflict in the Third World would disappear in a flood of virtually uncontrollable violence.

The second strategy of ethnic assimilation and its corollary, the deliberate ignoring of minority cultural and political rights, has not solved the ethnic problem even in societies that have one clearly dominant ethnic group. Such forced assimilation has usually fueled minority resentment and ethnic strife. The Kurdish insurgency in southeastern and eastern Turkey and the Malay Muslim insurgency in southern Thailand show the remarkable resilience of ethnic defiance when minorities are faced with forcible assimilation on terms they consider to be culturally and politically unacceptable.[13]

The third option, that of killing off or expelling by force members of minority ethnic groups, prescribes a remedy that is far worse than the disease. It would surely lead to bloodshed on a scale before which current violence in the Third World, by both ethnonational insurgents and states, will pale into insignificance. The Bosnian tragedy is sufficient to demonstrate not only the morally reprehensible nature of this strategy but its political futility as well. Massacres of genocidal proportions in the name of "ethnic cleansing" leave behind such deep hatred between ethnic communities doomed to live next to each other that the stability of regions they inhabit is bound to be imperiled for decades, if not generations. It takes a brave analyst to argue that "once the fighting stops, all former Yugoslav republics will quickly discover that economic considerations dictate the restoration of severed links. Those small states must become building blocks for a new regional order."[14]

The second problem with ethnonational self-determination relates to the definition of the ethnic group that is trying to determine its future. The self-definition of ethnicity is usually subject to change depending upon the context in which it operates at any point in time. As a leading scholar of South Asian ethnicities pointed out, ethnicity is a fluid and flexible concept: "Its boundaries expand or contract. Its multiple attributes assume a different order of pre-eminence in diverse situations."[15] This flexibility is what Crawford Young has referred to as "the dynamic and changing character of contemporary ethnicity: far from representing a fixed and immutable set of static social facts, cultural pluralism is itself evolving in crucial ways, and is in major respects contextual, situational, and circumstantial."[16] Moreover, "The intensity of ethnic conflict [also] varies greatly with changing social and political conditions."[17]

To give one past example of the fluid nature of ethnicity, in 1946 and 1947, during the last days of the British Raj in India, the Bengali Muslims defined their ethnic identity in ethnoreligious terms as Muslims rather than in ethnolinguistic terms as Bengalis, even though Muslim Bengalis formed a clear majority in the British Indian province of Bengal. East Bengal, the predominantly Muslim part of Bengal, therefore, opted to become a part of the geographically divided state of Pakistan. Soon thereafter, the Muslim Bengalis became disenchanted with the predominantly Muslim state of Pakistan and began to stress their Bengali identity compared to the identity of the numerically inferior but politically predominant West Pakistanis, especially the Punjabis. This process culminated in 1971 with the separation of East Pakistan from West Pakistan and the transformation of the former into the sovereign state of Bangladesh (literally, the land of the Bengalis). In short, most East Bengalis defined their ethnic identity in 1971 in terms radically different from those they had used twenty-five years earlier because the political context had changed dramatically during the intervening period.[18]

The current example of this phenomenon is the transformation of Somalia—once considered the only nation-state in Africa because it is inhabited almost exclusively by a single ethnolinguistic and ethnoreligious group—into a virtual anarchy, pitting clans and subclans against each other. Northern Somalia, the former British Somaliland, announced its secession from Somalia in May 1991, although this has not been recognized by any other state. The rest of the country has slid into such an acute state of ungovernability that it has become the prime contemporary example of the failed state. Somali identity, which in the late 1970s had even led to an irredentist war against neighboring Ethiopia over Ethiopia's possession of the Somali-inhabited Ogaden, now lies in shambles, which demonstrates how superficially constructed it was in the first place.[19]

Somalia is not the only example that demonstrates the transitory nature of many ethnic self-definitions in the Third World. Once again, Pakistan comes to mind. Self-consciously created on the basis of an ethnonational identity ascribed to the Muslims of the Indian subcontinent through dubious logic, Pakistan is riven with ethnic fissures, even in the rump form in which it exists today. This situation has led one observer to remark, "Once Pakistan was created the tables were turned. Religion was no longer paraded as ethnicity but was charged with the task of containing it. . . . Built on the basis of a confluence of Islam and ethnicity, the state is besieged by a stand-off between the two."[20]

Therefore, to link such a potent ideology as self-determination to a malleable idea such as ethnicity and then to legitimize this combination by referring to the principle of human rights of groups is bound to introduce even greater disorder in the Third World by endowing every disgruntled ethnic group with the legitimacy of the ideal of national self-determination. The danger is that this is exactly what the renewed popularity of the idea of ethnonational self-determination may end up doing, to the great detriment of order and justice in the Third World.

Quasi-States to Failed States

The issue of ethnonational self-determination is connected to the failed states phenomenon.[21] Jack Snyder succinctly linked the two by describing ethnic nationalism as "the default option." According to Snyder, ethnic nationalism "predominates when institutions collapse, when existing institutions are not fulfilling people's basic needs and when satisfactory alternative structures are not readily available."[22] This may not provide the total explanation for the revival of ethnonationalism, but it does capture a major ingredient—the lack of effective statehood—that has contributed to the recent popularity of ethnonationalist ideology. This is true not only in the components of the former Soviet Union and of the former Yugoslavia but in many parts of the Third World as well. It was the lack of effective statehood, or "empirical statehood," in Robert Jackson's words, that was responsible for the emergence of "quasi-states" in the Third World, a phenomenon I discussed in Chapter 2.[23] These quasi-states are clearly the precursors of failed states.

The end of the Cold War has helped transform some of these quasi-states into failed states. This is especially true in the case of states that had witnessed high levels of superpower military involvement, including arms transfers, during the Cold War. At the height of the Cold War, the superpowers often attempted to shore up client governments in internally fragmented states in order to maintain a semblance of stability in countries that were their allies. One major instrument of this support was the transfer of large quantities of relatively sophisticated arms to friendly regimes. Such arms transfers frequently led to countervailing transfers of weaponry by the rival superpower to forces opposed to the central authorities. During the 1980s Afghanistan epitomized this action-reaction phenomenon.[24]

Superpower policies of pouring arms into fragmented polities became a major source of instability in the post–Cold War period. As one observer has pointed out in relation to Somalia, "Today the prevalence of modern weapons, Somalia's most significant legacy of superpower involvement during the Cold War, has undermined the very foundation for order in Somalia's society—the authority of clan elders."[25] The presence of large quantities of sophisticated weaponry, ranging from AK-47s to Stinger missiles, combined with the withdrawal of superpower support to weak regimes—support that prevented the central authorities from being overwhelmed by domestic rivals who, in turn, were divided among themselves—has created near-total anarchy in countries such as Afghanistan and Somalia. In these places, central authority has completely collapsed, turning these quasi-states into failed states.

Whereas the human toll in Afghanistan has continued to mount even six years after the Soviet withdrawal,[26] the starvation in Somalia during 1991 and 1992 was "by some measures worse than the 1984–1985 Ethiopian famine—the universal benchmark for incomprehensible human suffering. The Ethiopian famine was somewhat limited to specific geographic pockets; in contrast, in July 1992 the International Committee of the Red Cross (ICRC) was estimating that 95 percent of the people in Somalia suffered from malnutrition, with 70 percent enduring severe malnutrition."[27]

Zaire—a major U.S. client in Africa during the Cold War, which was used to supply arms to Angolan factions fighting the Soviet-supported MPLA regime in Luanda—is on the verge of becoming a massive case of state failure as well. Since the United States lost interest in propping up the corrupt Mobutu regime after the end of the Cold War, the situation in Zaire over the past several years has become increasingly anarchic. The U.S.

State Department has even warned in a confidential memorandum that Zaire could develop into "Somalia and Liberia rolled into one."[28]

The recent Lebanese[29] and the current Somali, Afghan, Liberian,[30] and Zairean experiences demonstrate clearly that the failure of the state in the Third World is a much greater source of human tragedy than the repression of their own people by even the most autocratic but functioning states such as Iraq and Syria. The combination of juridically sovereign but empirically nonfunctioning central authority, for which the term *failed state* is used as shorthand, could well be the major source of suffering and disorder in the Third World, and possibly in the entire international system, well into the twenty-first century.

The Transformation of International Norms

The withdrawal of superpower support from vulnerable regimes and the availability of large quantities of arms in fragile and divided polities account, however, for only part of the reason for the failure of states in the Third World. Another cause involves the transformation of an important international norm in the past few years. Since the end of World War II, a major norm of the international system has been that once a postcolonial state acquired juridical sovereignty and received international recognition, it could not alienate its sovereignty over even a part of its territory, even if in practice the state was not fully viable. This norm assured the territorial integrity of fragile Third World states, thereby helping many of them through the crucial initial stages of state survival. Without the protection of this international norm, several of these states, especially in Africa but also in the Middle East and Asia, would have come apart very early in their postcolonial existence.

The stability of the Cold War period helped augment this norm because both superpowers were wary of states breaking apart in unpredictable ways that might work against them or involve them in messy traps in the Third World. However, the events of the past few years have undermined the norm.

The disintegration of the Soviet Union demonstrated that even a superpower could not remain immune to centrifugal pressures and fragmentation. Also, the relaxation in international tensions and the end of bipolarity have meant that the remaining superpower and the other great powers have less stake in maintaining the territorial status quo in the Third World or even in the peripheral areas of Europe such as the Balkans. The major capitals of the world now take a more relaxed view of transformations in boundaries and even of the failure of states in the Third World and in the Balkans than they did when they still had to worry about the impact of such shifts on the global balance of power.

The breakup of the Soviet Union, Yugoslavia, and Czechoslovakia; the secession of Eritrea from Ethiopia; and the prompt admission of the breakaway states to the United Nations have sent the message to prospective Third World separatists that the international community is no longer committed to the maintenance of existing state boundaries. We can argue that the current international toleration of state breaking is limited and is a product of the circumstances that accompanied the end of the Cold War, especially the demise of the Soviet Union, rather than being a long-term trend. However, the visible examples of established states disintegrating already may have damaged the more fragile Third World states, especially by making a strong impression on groups agitating for their fragmentation. At a minimum, as a Carnegie Endowment study has stated, "The old assumption that the boundaries set after World War II were permanent has been shaken by events in the Soviet Union and Yugoslavia."[31] Even the temporary diversion from the principle that the political boundaries of established states are guaranteed by the international community is likely to exacerbate the security problems of insecure Third World states faced with secessionist challenges.

The combination of the end of the Cold War and the erosion of the international norm that guarantees the integrity of states could invite a spurt of secessionist challenges to established states and a proliferation of failed states, especially in Africa and Central Asia. This situation, in turn, could require a major international effort to help impose order on increasingly anarchic situations. In the absence of interest or resources brought to this task by the international community, a lesson driven home by the Somalian episode, several inviable states in the Third World may be left in nearly perpetual anarchy. However, since no state lives or dies in complete isolation, what happens within the borders of a failed or failing state can have major implications for nearby states. As Liberia, Afghanistan, and Somalia demonstrate, anarchy within individual Third World states is bound to spill over state boundaries in the form of refugees, sanctuaries for warring groups, gun running, drug trafficking, and other fallouts that are likely to heighten tensions between neighbors.

To cite the figures, according to the UN High Commissioner for Refugees, the combination of ethnic strife and failed statehood pushed the number of refugees to 44 million worldwide in 1993. Of these, close to 20 million were driven across international boundaries, and approximately 24 million were forced into exile within their own countries.[32] By the summer of 1994, at the height of the exodus from Rwanda, the number of refugees had reached the staggering level of 49 million, of whom 26 million were internally displaced and 23 million driven across international boundaries.[33] Human dislocations of such tremendous proportions are bound to push entire regions toward chronic high instability, as has been demonstrated across Asia, Africa, and Latin America in the past several decades.

Refugee flows have intensified during the past few years as more states in the Third World have failed to assert control over their territories and to protect their citizens. Currently, Central Asia, the Balkans, and several parts of Africa are leading contenders for regional instability that may be connected with large-scale human movements across and within state boundaries. But other parts of the Third World, as earlier experiences have demonstrated, are not immune to the negative effects of this problem, which is both a consequence and a cause of instability and conflict in the Third World.

Proliferation of Ministates

Any acceleration of state failure in the Third World is likely to be very dangerous for international and regional stability because in the 1990s, the outcome of state failure is expected to be dramatically different from the outcome for European states in the seventeenth, eighteenth, and nineteenth centuries. During that earlier period, conquest and annexation were permissible under the norms then governing the international system. Consequently, many inviable states were annexed by, or partitioned among, their stronger neighbors. This situation led to a dramatic reduction in the number of political entities in the European international system, from about five hundred entities in 1500 to twenty-five entities in 1900.

Annexation and conquest are no longer feasible in the international system for two reasons. First, conquest and annexation are likely to remain impermissible under international law even if the norm supporting territorial integrity of postcolonial states is relaxed. Second, now that the era of formal colonialism is over, conquest and annexation can be undertaken only by neighboring states. Such ventures can largely be ruled out, because neighbors of failing Third World states usually have neither the capability nor the will to annex failed states. Several Third World states may be willing to dismember hostile neighbors if the international environment becomes more permissive. However, as the Indian involvement in the 1971 Pakistani crisis demonstrated, dismemberment is one thing and annexation is quite another. Whereas some Third World states may profess irredentist designs against neighboring states, most would not be interested in annexing large chunks of their neighbors' territories, because this would immensely complicate the already acute problems of ethnicity and ethnonationalism they themselves face.

Failed states will, therefore, be left with only two options: to continue to revel in their anarchy and the suffering this will cause their populations or to splinter into ministates based on the dominant ethnic groups in particular regions of the failed states. Ethnic self-definitions are likely to be used as surrogates for failed political institutions, thus providing further evidence that ethnicity "has now become the ultimate resort of the politically desperate."[34] These ministates will seek recognition as full members of the international community, a status the established states will find difficult to refuse because of the precedents set in the Balkans, the former Soviet Union, and the Horn of Africa.

If this condition comes to pass, it is likely to lead to a situation against which Hurst Hannum has warned forcefully.

> Full exercise of ethnic self-determination, grounded on linguistic, religious, or other self-defining criteria, might better protect current incarnations of "nationalities," "minorities," and "indigenous peoples." Nevertheless, the prospect of 5,000 homogeneous, independent statelets which define themselves primarily in ethnic, religious, or linguistic terms is one that should inspire at least as much trepidation as admiration. As frontiers are shifted and minorities displaced to make way for greater purity, a new age of intolerance is more likely to follow than is an era of mutual respect and tolerance for all.[35]

Even if the number of states increases to 500 instead of the 5,000 envisaged by Hannum, a much more anarchic situation would be created than the one that is prevalent today, in which full membership in the system of states has already been bestowed on over 180 states. This situation would be aggravated by the fact that most of the newcomers would be even more insecure than the most insecure states that emerged in the wake of decolonization. Moreover, some may have access to weapons of mass destruction. Problems of containing nuclear proliferation in the aftermath of the disintegration of the Soviet Union will pale before those that are likely to arise if this scenario unfolds.

Democratic Virtue as a Necessity

Because of the tremendous problems that would accompany the failure of states or the widespread application of ethnonational self-determination, it is imperative for Third World state elites to find a way to successfully reconcile the task of state making with the demands for the human and political rights of groups. The competing pull of the demands associated with state making and those associated with the preservation of human rights often leads to internal conflicts within states and paves the way for either indiscriminate repression or state failure.

This contradiction between the territorial integrity of postcolonial states (including those of Central Asia, the Caucasus, and the Balkans, as well as of the established Third World) and the desire to assure the human and political rights of groups within these states inspired this statement by UN Secretary-General Boutros Boutros-Ghali.

> If every ethnic, religious or linguistic group claimed statehood, there would be no limit to fragmentation, and peace, security and economic well-being for all would become ever more difficult to achieve. One requirement for solutions to these problems lies in the commitment to human rights with a special sensitivity to those of minorities, whether ethnic, religious, social or linguistic. . . . The sovereignty, territorial integrity and independence of States within the established international system, and the principle of self-determination for peoples, both of great value and importance, must not be permitted to work against each other in the period ahead.[36]

This statement sums up the most fundamental dimension of the security predicament Third World states, many lacking effective statehood, face in the post–Cold War world. It implies that the imperatives of state building frequently clash with the demands for human and political rights, especially of ethnic minorities who may not be reconciled to the existence of postcolonial states within their colonially imposed boundaries.

However, despite the daunting nature of the task, ruling elites in individual Third World states must make every effort to reconcile these contradictory demands by charting a course for a political order that is both effective and legitimate; otherwise, the Third World's security predicament will become more acute in the post–Cold War era. This problem could lead to worse interethnic strife, near-total political anarchy, and the dismemberment or failure of vulnerable Third World states.

This task must be performed domestically, a fact that has been driven home by the failure of international efforts to impose order when ethnic strife has become acute or when the state has failed to perform even the minimum security function. Whether they are undertaken by regional organizations, as in Liberia, or by the United Nations, as in Cambodia and Somalia, international efforts can at best be only temporary, as all these cases have demonstrated. At worst, they may further exacerbate conflict among warring factions within failing states by trying to implement policies that are partisan (as in Liberia), insensitive to local realities (as in Somalia), or totally ineffective (as in Bosnia).

Experience demonstrates that if states approach complete failure, or if the forces of ethnonationalism—the last refuge of the politically desperate—alienate large segments of the population from the concept of the multiethnic state, external or internal parties can do little to salvage the situation. Therefore, to have even a moderate chance of success, a rescue strategy has to be preventive, coming into operation before the situation passes the point of no return. Moreover, such a strategy must be implemented indigenously, because no amount of external intervention can preserve the social and political order within a state if the will to preserve that order is missing among the major domestic actors.

A preventive strategy must recognize that political sagacity and international political morality demand that Third World state elites sincerely try to accommodate the interests of minority groups, assure basic human rights for individuals, and guarantee political participation for all or most citizens. Such a political strategy often runs directly counter to the impulses of political leaders, who are engaged in "primitive central state power accumulation."[37] The attempt to accumulate such power entails a certain degree of coercion of the state's population, especially of its more recalcitrant elements, who are often ethnic minorities that inhabit what Walker Connor has called their "ethno-national homelands, regions whose names reflect a special claim upon the territory by a people—Baluchistan, Nagaland."[38]

This state-building requirement must, however, be weighed against other political realities of the late twentieth century. These include the global dissemination of the ideas of democracy and human rights, including group rights, and the changed international sensibility toward these principles in the political lives of states, including those in the Third World. The revolution in communications technology has given Third World populations easy access to the ideas of human rights and democracy. Simultaneously, the popularity of self-determination, especially when combined with the strategic interests of neighboring states, has led to a rapid increase in moral and material assistance from outside states to those who claim to fight for self-determination. Pakistani support of the anti-Indian insurgency in the Kashmir Valley, which was extended far more brazenly in the 1990s than it would have been a decade ago, is an example of this trend. This trend also shows the changed international climate, which is more tolerant of aid to ethnic separatists who invoke self-determination.

In such a context, repression of separatist groups unaccompanied by concessions on democracy and human rights can be counterproductive, even for Third World elites who are self-consciously engaged in consolidating the political capacity of the central state. In short, repression alone is no longer sufficient to maintain the fragile fabric of political unity within Third World states and to attain the goals of the state-making process.

This political reality has also been driven home by the change in the attitudes of the major powers toward issues of human rights and democracy. Now that the Cold War no longer determines foreign aid and trade preferences, Western powers are emphasizing democratization and human rights as preconditions for assistance and preferential treatment in bilateral trade. Especially in the case of the United States, it is becoming conventional wisdom to argue that "the protection and promotion of human rights is both a normative imperative and an interest for U.S. policy . . . for failure to address it effectively can threaten both order and peace in the international system."[39] The fact that in 1994 the renewal of most-favored-nation (MFN) trading status for China became subject to human rights considerations by the United States shows the growing importance of this issue in Washington from both the idealist and the realist perspectives.[40] Although not invoked uniformly in all cases,[41] this change in priorities by states that control decisionmaking in the World Bank and the International Monetary Fund is perceptible enough to signal Third World state elites that it is time for them to move toward more participatory forms of governance and to pay greater heed to rights of individuals and groups.

Evidence of this new international sensibility can also be seen in the writings of some Western legal scholars, who have recently begun to argue that "entitlement" to democracy is emerging as a principle of international law.[42] Evidence is also demonstrated in intergovernmental documents such as the one produced by the Conference on Security and Cooperation in Europe (CSCE) in its meeting in Copenhagen in 1990. This document stated that "the will of the people, freely and fairly expressed through periodic and genuine elections, is the basis of the authority and the legitimacy of all government."[43]

In the climate of these changed domestic and international attitudes, the move toward democratization is no longer merely a laudable goal for states in the Third World; it has become a political precondition for establishing legitimate state structures and regimes that enjoy the acquiescence, if not the enthusiastic support, of their populations. This is a major reason for the new wave of democratization that has been visible in the Third World during the past several years.[44] Although this trend may be reversible, it demonstrates the growing internal and external pressures on Third World state elites to conform to what has become a major international and domestic expectation. The trend also demonstrates the increasing realization by Third World ruling elites that they cannot build credible states and legitimate regimes without guaranteeing minimum civil and political rights and at least some political participation for their citizens.

The need for political systems that guarantee political participation, even in Third World states without major secessionist challenges, has also been emphasized by recent events ranging from those in Mexico[45] to Algeria.[46] In the absence of political participation and governmental responsiveness to the people, opposition to state authority can easily take the form of violent insurrection justified on ideological grounds—Islamic, Marxist, or other—rather than on ethnic grounds. This is not a new phenomenon; it occurred during the Cold War in Iran, Nicaragua, and Peru. Such movements posed, and continue to pose, challenges to the legitimacy of regimes more than to the integrity of states.

In the post–Cold War period, beleaguered Third World regimes cannot readily call upon external great powers for support to crush opposition insurgencies, and insurgents are often incapable of overthrowing regimes; they can, however, paralyze their ability to function. In such a climate, the specter of anarchy has come to haunt states such as Algeria and Egypt that suffer primarily from political and social rather than ethnic divisions.[47] Such divisions can eventually paralyze the state, as in Algeria and potentially in Egypt, rather than cause its disintegration. However, both paralysis and fragmentation eventually lead to state failure and the attendant miseries this is likely to inflict on the failed state's population.

Many state elites in the Third World seem to have realized that the only way to prevent state making from turning into state failure is to allow greater political participation by sectors of society that were previously excluded from political power. The recent wave of democratization in the Third World arose largely from the realization by ruling elites that the survival of their states and regimes depends upon defusing the crisis of legitimacy they face. Others, such as the rulers of Egypt and Algeria, have resisted this trend at what may turn out to be great cost to their states and their societies.[48] They refuse to countenance political participation largely because they know they will lose power if the political systems in their countries become genuinely participatory. In such cases, considerations of regime security—which are shortsighted even for the interests of the ruling elites—clash directly with those of state security and, in the view of ruling elites, take precedence over state security. This situation threatens the survival of the state.

Self-Determination Without Secession

With the spread of democratization, even in imperfect forms,[49] it has become essential to separate self-determination from secession and to link self-determination to political participation within postcolonial states if a tolerable amount of order is to be preserved in the international system in general and in the Third World in particular. As the Carnegie Endowment study on self-determination pointed out, "The principle of self-determination is best viewed as entitling a people to choose its political allegiance, to influence the political order under which it lives, and to preserve its cultural, ethnic, historical, or territorial identity. Often, although not always, these objectives can be achieved with less than full independence."[50] The goal of delinking self-determination from secession can only be achieved if all or most segments of a state's population believe they are no longer politically powerless, particularly given the history of monoethnic control of state power in many multiethnic Third World states. The current composition of ruling elites and the monoethnic definition of national identity in many multiethnic states show that monoethnic control of state power is very much alive.

The ideal strategy for Third World elites in order to preserve their states and to bolster the legitimacy of state structures and regimes is to help their populations shift from being subjects to being citizens, politically as well as legally. In most cases, even a move halfway on the continuum from subject status to full citizen status, defined as political empowerment, can be a giant step toward defusing many internal security problems. Although, as one observer has said, "political democracy is not always a solution to ethnic conflict,"[51] the total lack of avenues for political expression in multiethnic societies can accentuate ethnic conflicts and escalate secessionist demands. Opening up avenues of political participation to all or most ethnic groups in a Third World state offers disgruntled segments of society the prospect that self-determination can take place within an existing state rather than being achieved only by destroying that state.

The separation of self-determination and secession can be boosted by constitutional guarantees to protect minority rights and to preserve or bestow autonomy on regions populated by minority ethnic groups that are likely to feel more secure under such an arrangement. As one scholar has observed, "Democratization can prevent or dampen ethnic conflicts if the forces pushing for democratization, first, recognize and acknowledge the ethnic differences that exist within the state and, second, if they can accommodate the interests of different groups in a way that is perceived to be fair and even-handed. Neither of these is automatic. . . . Yet, this suggests that the democratization process provides a window of opportunity to allay potential ethnic problems."[52]

Although such a sagacious strategy may not eliminate the tension between state making and self-determination, it has the potential to ease the most fundamental problem that has bedeviled the process of state making in the Third World: how to make the postcolonial state the focus of political loyalty from the population in a drastically short time without extensive coercion. Coercion in any case is likely to be severely circumscribed because of the internal and external variables, discussed earlier in this chapter, that will not allow the unrestrained use of force in the cause of state building in the late twentieth century.

It would be too naive to suggest that by itself, democratization would neutralize ethnic separatism. As the example of the Congo demonstrates, holding elections without adequate sensitivity to ethnic fissures can be counterproductive, especially if the fairness of the elections is in doubt and if the postelection regime has a distinctive ethnic hue. Such an outcome may widen ethnic rifts and heighten internal tensions and conflicts, as has happened in the Congo since the overthrow of the one-party Marxist-Leninist regime in Brazzaville in 1991 and the elections in the fall of 1992.[53]

The success of the democratic experiment in defusing ethnic tensions will depend upon a number of factors. These have been identified by Renee de Nevers as "the speed with which ethnic issues are recognized; the level of ethnic tension when the democratization process begins; the size and power of different ethnic groups within the state; the ethnic composition of the previous regime and its opposition; the political positions of the leaders of the main ethnic groups; the presence or absence of external ethnic allies; and the ethnic composition of the military."[54]

Despite the relevance of all of these factors to the problems of state and regime legitimacy in multiethnic societies, attempts at democratization still constitute the first crucial step. In the absence of this step all of the other variables, even if important, will remain of academic interest. In this sense democratization can be considered the necessary, although not the sufficient, condition to contain challenges to state boundaries, state institutions, and governing regimes in the Third World.

Democratization and the Consolidation of State Power

However, the demands of state building and democratization can be reconciled only if the democratizing state can monopolize the instruments of violence and prevent dissident groups from changing the state's boundaries when political controls are eased. These conditions are essential, because "often the first act of forces liberated by the introduction of democracy is to seek some permanent escape from the state they see as having oppressed them."[55]

Therefore, the trajectories of democratization and the consolidation of coercive power in the hands of the state must not diverge radically. Most important, the two processes should not be allowed to become the polar opposites of each other. Faced with a stark choice between the territorial integrity of the state and democratization, state elites will invariably opt for territorial integrity over democratization. This fact is borne out by Myron Weiner's observation that even in India, the most consistently democratic major Third World state, "faced with the choice of exercising coercive authority to maintain a single country or remaining democratic, most of the elite would choose the former over the latter. If need be, the center would exercise all the force at its command to prevent secession even if it meant a suspension of democratic rights."[56] The events of the past several years in Punjab and Kashmir bear testimony to this statement.

It is, therefore, all the more important that other, less democratic and more fragile states should not be forced to make a stark choice between territorial integrity and democratization, because they are bound to reject democratization. When the processes of territorial integrity and democracy collide, democratization cannot prevail without the disintegration of the state. Therefore, in order for the strategy of democratization to work successfully without threatening such disintegration, the state elites' decision to democratize must be linked firmly to the surrender of separatist groups and should be contingent upon disarming these groups.

It is in this area that the most severe problems are likely to arise, even if democratic political systems become the norm rather than the exception in the Third World. Democratic regimes cannot afford to be seen as weak when confronted by separatist challenges, and they cannot give up their right to lay down and enforce the rules by which the game of politics is played within their states. Otherwise, "a democratic center may be questioned for its inefficiency in creating or its weakness in handling the secessionist crisis, opening the way for military intervention."[57]

This point is not well understood by most proponents of democratization in the Third World, who tend to equate democratic states with weak states on the assumption that strong states are bound to be autocratic.[58] This assumption ignores the European experience in which democracy emerged as the final stage of the state-building process and not at the expense of that process. Even if democratization cannot wait until state building is completed, it cannot thrive in the absence of the political order only a strong state can provide. Democratization, therefore, must complement rather than contradict the process of state making. Without the political order that can only be provided by effective and legitimate states, the gains of democratization cannot be sustained. Anarchies, as Lebanon, Somalia, Liberia, and Afghanistan clearly demonstrate, are no respecters of democratic values. This truth prompted a perceptive scholar of the Middle East to say about the failure of the Lebanese state, "'Seek ye the political kingdom first'—not because it matters more, but because, in the lack of political order, no normal social development is possible. The state cannot replace society, but it must protect society. In the lack of political order, social and individual values are meaningless; they cannot be realized, nor can they be protected from assault, violence and chaos."[59]

Reconciling the two imperatives of the consolidation of state power and democratization is not an easy task, even if tremendous goodwill is present on all sides. Major problems are bound to arise between state elites and ethnic and political opponents who would like to curb the power of the central state. In addition, when separatist insurgencies are already underway, major problems between separatists and democratizing central governments are likely to center around two basic questions. First, what is the guarantee that groups espousing separatism will surrender all arms and reconcile themselves to autonomous or semiautonomous status that will depend upon the good faith and wisdom of the central government? Second, what is the guarantee that central authorities, after persuading separatist ethnic groups to lay down their arms, will abide by their commitment to popular political participation, the constitutional protection of minority rights, and regional autonomy?

The answers to these questions provided by the history of the Third World leave little room for optimism. Furthermore, the earlier European experience leads us to conclude that the historical juncture at which most Third World states find themselves today is unlikely to permit a great deal of ethnic accommodation and political participation. These two processes usually run counter to the overriding imperatives of the consolidation of state power and the fashioning of a national state. However, the late-twentieth-century context is so dramatically different from the late-eighteenth or even the late-nineteenth-century context that radically new solutions must be found for this dilemma.

In other words, the problem of reconciling the demands of state making with those of democratization and human rights will have to be addressed much more creatively, and mutually acceptable solutions will have to be found, if the twin specters of failed states and destructive ethnonationalisms are to be kept at bay. However, we must be realistic enough to recognize that even in cases in which there is no dearth of goodwill and creative thinking, the imperatives of state building and the demands for human rights and democracy may be irreconcilable. Given the stage of state making at which most postcolonial states find themselves, this fact should not come as a surprise to seasoned observers of the Third World. It means we should be prepared for a future in which internal conflicts based on ethnic, social, and ideological divisions will be further accentuated in many Third World regions, leading to state repression or state failure and often to a combination of the two.

This combination is sure to spill over political boundaries and increasingly fuel interstate conflict. Together, intrastate and interstate conflicts will continue to perpetuate the vulnerabilities and insecurities from which the Third World has traditionally suffered. The only difference will be that these vulnerabilities and insecurities are likely to become more acute in the post–Cold War era because of the transformations that have occurred, and are likely to occur, both in the nature of great power relations and in some of the norms that govern the international system and that are crucial to the security and integrity of Third World states. I return to some of these themes in the concluding chapter.

Notes

1. For a historical discussion of ethnic cleansing, see Andrew Bell-Fialkoff, "A Brief History of Ethnic Cleansing," *Foreign Affairs* 72, no. 3 (Summer 1993): 110–121.

2. Ashutosh Varshney, "Contested Meanings: India's National Identity, Hindu Nationalism, and the Politics of Anxiety," *Daedalus* 122, no. 3 (Summer 1993): 230.

3. Amitai Etzioni, "The Evils of Self-Determination," *Foreign Policy,* no. 89 (Winter 1992–1993): 21–22.

4. Christopher Cviic, *Remaking the Balkans* (New York: Council on Foreign Relations Press, 1991): 7, 9.

5. Hurst Hannum, *Autonomy, Sovereignty, and Self-Determination: The Accommodation of Conflicting Rights* (Philadelphia: University of Pennsylvania Press, 1990): 49.

6. It is instructive to note that Wilson's secretary of state, Robert Lansing, was extremely distressed over Wilson's espousal of the principle of self-determination at the 1919 Paris Peace conference. According to Lansing, "The phrase is simply loaded with dynamite. It will raise hopes which can never be realized. It will, I fear, cost thousands of lives. . . . What a calamity that the phrase was ever uttered! What misery it will cause!" Robert Lansing, *The Peace Negotiations: A Personal Narrative* (Boston: Houghton Mifflin, 1921): 98.

7. Lloyd N. Cutler, "Foreword," in Morton H. Halperin and David J. Scheffer, with Patricia L. Small, *Self-Determination in the New World Order* (Washington, D.C.: Carnegie Endowment for International Peace, 1992): xi.

8. Gidon Gottlieb, *Nation Against State: A New Approach to Ethnic Conflicts and the Decline of Sovereignty* (New York: Council on Foreign Relations Press, 1993): 2.

9. Charles Tilly, "National Self-Determination as a Problem for All of Us," *Daedalus* 122, no. 3 (Summer 1993): 30.

10. William Pfaff, "Invitation to War," *Foreign Affairs* 72, no. 3 (Summer 1993): 99, 101.

11. Rupert Emerson, *From Empire to Nation* (Boston: Beacon Press, 1960): 307.

12. John Zametica, *The Yugoslav Conflict,* Adelphi Paper no. 270 (London: International Institute for Strategic Studies, Summer 1992): 81.

13. For the Turkish policy toward the Kurds in Turkey and the Kurdish reaction, see Nader Entessar, *Kurdish Ethnonationalism* (Boulder: Lynne Rienner Publishers, 1992): 81–111; also see Henri J. Barkey, "Turkey's Kurdish Dilemma," *Survival* 35, no. 4 (Winter 1993–1994): 51–70. For the Thai policy toward the Malay Muslim minority in Thailand and the Muslim reaction, see Astri Suhrke, "Thailand," in Mohammed Ayoob (ed.), *The Politics of Islamic Reassertion* (London: Croom Helm, 1981): 233–255.

14. Dusko Doder, "Yugoslavia: New War, Old Hatreds," *Foreign Policy,* no. 91 (Summer 1993): 23.

15. Urmila Phadnis, *Ethnicity and Nation-Building in South Asia* (New Delhi: Sage, 1990): 241.

16. Crawford Young, "The Temple of Ethnicity," *World Politics* 35, no. 4 (July 1983): 659.

17. Jack Snyder, "Nationalism and the Crisis of the Post-Soviet State," *Survival* 35, no. 1 (Spring 1993): 5.

18. For details, see Rounaq Jahan, *Pakistan: The Failure of National Integration* (New York: Columbia University Press, 1972).

19. For a concise discussion of Somalia's slide into anarchy, see Samuel M. Makinda, *Security in the Horn of Africa,* Adelphi Paper no. 269 (London: International Institute for Strategic Studies, Summer 1992): 24–37. For a more detailed analysis of the breakdown of the Somali state and the resulting anarchy and starvation, see Jeffrey Clark, "Debacle in Somalia: Failure of the Collective Response," in Lori Fisler Damrosch (ed.), *Enforcing Restraint: Collective Intervention in Internal Conflicts* (New York: Council on Foreign Relations Press, 1993): 205–239.

20. Seyyed Vali Reza Nasr, "Pakistan: Islamic State, Ethnic Polity," *Fletcher Forum of World Affairs* 16, no. 2 (Summer 1992): 83, 89.

21. For a discussion of failed states, see Gerald B. Helman and Steven R. Ratner, "Saving Failed States," *Foreign Policy,* no. 89 (Winter 1992–1993): 3–20.

22. Snyder, "Nationalism and the Crisis of the Post-Soviet State," 12.

23. Robert H. Jackson, *Quasi-States: Sovereignty, International Relations and the Third World* (Cambridge: Cambridge University Press, 1990).

24. For details of the situation in Afghanistan in the 1980s during the height of

superpower involvement in that country's civil war, see Olivier Roy, *Islam and Resistance in Afghanistan,* 2d ed. (Cambridge: Cambridge University Press, 1990).

25. Clark, "Debacle in Somalia," 207–208.

26. For details of the civil war in Afghanistan after the Soviet withdrawal and the disintegration of the Afghan state, see Barnet R. Rubin, "Post–Cold War State Disintegration: The Failure of International Conflict Resolution in Afghanistan," *Journal of International Affairs* 46, no. 2 (Winter 1993): 465–492.

27. Clark, "Debacle in Somalia," 212.

28. Quoted in Kenneth B. Noble, "Mobutu Overture to U.S. Reported," *New York Times* (January 16, 1994): 7.

29. For an analysis of the failure of the state in Lebanon, see David Gilmour, *Lebanon: The Fractured Country* (New York: St. Martin's Press, 1983).

30. For Liberia, see David Wippman, "Enforcing the Peace: ECOWAS and the Liberian Civil War," in Damrosch (ed.), *Enforcing Restraint,* 157–203.

31. Halperin and Scheffer, with Small, *Self-Determination in the New World Order,* 119.

32. Paul Lewis, "Stoked by Ethnic Conflict, Refugee Numbers Swell," *New York Times* (November 10, 1993): A6. For a detailed analysis of the nexus between conflict and the refugee problem in the Third World, see Aristide R. Zolberg, Astri Suhrke, and Sergio Aguayo, *Escape from Violence: Conflict and the Refugee Crisis in the Developing World* (New York: Oxford University Press, 1989).

33. John Darnton, "UN Faces Refugee Crisis that Never Ends," *New York Times* (August 8, 1994): A1, A5.

34. John Chipman, "Managing the Politics of Parochialism," *Survival* 35, no. 1 (Spring 1993): 143.

35. Hannum, *Autonomy, Sovereignty, and Self-Determination,* 454–455.

36. Boutros Boutros-Ghali, *An Agenda for Peace: Preventive Diplomacy, Peacemaking and Peacekeeping* (New York: United Nations, June 1992): paragraphs 17–19.

37. Youssef Cohen, Brian R. Brown, and A. F. K. Organski, "The Paradoxical Nature of State Making: The Violent Creation of Order," *American Political Science Review* 75, no. 4 (1981): 902.

38. Walker Connor, "Ethnonationalism," in Myron Weiner and Samuel P. Huntington (eds.), *Understanding Political Development* (Boston: Little, Brown, 1987): 208–209.

39. J. Bryan Hehir, "The United States and Human Rights: Policy for the 1990s in Light of the Past," in Kenneth A. Oye, Robert J. Lieber, and Donald Rothchild (eds.), *Eagle in a New World: American Grand Strategy in the Post–Cold War Era* (New York: Harper Collins, 1992): 234. For a thoughtful and balanced analysis of the importance of the concern for democratization in the post–Cold War U.S. foreign policy, see Brad Roberts, "Democracy and World Order," in Brad Roberts (ed.), *U.S. Foreign Policy After the Cold War* (Cambridge: MIT Press, 1992): 293–307.

40. For one analysis of this issue, see Elaine Sciolino, "U.S. Again Warns Beijing on Rights: Christopher, on Eve of Talks, Says Favored Trade Status Is in Serious Jeopardy," *New York Times* (January 24, 1994): A3.

41. For one exception, that of U.S. soft-pedaling of human rights violations in Morocco for reasons of realpolitik, see Roger Cohen, "King's Wrath: Morocco Family Tale of 2 Decades," *New York Times* (January 25, 1994): A3.

42. For example, Thomas M. Franck, "The Emerging Right to Democratic Governance," *American Journal of International Law* 86, no. 1 (1992): 46–91.

43. Quoted in Gottlieb, *Nation Against State,* 20–21.

44. For a detailed analysis of this phenomenon, see Larry Diamond, "The Globalization of Democracy," in Robert O. Slater, Barry M. Schutz, and Steven R. Dorr (eds.), *Global Transformation and the Third World* (Boulder: Lynne Rienner Publishers, 1993): 31–69.

45. For an analysis of the Zapatista uprising in Mexico in January 1994, see Tim Golden, "Old Scores: Left Behind, Mexico's Indians Fight the Future," *New York Times* (January 9, 1994): section 4, 1, 6.

46. For one report on the Islamic opposition to Algeria's military rulers, see Chris Hedges, "Islamic Rebels Gain in Fight Against Army Rule in Algeria," *New York Times* (January 24, 1994): A1, A6.

47. For example, according to one long-time observer of Egypt, "President Mubarak is facing the most serious challenge since he took over the government following the assassination of Anwar Sadat in October 1981. The danger is not so much that the Gamaa [Gamaa al-Islamiya, or Islamic Group] will seize power. They lack the popular appeal and the talent to take over anytime soon. But they could cripple Mubarak's ability to deal with economic and political challenges that are daunting enough without the added complication of an armed insurrection." Stanley Reed, "The Battle for Egypt," *Foreign Affairs* 72, no. 4 (September–October 1993): 94.

48. Whereas the main challenge to both the Algerian and Egyptian regimes comes from Islamic political movements, often incorrectly described as "fundamentalists" in the West, the popularity of Islamism in these countries rests on the fact that "more than any other force in the region, it has articulated the deep-rooted malaise of repressed populations and proffered alternative visions of a more moral society." Claire Spencer, *The Maghreb in the 1990s,* Adelphi Paper no. 274 (London: International Institute for Strategic Studies, February 1993): 57. This theory is corroborated by Ghassan Salame's conclusion that "in most Muslim countries, decades of repression of nationalist, liberal, and Marxist trends left a wide-open, depoliticized society, a political and intellectual vacuum, that is now filled mostly by Islamic militants." Ghassan Salame, "Islam and the West," *Foreign Policy,* no. 90 (Spring 1993): 30.

49. For one analysis that makes the point about imperfect democratization in relation to Latin America, see Nathaniel C. Nash, "A New Breed of Strongman in the South," *New York Times* (January 16, 1994): section 4, 4. According to Nash, "Now that all countries in the region except Cuba have ushered in democratic reform, the Latin American strongman hasn't vanished, he's evolved. . . . The new breed of authoritarian democracy appears to be acceptable to the people it governs so long as it fosters economic progress as it insures law and order." Nash quotes an Argentinean political adviser to the effect that "people will give their consent to greater power for politicians, but they have stricter requirements. . . . People feel they can take power away from politicians now if they misbehave."

50. Halperin and Scheffer, with Small, *Self-Determination in the New World Order,* 47.

51. Martin Slann, "Introduction: Ethno-nationalism and the New World Order of International Relations," in Bernard Schechterman and Martin Slann (eds.), *The Ethnic Dimension of International Relations* (Westport, Conn.: Praeger, 1993): 7.

52. Renee de Nevers, "Democratization and Ethnic Conflict," *Survival* 35, no. 2 (Summer 1993): 31.

53. For details of the Congo case, see Kenneth B. Noble, "Democracy Brings Turmoil in Congo," *New York Times* (January 31, 1994): A3.

54. de Nevers, "Democratization and Ethnic Conflict," 31–32.

55. Chipman, "Managing the Politics of Parochialism," 168.

56. Myron Weiner, *The Indian Paradox: Essays in Indian Politics* (New Delhi: Sage, 1989): 37.

57. Larry Diamond, Juan J. Linz, and Seymour Martin Lipset, "Introduction: Comparing Experiences with Democracy," in Larry Diamond, Juan J. Linz, and Seymour Martin Lipset, *Politics in Developing Countries: Comparing Experiences with Democracy* (Boulder: Lynne Rienner Publishers, 1990): 29.

58. For example, Rajni Kothari, *State Against Democracy: In Search of Humane Governance* (Delhi: Ajanta Publications, 1988).

59. Gabriel Ben Dor, *State and Conflict in the Middle East: Emergence of the Post–Colonial State* (New York: Praeger, 1983): 244.

■ 9 ■

The Security Problematic of the Third World

The Third World's security problematic can be described as a multilayered cake in which the flavors have mingled; even though each layer has maintained its own distinctive flavor, it has lost its purity by mixing with the other flavors. The three main layers of this cake are the domestic, regional, and global dimensions of security. Although these three dimensions of the Third World's security problematic have influenced each other, the primary dimension—the layer that flavors the entire cake—is the domestic one.

The internal vulnerabilities of Third World states are primarily responsible for the high level of conflict in many parts of the Third World.[1] These internal fissures have helped many domestic conflicts mutate into interstate conflicts by providing the opportunity for neighboring states to intervene in internal disputes. Furthermore, the internal weaknesses of Third World states, and the conflicts these weaknesses have generated within and between states, have also permitted global rivalries to permeate the Third World. If the internal sources of conflict had been absent, or present on a much reduced scale, Third World states would have been more immune to external involvement by regional and global powers.

There are, however, autonomous dynamics of interstate conflict within Third World "security complexes."[2] These regional dynamics attain greater prominence because of the internal vulnerabilities of Third World states, since they feed upon the internal weaknesses of these states. This situation opens the door to both external involvement and interstate conflicts arising from domestic problems.

Similarly, global dynamics, including the global balance of power and the operations of international norms, would have had a smaller impact on Third World security if Third World states had been more cohesive and if their regimes possessed greater popular legitimacy. In the absence of cohesion and legitimacy, the major ingredients of "security software," Third World states were open to a high degree of interference, especially from the great powers in the international system.[3] This situation was manifested dramatically in superpower involvement in Third World affairs during the Cold War.

Third World states are also vulnerable to changes in international norms that guarantee their juridical statehood and territorial integrity. Unlike the states of the industrialized world, many Third World states, which Robert Jackson has called "quasi-states," depend upon international norms to preserve their sovereign status.[4] Their sovereignty and integrity are guaranteed primarily by the recognition they receive from the international community rather than by their effectiveness at home.

The Political Core of Security

The low level of social cohesion and of state and regime legitimacy is the root cause of domestic insecurity in Third World states. This low level is the product of the early stage of state making in which these states find themselves and of the lack of time to complete this process in sequential phases, as occurred in the cases of Western Europe and North America.[5] The discontinuities colonialism introduced into the evolution of Third World states, whether by imposing arbitrary boundaries or by clubbing together disparate ethnic groups, have further complicated state making in the Third World, making legitimacy and cohesion even more difficult to attain. State making and its attendant complications have become the centerpiece of the Third World security problematic. However, the task of state making is not undertaken in isolation from regional and global dynamics; these dynamics impinge upon the process and strongly influence its outcome.

To make this case intelligible and to preserve the analytical usefulness of the concept, the term *security* is defined in Chapter 1 in political terms—that is, in relation to threats to state boundaries, state institutions, and governing regimes. I am aware of the link between the political realm and other societal realms, ranging from the economic to the ecological. However, I have adopted the position that issues such as economic deprivation and environmental degradation do not automatically become part of the security calculus of Third World states; they do so only when they gain enough prominence to be able to produce political outcomes that can threaten the survival or effectiveness of states and regimes. In other words, nonpolitical issues that have the potential to endanger the well-being of Third World states and regimes become security problems only when they are able to intrude into the political arena.

A spate of recent writings warns that environmental degradation, resource scarcity, and the skewed distribution of resources are likely to lead to conflict in the Third World.[6] However, the more incisive authors on this subject recognize that these variables will have to be filtered through the political realm before they can become threats to the security of states. For example, Thomas Homer-Dixon, a leading analyst in this field, has listed "the perceived legitimacy of the regime, the role of *politics* in shaping a society's response to social stress, [and] the nature and rate of change of power relations among states" as crucial variables in the relationship between environmental degradation and state conflict.[7] All of these variables are political in character.

The definition of security used in this book accepts the primacy of the political realm and also adopts a distinctively state-centric approach to defining security issues. In doing so, the definition attempts to attain two objectives. First, it aims to preserve the fundamental link between the concept of security and that of the state in order to prevent the concept of security from being so diluted it loses all analytical utility. Second, this definition emphasizes the role played by the political elites in defining issues that affect the security of Third World states. Since the political elites are ultimately responsible for meeting challenges to state and regime security, their perceptions are important in defining the security problems faced by Third World states. If they consider an issue to affect the security of states or regimes and act accordingly, that issue becomes part of the security calculus. Any other way of defining the security realm would distort the Third World's security problematic, especially the priorities in the security arena of ruling elites and their political opponents.

Security: The Key Variable

Any formulation that does not make security its centerpiece will inadequately explain Third World state behavior, domestically and internationally. This is the case because the elites who make and implement domestic and foreign policies in the Third World are preoccupied, if not obsessed, by state and regime security, and they shape their policies accordingly. The Third World states' collective concern regarding their status in the international system is largely an extension of the internal security situation as far as Third World elites are concerned. To many of these elites, security and status are virtually indistinguishable. The Third World leaders' preoccupation with the security of states and regimes, and their concern with the status of their states as a group in the international system, are functions of vulnerabilities that, in turn, are related to their present stage of state making. In the international sphere, this is reflected in their lack of power to influence the outcome of most important political and economic issues.

Security considerations dominate domestic as well as the foreign policies of Third World states. Despite the routine rhetorical commitment of Third World state elites to development (defined as economic growth plus some distributive justice), for most of these elites development is a tool to help them achieve political legitimacy and state and regime security. This is the reason, despite Nicole Ball's lament that "available evidence . . .

[suggests] that expenditure in the security sector is more likely to hinder than to promote economic growth and development in the Third World,"[8] the security apparatuses of Third World states continue to corner a substantial proportion of those states' scarce resources. According to estimates provided by the U.S. Arms Control and Disarmament Agency, the military expenditure of developing countries as a group in 1989 was 18.6 percent of their total central government expenditures.[9] SIPRI has estimated Third World military expenditure for 1991 at over 16 percent of central government expenditures.[10] Although military expenditures vary by regions, these gross figures give us some idea of the importance of the military in the life of Third World states. It should also be noted that states normally understate expenditure on the military by a considerable margin and often hide security expenditures under different budget headings. Therefore, we can assume that the actual expenditures on security in Third World states are likely to be appreciably higher than those presented explicitly as military spending.[11]

Moreover, as Ethan Kapstein has pointed out, not only does security absorb a considerable share of resources, but "national security concerns have influenced the scope, timing, and trajectory of economic development. National security has also played a role in determining the geographical location and ownership of those capital-intensive projects which are important to the military, and the choice of technology employed in the project."[12] Furthermore, domestic political and security concerns frequently determine Third World states' resource allocations, even those earmarked for economic development. Such resources are often apportioned either as rewards to loyal groups or as pacifiers to disgruntled groups.

However, expenditures on military forces alone do not indicate the Third World state elites' obsession with security. This obsession is visible in the role played by the military in the political process of many Third World countries, from Indonesia to Egypt. The overt as well as implicit agreements worked out between civilian leaders and their military counterparts, from Chile to Pakistan, that have permitted the democratization of several Third World countries previously under military rule also indicate the continuing importance of the military in the political processes of many Third World countries.

The military is important in the political process because no other institution is more involved in the connection between issues of state making and security. As the early modern European experience demonstrated, the role of military coercion in the early phase of state making is considerable.

The problem for most Third World states has been compounded by two further factors. The first is the weakness of civil society and of political institutions, which precludes the emergence of strong checks on the security apparatuses' proclivity to usurp state power and resources. Second, the telescoping of the phases of state building into one phase, and the curtailment of the time available to complete the process, enhance the political importance of the coercive functions and of the agencies that perform these functions. Even in a country such as India, where a democratic political system has operated more successfully than probably anywhere else in the Third World, the important role of the security apparatus is visible in states such as Punjab and Kashmir, where the Indian state faces major challenges to state building.

Security Expenditures and State Making

A breakdown of Third World security expenditures clearly demonstrates that much of the insecurity faced by states and regimes is internal and is, therefore, linked to the state-making process. Such a breakdown, as Nicole Ball has shown, leads to the conclusion that whereas arms transfers from the North to the South are important for state security, these transfers do not account for the bulk of Third World security expenditures. After examining the evolution of operating costs—including salaries and compensation for troops—as a percentage of total security expenditures of twenty selected Third World countries from 1951 to 1979, Ball found that in all cases except one, operating costs dominated the mix of security expenditures.[13] Working with Ball's figures, Keith Krause tabulated that in the late 1970s, eighteen Third World countries spent an average of 79 percent of their military budgets on operating costs.[14] The high percentage of operating costs, Ball suggested, is connected to the fact that "the internal security role of the armed forces is considerable throughout the Third World and, in many cases, is their primary function."[15]

The positive relationship between high operating costs and internal security is true for most Third World countries. This fact shows the low level of technology and the high level of manpower required by Third World states in order to maintain internal control. But it also indicates where these countries are located on the state-making continuum. As the European experience has shown, three areas—imposing order, extracting resources, and controlling disputed territory—all of which are aimed at accumulating state power, comprise most of the activities of early state makers.[16] These are all labor-intensive tasks; they engage large numbers of persons and raise the ratio of operating costs relative to total expenditures on security. Security-sector costs in the Third World are understandably linked to the performance of these essential functions in the current early stage of state making, with the state-making variable determining much of the security cost.

There seems to be little difference in the allocation of resources to the security sector between the overtly military-dominated polities in the Third World and those under civilian control. This fact is demonstrated by Ball's data, which show that several states under civilian rule fall among the heaviest spenders on security.[17] The point is also corroborated by a study of defense spending by the members of ASEAN that, despite several caveats and qualifications, concluded that "the countries [in ASEAN] in which the military has the largest political role (Thailand and Indonesia) are the ones in which defense spending has grown more slowly than the ASEAN average."[18] State making and the violence that accompanies it seem to cut across the distinction between military-dominated and civilian-ruled polities in the Third World.

My analysis here reinforces the conclusion that it is important to make security the central focus of any explanation of Third World state behavior. At the same time, it is essential to consider state making the point of departure from which to study Third World security. Analyses based on the centrality of the security variable and on the importance of state making within that variable will provide richer comparative data and less ephemeral conclusions than analyses that adopt development or dependency as their basic organizing concepts. The explicitly political variables of state making and state and regime security must be studied in their own right rather than as corollaries of development and dependency theories if we are to clearly visualize where the Third World is headed. A clear understanding of this fact is the beginning of wisdom for scholars of the Third World.

Limits of Peace Through Democracy

Analyses that focus primarily on state making and on state and regime security are also likely to furnish more realistic assessments of democracy's chances in postcolonial societies. Democratization of Third World states is crucial to resolving significant internal security problems in these states and could also be important to their external behavior if we accept the argument of scholars such as Michael Doyle that democracies do not fight each other.[19] This argument is very different from the assertion that democracies are less prone to interstate conflict than are nondemocratic states. In fact, Steve Chan assembled data from 1816 to 1980 that demonstrate that democracies have been associated with more, not less, interstate conflict.[20] In a study that attempted to correlate regime types with international conflict between 1816 and 1976, Zeev Maoz and Nasrin Abdolali concluded that even though democratic states have never gone to war with one another, they are neither more nor less prone to conflict than are nondemocratic states.[21]

In light of these data, one wonders whether the latest wave of democratization in the Third World will make these states more pacific, even if more of the long-standing enemies among the developing countries become democratic. Specifically, it raises the question of whether countries such as India and Pakistan, both of which are now democracies, will desist from warring with each other. Again, even if India and Pakistan do not go to war with each other, can this fact be attributed to the democratic nature of their regimes or to other factors, such as their possession of nuclear weapons.

These assertions and the corresponding doubts about the role of democracy raise the fundamental question of whether democracy is the independent variable in determining the warlike character of states. Alternatively, we can argue that democracy is a dependent variable itself, and its presence or absence is determined by factors that also may have more to do with determining whether a state is conflict-prone.

I conclude that states can afford the luxury of stable, liberal democratic governance only if they are territorially satiated—that is, finished with the process of state building—are socially and politically cohesive, and have reached a high level of industrialization and, therefore, of affluence that is distributed relatively evenly. They can do so because only marginal differences in the population remain on the fundamental issues of political and economic organization of the society and on the basic identity of the state. This absence of major differences on fundamental issues explains why "political struggles in a democracy do not need to degenerate into an all-or-nothing fight for the control of the state; prosperity and the enjoyment of economic and political rights do not depend on a life-and-death conflict over which group controls the government."[22]

The historical evolution of the industrialized democracies also explains the absence of conflict among them. These states have completed their process of state making over a period of three hundred to four hundred years and are territorially satiated in relation to one another. They have no residual state-making claims outstanding against each other.[23] Also, they have too much at stake in the global capitalist economy to go to war with each other, thereby upsetting the global economic apple cart. The nuclear factor, which has ruled out war in the global strategic heartland where most industrial democracies are located, provides further explanation for their pacific behavior toward each other and toward the members of the erstwhile Warsaw Pact. Furthermore, the industrial democracies' habit of politically cooperating with each other was enhanced during the Cold War by the formation of a grand alliance of the major democracies that was pitted in "mortal" combat against a totalitarian superpower and its satellites.

The comparison with the industrialized democracies raises the question of whether these variables can come together in the same mix for most Third World countries so they can also become stable democracies and maintain pacific relations with each other. Even if some or many Third World states formally adopt democratic forms of governance for a significant length of time, this will not signal that their state-making process is complete nor necessarily reduce their vulnerabilities to the extent that they can be considered internally stable and externally pacific. They may be democracies, but they will be neither satiated nor stable democracies.

Territorial satiation, societal cohesion, and political stability—all part of successful state making—have determined the generally pacific nature of the industrial democracies' relations with each other. In Western Europe and North America, liberal democracy is a function, rather than a cause, of these factors when they are present in the right combination. As long as Third World states are unable to achieve these three goals, their democratic institutions will continue to be vulnerable to internal challenges, and the gains of democratization could be reversed.[24] This is the reason it is wise to heed Robert Rothstein's warning that "it is a mistake to jump too easily from the observation that democracies do not fight each other to the notion that a world of mostly democracies (many of them weak and potentially unstable) will necessarily be more peaceful, either internally or internationally."[25]

The Contagion of Instability

If the Third World continues to suffer from conflict, insecurity, and instability, that situation can harm the international system as a whole. Contrary to certain prognoses,[26] the components of the international system are so closely intertwined today that a Hobbesian periphery and a Lockeian core cannot coexist without the periphery exporting some instabilities to the core. It would be foolhardy to assume that a core of about thirty or thirty-five states could remain free of the turmoil that exists in a group of states four times its number, especially when some, such as those in the Gulf, possess strategic resources and others, such as those in Central Asia and the Caucasus, could enmesh great powers in their conflicts. Others, such as Israel, India, and Pakistan, have acquired nuclear capabilities that can wreak havoc on a frightening scale.

More generally, conflict in the Third World could lead to refugee flows not only into neighboring states but also into the developed countries, aggravating racial tensions in the industrialized democracies.[27] Since most members of the international system are still undergoing the trauma of state making, and since the international environment complicates the task of imposing political order on fragmented societies, conflict is likely to be the rule rather than the exception in the Third World in the foreseeable future. In this era of nuclear weapons and jet travel, industrialized democracies cannot insulate themselves from conflicts in the global periphery. There may be an element of poetic justice in this outcome after all.

Notes

1. According to data published by SIPRI, in 1992 "major armed conflicts were waged in 30 locations around the world. All of these conflicts except one (India-Pakistan) were intrastate. A major armed conflict is characterized by prolonged combat between the military forces of two or more governments or of one government and at least one organized armed group, and incurring the battle-related deaths of at least 1000 persons during the entire conflict." Ramses Amer et al., "Major Armed Conflicts," in *SIPRI Yearbook 1993: World Armaments and Disarmament* (Oxford: Oxford University Press, 1993): 81. Almost all of these conflicts were located in the old or new Third World.

2. For a discussion of security complexes, as defined by Barry Buzan, see Chapter 3.

3. For a discussion of security software, as defined by Azar and Moon, see Chapter 1.

4. For a discussion of quasi-states, as defined by Robert Jackson, and the role of international norms in assuring many Third World states juridical statehood and territorial integrity, see Chapter 4. For likely changes in such norms, see Chapter 8.

5. For a discussion of state making in a comparative framework, see Chapter 2.

6. For some of the best examples of this genre of writing, see Andrew Hurrell and Benedict Kingsbury (eds.), *The International Politics of the Environment* (Oxford: Clarendon Press, 1992); and Nazli Choucri (ed.), *Global Accord: Environmental Challenges and International Responses* (Cambridge: MIT Press, 1993).

7. Thomas F. Homer-Dixon, "On the Threshold: Environmental Changes as Causes of Acute Conflict," *International Security* 16, no. 2 (Fall 1991): 114–115. Emphasis in the original.

8. Nicole Ball, *Security and Economy in the Third World* (Princeton: Princeton University Press, 1988): 388. According to Ball, security expenditure "absorbed more than 15 percent of central government expenditure in about 40 percent of the developing countries between 1973 and 1983" (p. 386). The highest spenders during this period—that is, those above the 25 percent mark—included China, Egypt, Iran, Iraq, Israel, Pakistan, Saudi Arabia, South Korea, and Syria. (For details, see Figure 10-1, 387.)

9. U.S. Arms Control and Disarmament Agency (USACDA), *World Military Expenditures and Arms Transfers, 1989* (Washington, D.C.: USACDA, 1990): Table 1, 31.

10. Saadet Deger, "World Military Expenditure," in *SIPRI Yearbook 1993,* 392.

11. Security expenditures include but go beyond the traditional notion of defense expenditures as reflected in defense budgets. Nicole Ball has pointed out that it is preferable in the context of the Third World to refer to the "security" sector rather than the "military" sector "in order to indicate the inclusion of paramilitary forces" and to reflect "the fact that Third World governments frequently use their armed forces to maintain themselves in power, that is, to promote regime security." Ball, *Security and Economy in the Third World,* footnote 2, xvi.

12. Ethan B. Kapstein, "Economic Development and National Security," in Edward E. Azar and Chung-in Moon (eds.), *National Security in the Third World: The Management of Internal and External Threats* (College Park: University of

Maryland, Center for International Development and Conflict Management, 1988): 137.

13. Ball, *Security and Economy in the Third World,* Appendix 1, 396–402.

14. Keith Krause, "Arms Imports, Arms Production, and the Quest for Security in the Third World," in Brian L. Job (ed.), *The Insecurity Dilemma: National Security of Third World States* (Boulder: Lynne Rienner Publishers, 1992): Table 6.5, 135.

15. Ball, *Security and Economy in the Third World,* 393.

16. For details, see Samuel E. Finer, "State- and Nation-Building in Europe: The Role of the Military," Rudolf Braun, "Taxation, Sociopolitical Structure, and State-Building: Great Britain and Brandenburg-Prussia," and David H. Bayley, "The Police and Political Development in Europe," in Charles Tilly (ed.), *The Formation of National States in Western Europe* (Princeton: Princeton University Press, 1975).

17. Ball, *Security and Economy in the Third World,* Fig. 10-1, 387.

18. David B.H. Denoon, "Defense Spending in ASEAN: An Overview," in Chin Kin Wah (ed.), *Defense Spending in Southeast Asia* (Singapore: Institute of Southeast Asian Studies, 1987): 49.

19. For details of this argument, see Michael Doyle, "Kant, Liberal Legacies, and Foreign Affairs," Parts 1 and 2, *Philosophy and Public Affairs* 12, nos. 3 and 4 (Summer and Fall 1983): 205–235 and 325–353, respectively. Also, Michael Doyle, "Liberalism and World Politics," *American Political Science Review* 80, no. 4 (December 1986): 1151–1169.

20. Steve Chan, "Mirror, Mirror on the Wall . . . : Are the Freer Countries More Pacific?" *Journal of Conflict Resolution* 28, no. 4 (December 1984): 617–648.

21. Zeev Maoz and Nasrin Abdolali, "Regime Types and International Conflict, 1816–1976," *Journal of Conflict Resolution* 33, no. 1 (March 1989): 3–35.

22. Robert L. Rothstein, "Weak Democracy and the Prospect for Peace and Prosperity in the Third World," in Sheryl J. Brown and Kimber M. Schraub (eds.), *Resolving Third World Conflict: Challenges for a New Era* (Washington, D.C.: United States Institute of Peace Press, 1992): 32.

23. It should be pointed out that in those instances in which industrialized states, such as Germany between the wars, were not territorially satiated, and when their democratic institutions were weak, they pursued policies that led to conflict with other industrialized states. It is instructive to note that Germany became a national state only around 1870. The weakness of democratic institutions in Germany in the interwar period could, therefore, be attributed to its relative newness as a national state that lacked societal consensus on fundamental issues of political and economic organization and was struggling to establish its legitimacy and complete its state-building process.

24. For one analysis of the latest wave of democratization, between 1974 and 1990, see Samuel P. Huntington, *The Third Wave: Democratization in the Late Twentieth Century* (Norman: University of Oklahoma Press, 1991). According to Huntington, "A wave of democratization is a group of transitions from non democratic to democratic regimes that occur within a specified period of time and that significantly outnumber transitions in the opposite direction" (p. 15).

25. Robert L. Rothstein, "Weak Democracy and the Prospect for Peace and Prosperity in the Third World," in Brown and Schraub (eds.), *Resolving Third World Conflict,* 24.

26. For example, Max Singer and Aaron Wildavsky, *The Real World Order: Zones of Peace/Zones of Turmoil* (Chatham: Chatham House Publishers, 1993).

Also James M. Goldgeier and Michael McFaul, "A Tale of Two Worlds: Core and Periphery in the Post–Cold War Era," *International Organization* 46, no. 2 (Spring 1992): 467–491.

27. For an insightful analysis of the nexus between international migration on the one hand and security and stability on the other, see Myron Weiner, "Security, Stability, and International Migration," *International Security* 17, no. 3 (Winter 1992–1993): 91–126. Also see Gerald Dirks, "The Intensification of International Migratory Pressures: Causes, Consequences, and Responses," in Gerald Dirks et al., *The State of the United Nations, 1993: North-South Perspectives,* ACUNS Reports and Papers, 1993, no. 5 (Providence: Academic Council on the United Nations System, 1993): 65–81.

Abbreviations

ANZUS	Australia–New Zealand–United States Pact
ASEAN	Association of Southeast Asian Nations
BRIE	Berkeley Roundtable on the International Economy
CENTO	Central Treaty Organization
CIA	Central Intelligence Agency
CIS	Commonwealth of Independent States
CMEA	Council on Mutual Economic Assistance
CSCE	Conference on Security and Cooperation in Europe
ECOWAS	Economic Community of West African States
FPDA	Five-Power Defense Arrangement
G-7	Group of Seven
G-77	Group of 77
GCC	Gulf Cooperation Council
IAEA	International Atomic Energy Agency
ICRC	International Committee of the Red Cross
IGO	intergovernmental organization
IMF	International Monetary Fund
IRBM	Intermediate Range Ballistic Missile
LDP	Liberal Democratic Party
LTTE	Liberation Tigers of Tamil Elam
MAD	mutual assured destruction
MFN	most-favored nation
MPLA	Popular Movement for the Liberation of Angola
MTCR	Missile Technology Control Regime
NAM	Non-Aligned Movement
NATO	North Atlantic Treaty Organization
NGO	nongovernmental organization
NICs	newly industrialized countries
NIEO	New International Economic Order
NNICs	near newly industrialized countries
NPT	Nuclear Non-Proliferation Treaty

NWFP	North-West Frontier Province (of Pakistan)
OAS	Organization of American States
OAU	Organization of African Unity
OECD	Organization of Economic Cooperation and Development
OPEC	Organization of Petroleum Exporting Countries
RENAMO	Mozambique National Resistance
SAARC	South Asian Association for Regional Cooperation
SEATO	Southeast Asia Treaty Organization
SIPRI	Stockholm International Peace Research Institute
SWAPO	South West African People's Organization
UN	United Nations
UNCTAD	United Nations Conference on Trade and Development
UNITA	National Union for the Total Independence of Angola
U.S.	United States
WTO	Warsaw Treaty Organization

Index

About the Book and Author

This book is a much-needed exploration of the multifaceted security problems facing the Third World in the aftermath of the Cold War.

Ayoob addresses what he perceives to be the major underlying cause of conflict and insecurity in the Third World—i.e., the early stage of state making at which postcolonial states find themselves—drawing comparisons with the West European experience. He argues that this approach provides richer comparative data and less ephemeral conclusions than approaches that adopt development or dependency as their basic organizing concepts.

Subsequent chapters analyze the dynamics of interstate conflict in the Third World, the role of Third World countries in the international system, and, especially, the critical impact of the end of the Cold War on the Third World security problematic. Ayoob concludes with a set of explanations intended to help students, scholars, and policymakers decipher the continuing profusion of conflicts in the Third World and the trends and problems that will likely dominate well into the twenty-first century.

MOHAMMED AYOOB is professor of international relations at James Madison College, Michigan State University. He was Ford Foundation Fellow in International Security at the Watson Institute for International Studies, Brown University, for the 1993–1994 academic year. A specialist on conflict and security in the Third World, he has been awarded a Rockefeller Foundation Fellowship in International Conflict and a Social Science Research Council-MacArthur Foundation Fellowship in International Peace and Security. He earlier held faculty appointments at the Australian National University, the National University of Singapore, and Jawaharlal Nehru University in India and visiting appointments at Princeton, Oxford, and Columbia Universities. His numerous books and articles include *Regional Security in the Third World* and *India and Southeast Asia.*

Emerging Global Issues

THOMAS G. WEISS, SERIES EDITOR

Third World Security in the Post–Cold War Era
edited by Thomas G. Weiss and Meryl A. Kessler

The Suffering Grass:
Superpowers and Regional Conflict in Southern Africa and the Caribbean
edited by Thomas G. Weiss and James G. Blight

State and Market in Development: Synergy or Rivalry?
edited by Louis Putterman and Dietrich Rueschemeyer

Collective Security in a Changing World
edited by Thomas G. Weiss

Humantarianism Across Borders: Sustaining Civilians in Times of War
edited by Thomas G. Weiss and Larry Minear

Changing Political Economies:
Privatization in Post-Communist and Reforming Communist States
edited by Vedat Milor

The Third World Security Predicament: State Making, Regional Conflict, and the International System
Mohammed Ayoob